IMAGES
of America

EDINBURG

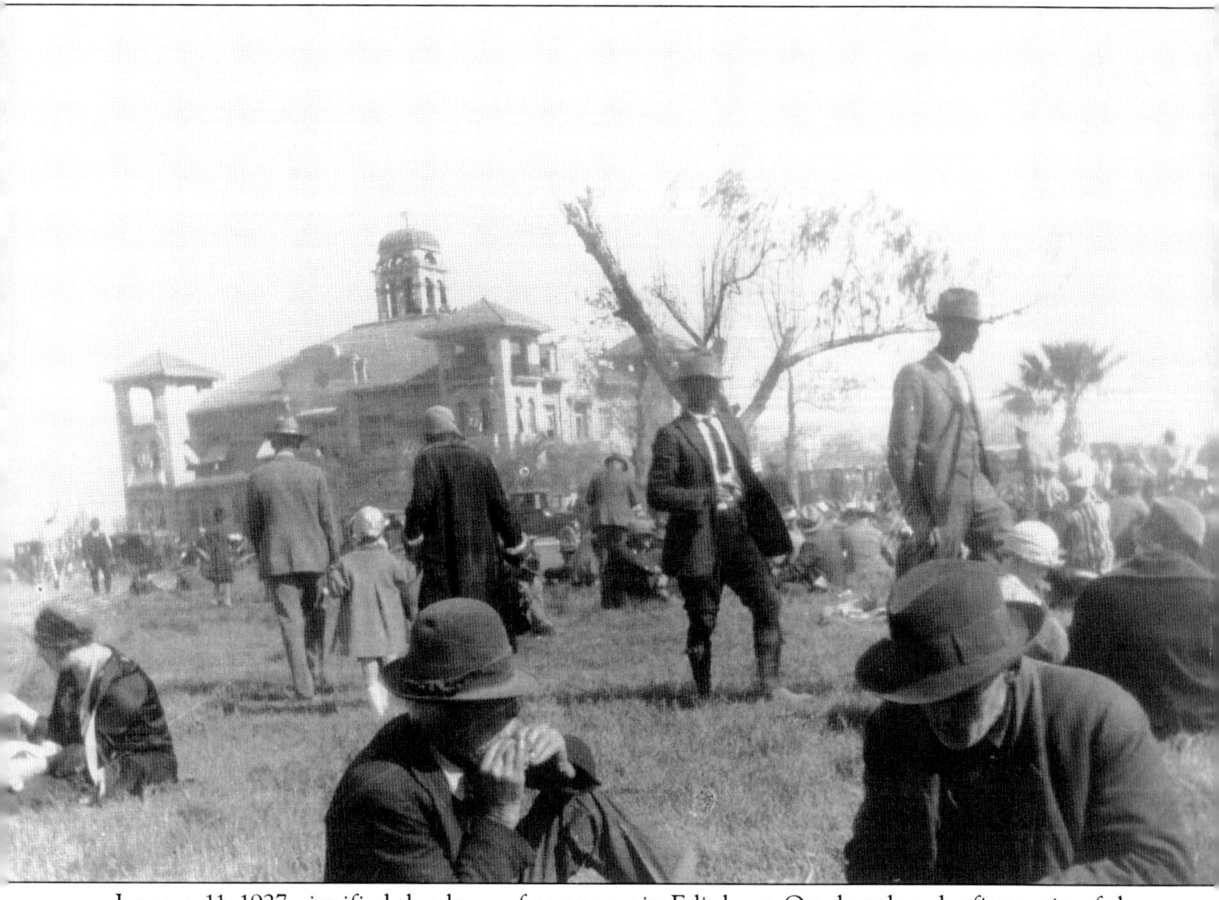

January 11, 1927, signified the dawn of a new era in Edinburg. On that day, the first train of the Southern Pacific Railroad arrived with Lower Rio Grande Valley and Southern Pacific dignitaries on board. A citywide celebration was held for thousands of people, schools were closed, and barbecue was served, with the courthouse square serving as a large picnic area. The 1910 courthouse shown above was torn down in 1955 after the current (1954) courthouse replaced it.

On the Cover: The Golden Jersey Creamery delivered milk, ice cream, and other dairy products to the citizens in Edinburg and other nearby towns. This photograph shows just one of the trucks that was used for deliveries with the telephone number of 181 clearly visible on the side. Long-term residents of Edinburg may remember the cow above the front door of the creamery building on the north side of the courthouse square. (Courtesy of The University of Texas–Pan American Library.)

IMAGES
of America

EDINBURG

Janette Garcia

ARCADIA
PUBLISHING

ISBN 978-0-7385-8477-5

Published by Arcadia Publishing
Charleston, South Carolina

Printed in the United States of America

Library of Congress Control Number: 2011927630

For all general information, please contact Arcadia Publishing:
Telephone 843-853-2070
Fax 843-853-0044
E-mail sales@arcadiapublishing.com
For customer service and orders:
Toll-Free 1-888-313-2665

Visit us on the Internet at www.arcadiapublishing.com

To my family, who helped make this book possible in so many ways.

Contents

Acknowledgments 6

Introduction 7

1. Water: The Essential Element 11
2. The County Seat: Three Locations, Four Names, Five Courthouses 29
3. A Town Grows Up: From a Ranch to a Branch Line 47
4. Edinburg: The Gateway to Education 87
5. Edinburg: Gateway City to the Valley 113

ACKNOWLEDGMENTS

The history of Edinburg is fascinating. In one sense I am sorry that this book is already being published, because just as I know there are many people I would like to thank for their help in finding information and photographs included in this publication, I also know that there are just as many people I didn't speak with, and photographs that didn't get published. I would like to thank my colleagues at The University of Texas-Pan American, especially the staff of Special Collections for their support and listening to me tell them all the interesting stories I found. Barbara Stokes and Steven Lomas at the Museum of South Texas History were also extremely helpful and knowledgeable. These two institutions serve as the largest source of materials in this book. Valerie Ramirez and Carlota Chapa were helpful with providing information and photographs, particularly regarding the Vela family and descendants. I am proud to be associated with this city of education, and would like to thank the staff who helped me from Region One Education Service Center, the Rio Grande Bible Institute, and the South Texas Independent School District. Early in my research, I determined that it would not be possible to include all of the historical and important businesses in Edinburg. I chose the Edinburg Citrus Association as one of the longest running successful businesses indicative of the citrus and the shipping industry so important to this region, and I would like to thank them as well for their help and wonderful photographs and packing labels I was able to copy. Finally, I would like to thank my family for their support, my parents for serving as a sounding board and offering their advice, and my husband and children for putting up with long nights and busy weekends.

Introduction

The seat of Hidalgo County had humble beginnings as pastureland for ranchers. It slowly grew from a place where cattle outnumbered people to a town on the Rio Grande in the newly formed Hidalgo County. When river waters once again threatened the courthouse, the county voters elected to move the county seat farther inland. A site was selected in the brush, and essentially, a town grew up around the courthouse. Today, the county seat is more than just a place where county records and laws are maintained. It is also known as a place where civic pride and community action have improved the city in countless ways over the years, as a gateway city for people and products to and from the Lower Rio Grande Valley and Mexico, and as the home of the University of Texas–Pan American and other educational institutions. What is not as well known is the number of places the county seat has been located and the number of names those locations have been called.

José de Escandón first settled this region in 1749 when the area was part of Mexico's Nuevo Santander Province. Under the guidance of the Spanish government, Escandón was selected to colonize and settle the lands around the Rio Bravo, or Rio Grande, as it is now known. Escandón founded over 20 towns, villas, and missions. Reynosa, in 1749, was one of the earliest settlements, along with Camargo, also in 1749. Mier was founded in 1750, and Revilla (now Guerrero) in 1752. Reynosa was originally located across the Rio Grande from present-day Penitas, Texas. Ranching was the primary means of support for the people of the region, and good pastureland was essential for a good economy. Each settlement was allocated communal pasturelands where the ranchers would let their cattle, sheep, and goats graze. Because Reynosa was built so close to the river, two leagues of common pasture or grazing lands for the ranchers were designated across the river in a place known as Ejidos de Reynosa. After repeated flooding, Reynosa was moved to higher ground to the east, its present location, in 1802.

The Spanish crown, and later, the Mexican government, divided the land north of the river by porciones and land grants among the first settlers. Porciones were long, thin strips of land, each with access to the river, so necessary for the livestock. Initially, there were few human residents on the northern side of the river. Cattle, sheep, and other livestock were pastured on this land. Across the river from Reynosa in what is now known as the town of Hidalgo, Texas, as far back as 1770, there was a small ranch or colony known alternately as La Habitación, "dwelling place;" El Corralón, "corral" or "yard;" and Rancho San Luis, or San Luisito. Initially the region was little more than a suburb of Reynosa. People would travel back and forth across the river on flat boat ferries.

The Mexican War, fought between 1846 and 1848, changed a lot more in the region besides creating the Texas border. Gen. Zachary Taylor's army marched through "the Valley" in 1846, supposedly along the route known as Old Military Road. Some of the first Anglo American inhabitants of the Lower Rio Grande Valley settled in the region, either directly or indirectly because of the Mexican War. In 1848, the Treaty of Guadalupe Hidalgo was ratified, and the river became the recognized border between the United States and Mexico. What had once belonged to Mexico was now part of Texas and the United States. In 1848, San Patricio County was formed out of all of south Texas. Later that same year, Cameron County was formed out of San Patricio County.

Also in 1848, gold was discovered at Sutter's Mill in California. Thousands of men sought to make their way to California. One of the lesser-known routes started in Brownsville and traveled up the river. More early Anglo American settlers were "miner '49ers" who ended their search for riches in the Rio Grande Valley. At the same time, more ranches were developed on the Texas side of the river. By 1850, there were about 39 ranches in the region of what later became Hidalgo County. Cattle, fruits, and vegetables grew well enough to allow for shipping and trading of those products. E.D. Smith moved to La Habitación opposite Reynosa and opened a store in 1848 for the growing number of travelers and ranchers. Smith is also reported to have brought the first cotton gin to the Valley. A year later in 1849, James McAllen from Londonderry, Ireland, arrived in Matamoros, possibly on his way to California for the Gold Rush where he met up with John Young. Smith, Young, and McAllen worked together running a store, trading hardware, guns, and foodstuffs and transporting hides, bones, wild mustangs, cotton, sugar, and salt to larger boats bound for Europe. Young shipped his hides out first by the steamboat *Ranchero*, and later the steamboat *Bessie* to Brazos Santiago, and by ocean-going clipper to London. The steamboats would stop once or twice a week to unload and load their freight.

The first location of what could reasonably be called a town was named Edinburgh, Texas. The name Edinburgh was chosen by E.D. Smith to honor John Young's birthplace in Edinburgh, Scotland. Edinburgh grew from simply a suburb of Reynosa to being a town in its own right. The store was popular and visited by famous men including Gen. José. M. Carvajal, Col. John Davis Bradburn, Capt. Richard King, Capt. E.J. Kenedy, Lt. Col. Robert E. Lee, and Ranger captain John S. "Rip" Ford. Rip Ford, in fact, married Addie Smith, E.D. Smith's daughter.

By 1852, the population of Cameron County had increased, and the need for a new county was acknowledged. In the area that was to become Hidalgo County, there were between 40 and 45 ranches. As the original land grants and porciones were split among heirs of the original grantees, and more people moved to the successful ranches and farms, more towns and settlements arose. The size and travel difficulties of Cameron County were readily apparent, especially to state senator Israel B. Bigelow. Bigelow had been a stage line operator out of Point Isabel (now Port Isabel), and also a mayor and a county judge. He recognized the difficulties of traveling 100 miles or more to Brownsville, Texas, either along the rough, hazardous roads or waiting for the intermittent steamboat in order to conduct tax, land, or other governmental business. Bigelow introduced the measure to create a new county to the 15th Texas State Legislature, which passed under Gov. P. Hansborough Bell. Hidalgo County was formed on January 24, 1852, by taking 2,343 square miles out of Starr and Cameron Counties, thereby creating the seventh largest county in Texas.

Besides naming the town of Edinburgh, E.D. Smith is also credited with naming the county of Hidalgo to honor the priest Miguel Hidalgo y Costillo (1753–1811), known as the "Father of Mexican Independence." Father Hidalgo began the movement to liberate Mexico from Spain when he gave an impassioned speech, "Grito de Dolores," to his parishioners. Hidalgo protested against the evils of "bad government" and through the symbol of the virtuosity of the Virgin of Guadalupe, he and his followers began the Mexican Revolution. The beginning of the revolution is still celebrated today as Diez y Seis de Septiembre (16th of September). Father Miguel Hidalgo was shot as a rebel in 1811.

The Edinburgh post office was established in 1876. In 1885, the name of the post office was changed to Hidalgo. One year later, in 1886, the settlement that had first been known as La Habitacion, and then later Edinburgh, and for one year, Hidalgo, was destroyed by flood. A description, however, written in 1893 in the book *Twin Cities of the Border*, which was primarily about Brownsville and Matamoros, also included a short description of the new town of Hidalgo by comparing it to the old town: "The town presents a very attractive appearance, and is especially remarkable for a scarcity of jacals (thatched-roof mud huts) and unsightly buildings of all descriptions.

This is owing to the fact that most of the old town, which was established during the Mexican War, has been washed away by the Rio Grande."

The new town of Hidalgo and a new courthouse were built on higher ground two miles north of the river in 1886. *Twin Cities of the Border* goes on to describe the new town as having broad streets and avenues with a number of handsome dwellings in the center of town. Jetties were built and the high bank of the river was "sloped to prevent further encroachments, if possible." In those days before dams had been built to control the Rio Grande, flooding was a constant worry. When the river flooded, it could rise as many as five feet, leaving only the housetops to be seen in low areas. After the floods receded, the course of the river could also change, so that the courthouse that had once been two miles away was now just a quarter mile from the river. The August 12 commissioner's meeting passed an issuance for bonds for $5,000 "to protect the courthouse and jail and other property from further erosion of the Rio Grande River courthouse."

In 1902 and 1904, a series of floods once again threatened the courthouse. The flooding was so severe that in some instances, the water made its way up to McAllen. Talk began that it would be necessary to move the courthouse much farther away. Besides the threat of the river, two other reasons were given for wanting to move the county seat. In 1903, the St. Louis, Brownsville and Mexico Railway had been established. The line to Brownsville was completed by July 1904 and through Harlingen and Mission to Sam Fordyce by 1905. Towns were being developed all along the railroad, and the area was developing quickly, but the railroad would not risk laying tracks so close to the river to reach Hidalgo. Finally, proponents of the move brought up a Texas law that stated that it was desirable that county seats be within five miles of the geographic center of the county.

The county leaders began searching for a new location for the county seat. Landowners around McAllen and other nearby towns had been approached; however, no one was willing to donate land for the courthouse to the county. John Closner, William F. Sprague, and Dennis B. Chapin had land interests north of McAllen. The land at that time was undeveloped and populated only by mesquite trees, brush, and cattle. They selected a site in an area known only as Section 272, Land scrip No. 137, originally issued to the Texas Mexican Railway Company. Section 272 had been part of the property of the public free school fund by the commissioner of the General Land Office of Texas. The three men designated an area in that section for a town and called it Chapin, after D.B. Chapin, one of the landowners and promoters.

On September 5, 1908, Judge Chapin (the same Chapin for whom the town had been named) called for a general election based on a petition that had been passed around Hidalgo County proposing the move of the county seat from the town of Hidalgo to the town of Chapin. During a vacation of the commissioners' court, Judge Chapin called for an election to move the county seat to Chapin. The date of October 10, 1908, one month hence, was selected for the election. Two days before the election was to take place, Judge Chapin resigned to prevent allegations of fraud. In his stead, the commissioners elected Judge S.P. Silver from Mercedes. The election was duly held on October 10, 1908, and on October 12, the votes were counted.

420 people voted to move the county seat to Chapin, 90 people voted against the move. There was little opposition except for the precinct near Mercedes, where 70 voted against moving the courthouse, and only 62 voted for the move. At that time Mercedes was a well-established town, and the voters in that area felt that Mercedes would serve as a better location for the county seat. On October 12, 1908, the same day the votes were counted, those opposed to the move sent a telegram to the Corpus Christi District Court requesting an injunction against the move. That same day the proponents of the move also decided to take action. A team was sent up to Chapin to begin clearing the brush and setting up tents. Early the next morning, October 13, 1908, men showed up with ox carts at the courthouse and began loading wagons with the deed records, court books, and all the other court documents. The men finished loading the carts around four o'clock in the afternoon and traveled through the night, reportedly reaching Chapin very early on the morning of October 14. They celebrated the move by shooting guns into the air and with freely flowing drinks as they placed the records into the tents, which were guarded day and night until a brick vault could be built.

In 1908 at just 56 years old, Hidalgo County was already on its third county seat and was about to build its third courthouse. This courthouse, the first to be built in Chapin, was a wooden two story "barn-style" courthouse with an adjacent brick vault built to protect the county records until a permanent courthouse could be constructed. In 1910, courthouse number four was completed. The courthouse that replaced the wooden building was an elegant building with rounded cupolas and a red tile roof. A dedication and the laying of the cornerstone took place on June 24, 1910.

The courthouse celebration was still fresh in people's minds when D.B. Chapin went to San Antonio on a business trip. During that trip, Chapin met Oscar J. Rountree, a former Texas Ranger, in Dan Breem's saloon in San Antonio. Chapin shot and killed Rountree, and although Chapin was later able to prove self-defense during his trial and was acquitted of all charges, the residents of Chapin and the county of Hidalgo did not want the name of their county seat sullied by his criminal reputation. On February 13, 1911, Chapin's trial started in San Antonio, and that same day, the post office changed its name from Chapin to Edinburg, as petitioned by the residents of the town. The following day, February 14, 1911, county judge James H. Edwards signed the order to change the name of the town from Chapin to Edinburg by resolution of the commissioner's court. The name of Edinburg, minus the final h, was chosen once again to honor the former name of the county seat, the hometown of John Young, and had the added advantage of also recognizing the hometown of John McAllen of the nearby town of McAllen, who had also been born in Edinburgh, Scotland.

The newly named town of Edinburg grew from a small town in the brush to a fast-growing technological and educational city. Its citizens worked together over the years to improve the city's facilities. In 1927, it became home to one of the first institutions of higher education in the Lower Rio Grande Valley, now known as the University of Texas–Pan American. In the 1930s, it became a major location for packing and shipping citrus and vegetables when farming was the major industry in Hidalgo County, and today it is known as the "gateway city" on the NAFTA corridor. The county grew so fast that within 44 years, it had already outgrown the 1910 courthouse and was in need of a fifth courthouse. In 1954, the current five-story courthouse was constructed.

One

WATER
THE ESSENTIAL ELEMENT

The Rio Grande dominated the lives and the landscape of the early settlers in the Lower Rio Grande Valley. The first settlements in the region were laid out along the river by colonizer José de Escandón including the town of Reynosa, which was established in 1749 on the southern side of the river. Later, a series of porciones and land grants were allocated to settlers along the northern side, first by the king of Spain, and later by the Mexican government. The porciones were long and thin, designed to allow each ranch owner access to the river for their livestock. The river also transported salt from the famous salt lake of the kings, Sal del Rey, and hides and tallow and other products from the ranches to Matamoros to be shipped south or across the ocean to Europe. The Rio Grande was both a giver and a destroyer, however. Long before dams and levees tamed the river, it could flood and wash away any structures humans chose to place in its path. Both the original towns of Reynosa and Hidalgo had to be moved to higher ground after repeated flooding. Threats from the river were also the reason the county seat was moved inland to its current location of Edinburg.

As the area became more settled, people began to think more about how to bring the water to themselves and their crops rather than how to get their livestock to the river. Irrigation canals and water wells were built inland, bringing water to newly planted farms. The land was rich with alluvial soil after years of flooding, and the warm climate was conducive to growing a large variety of crops year-round. Monte Christo, northeast of present-day Edinburg, was one such town. The developers of Monte Christo promoted their deep artesian wells to farmers, and canals and irrigation systems were developed all along the river. The first local canals were built south of Edinburg around San Juan, McAllen, and Mission, and eventually were expanded to include Edinburg.

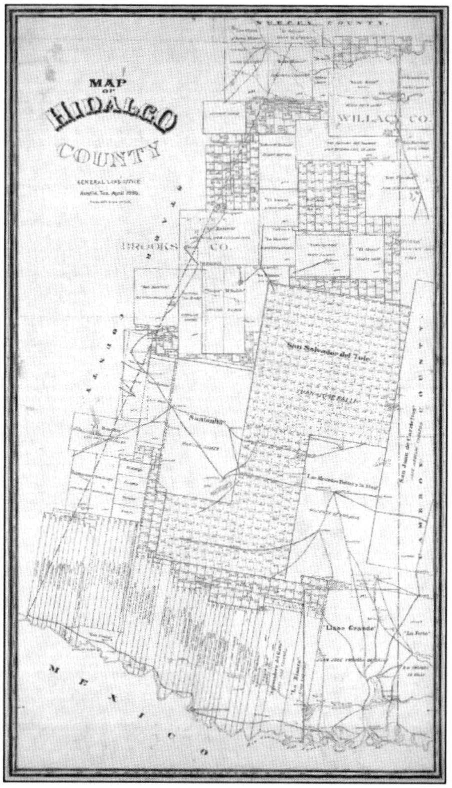

The map of Hidalgo County (left) and the close-up section of this region (below) show some of the earliest settlements. The settlement of Reynosa, now called Reynosa Vieja, was one of the first towns along the Rio Grande in this region. The old town was located across the river from present-day Peñitas, Texas. The earliest settlers let their livestock graze on shared lands north of the river known as Los Ejidos de Reynosa. First the Spanish and later the Mexican governments divided the land into long thin strips of land called porciones and larger land grants. In 1802 after repeated flooding, Reynosa was moved to its current location. Also shown on this map are Edinburgh, renamed Hidalgo, Chapin, and later, Edinburg. (Courtesy of the Texas General Land Office, Austin.)

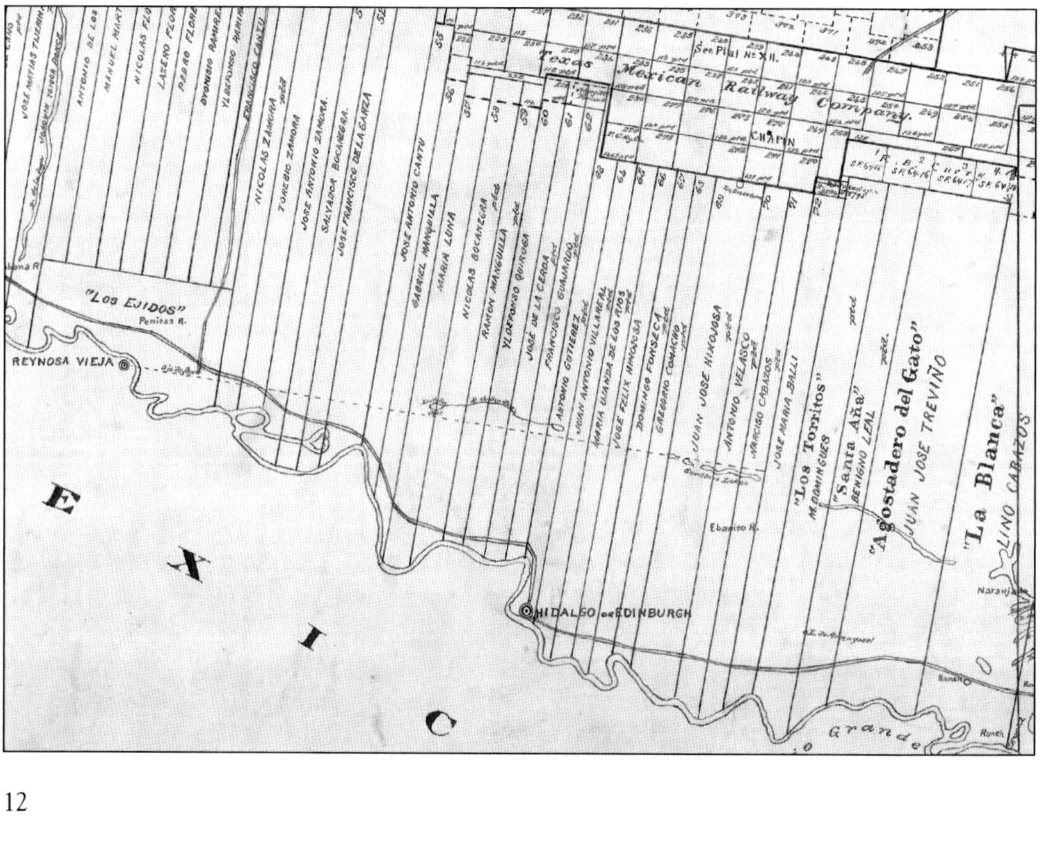

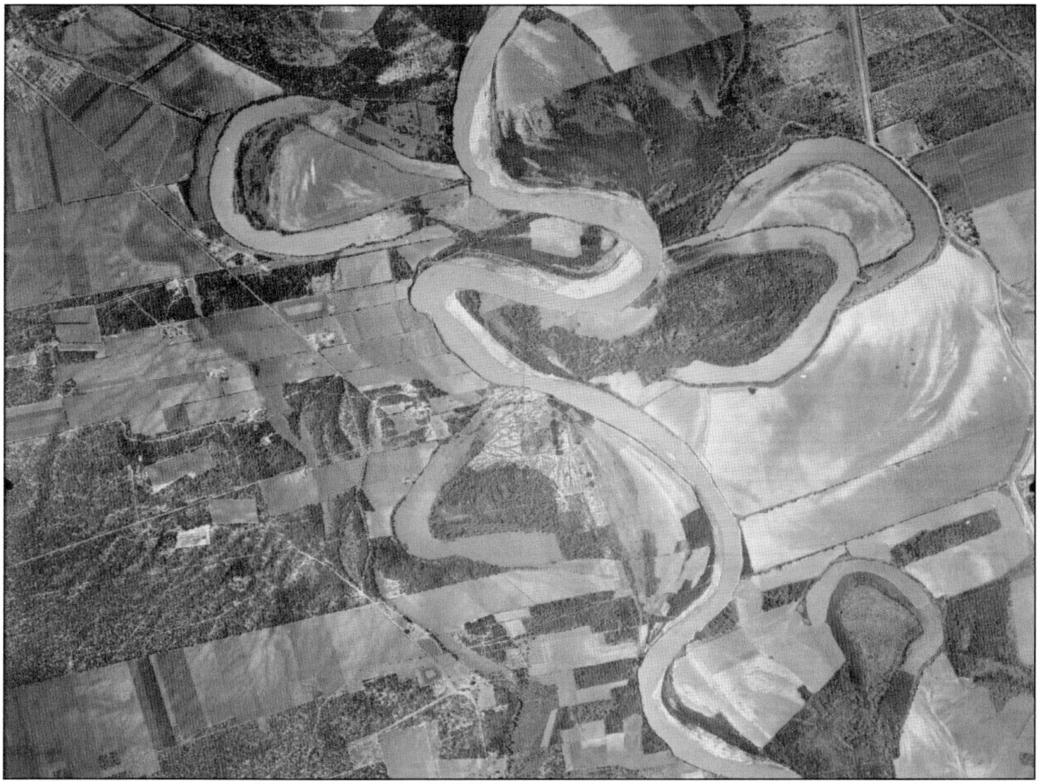

The location of the town now known as Hidalgo was originally closer to the river across from Reynosa. Originally just a settlement alternately known as La Habitación, "dwelling place;" El Corralón, "corral" or "yard;" and Rancho San Luis, or San Luisito, the town finally settled on the name of Edinburgh. In 1886, it was relocated because of the river. The Valley is really a flat delta, and the river meanders through the region as shown in the aerial photograph above. Any flooding can result in a change in the river course, creating cutoffs and horseshoe-shaped bancos as can be seen in the aerial photograph below. (Courtesy of the Texas Department of Transportation housed at The University of Texas–Pan American Library.)

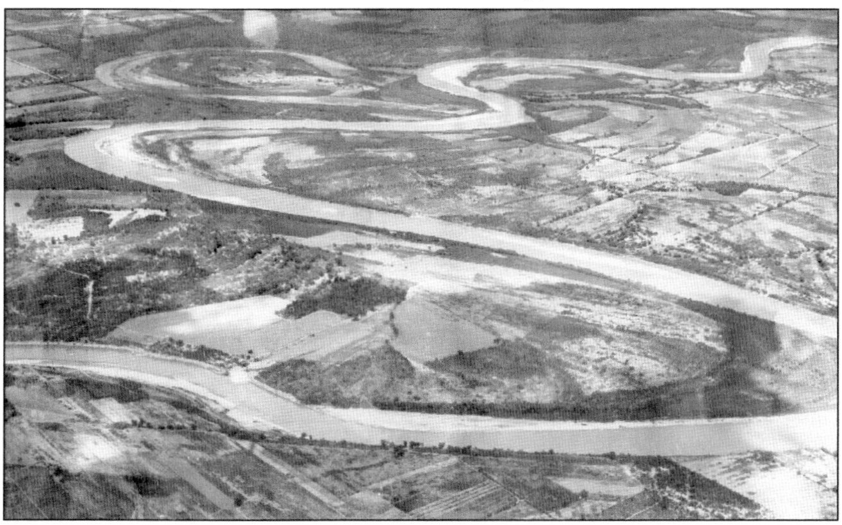

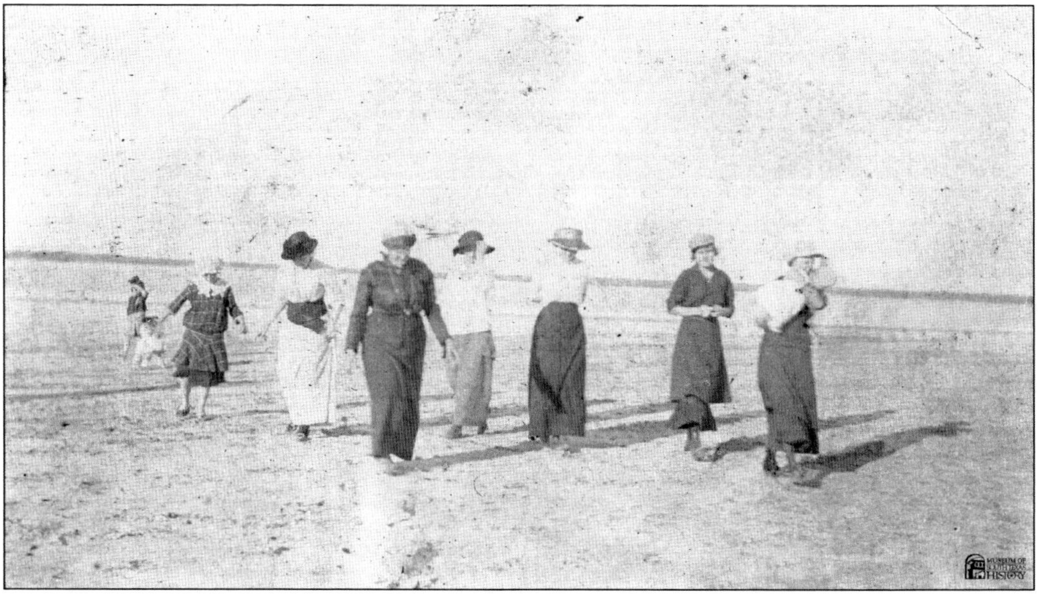

Almost as important as the river were the salt lakes located 22 miles north of present-day Edinburg. The largest lake, La Sal del Rey, "the King's Salt," is one of three naturally occurring salt lakes in the south. The lake has drawn visitors and salt traders since prehistoric times. The source of the salt is unknown, but salt removed from the lake is quickly replenished. It is estimated that the lake holds four million tons of salt. It has been a popular spot for both tourists and locals. Wading in its salty waters was reported to cure arthritis, and visitors could take home their own sparkly, salt-encrusted keepsakes that were left in the lakes overnight. These two photographs show visitors to La Sal del Rey. (Courtesy of the Museum of South Texas History.)

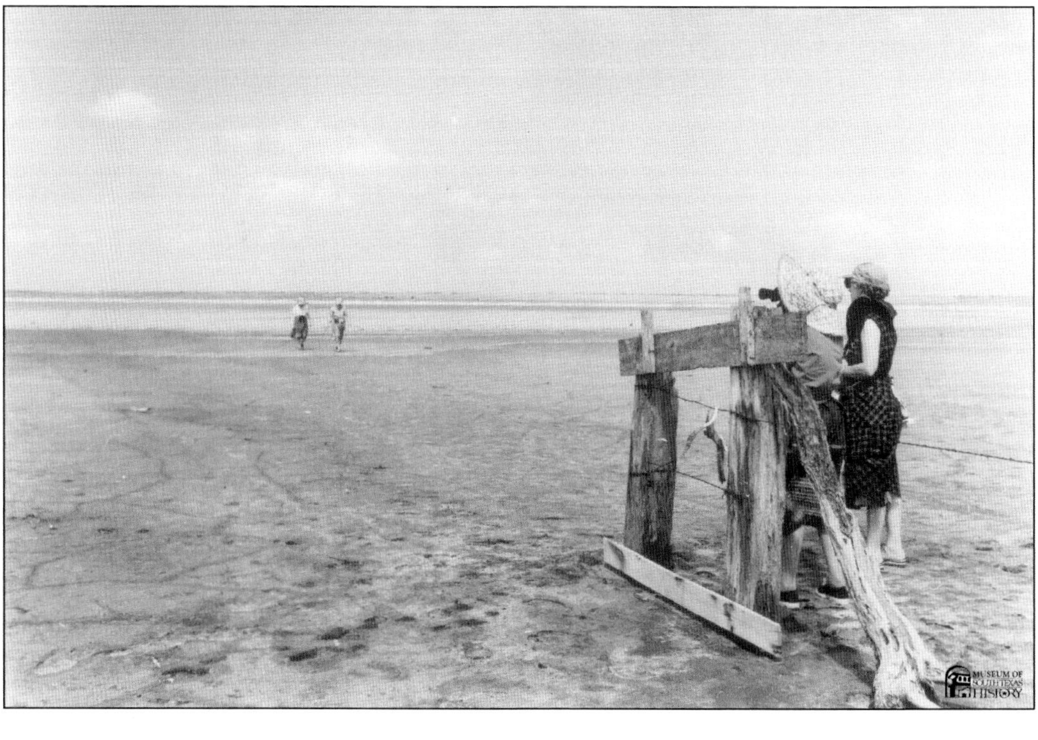

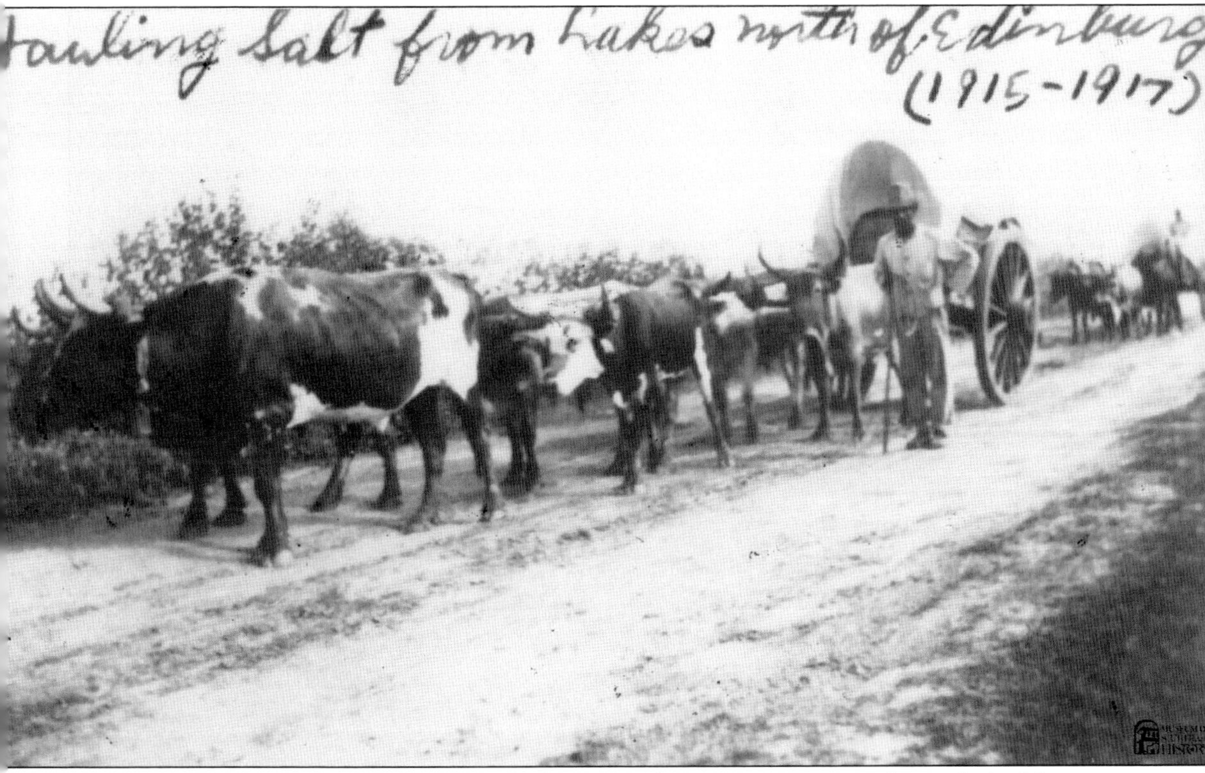

The salt in La Sal del Rey has been traded since prehistoric times, providing salt for Native Americans, Spanish explorers, and early settlers of the region. The lake is seven times saltier than the ocean. With purity at 99.0897 percent sodium chloride, it is second only to mines in Bavaria, Germany. The salt was transported as far away as Spain. The lake salt was free but entrepreneurs would charge 50¢ to dig and load the salt onto wagons. During the Civil War, salt was transported via camel caravans, each camel carrying 600 pounds. The caravans, however, proved too seductive to thieves, and the camel project was eventually abandoned because of the high theft rate. This photograph shows oxcarts being used to transport salt. (Courtesy of the Museum of South Texas History.)

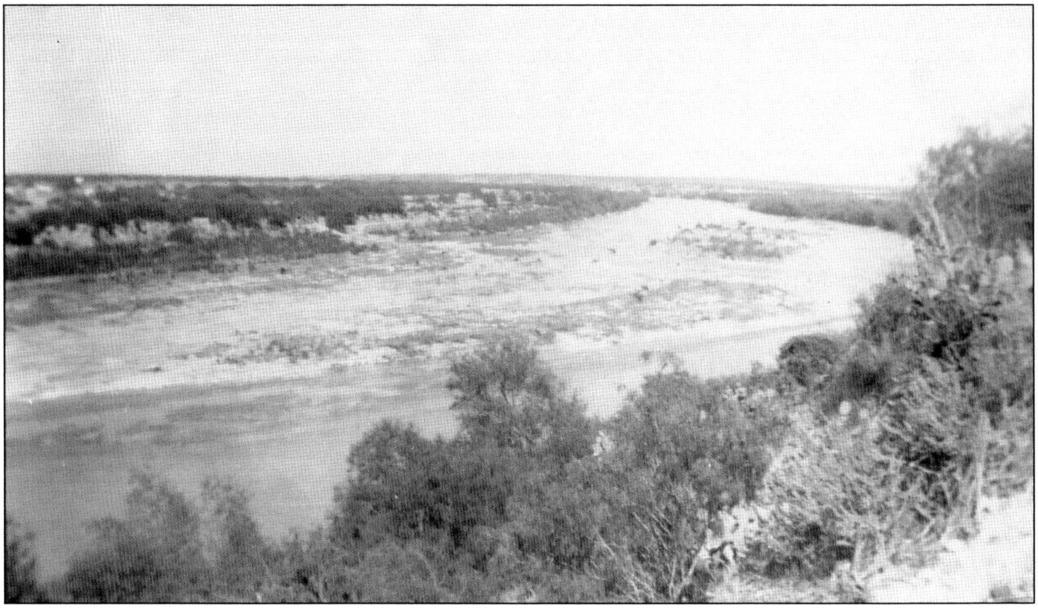

The waters of the Rio Grande ruled people's lives in the region until the river was tamed through a system of dams, levees, and floodways and direct access to the river was made no longer necessary because of a series of canals. Water was so imperative to early ranchers that the first land divisions were established to allow equal access to the river's banks. In the early 1900s, canals were built all along the river to pump the life-giving water to newly planted fields and farms. The same river that provided essential water to ranchers and farmers, however, could also destroy their homes when it flooded. When the river would flood, it could rise as many as five feet, leaving only the housetops to be seen in low areas. (Courtesy of The University of Texas–Pan American Library.)

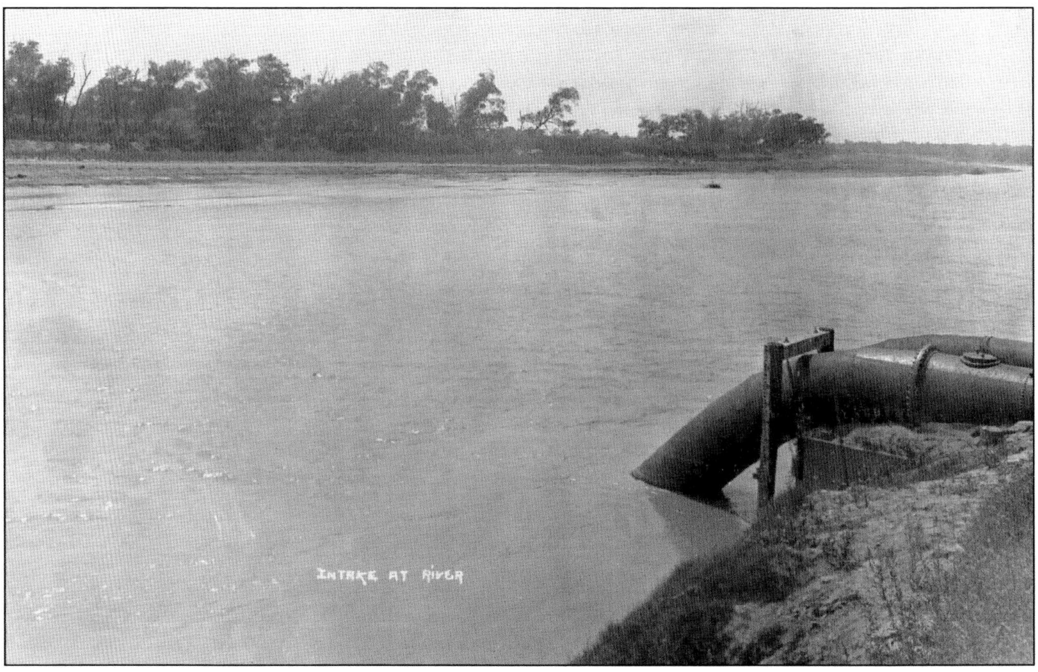

Flat boats and ferries were the sole means of getting between Hidalgo and Reynosa for many years until the first bridge was built in 1926. Ferries were so important that the very first order of business conducted by the county of Hidalgo was to issue licenses and set fees for ferries. Boats on the Rio Grande were typically flat bottom boats built for shallow banks and low waters in times of drought. The photograph on the right shows a typical flat-bottomed boat. What some may argue was also typical are the two smugglers caught in the photograph. John Peavey included the photograph in his scrapbook from his years in the US Border Patrol. The photograph below shows another boat on the Rio Grande. (Courtesy of The University of Texas–Pan American Library.)

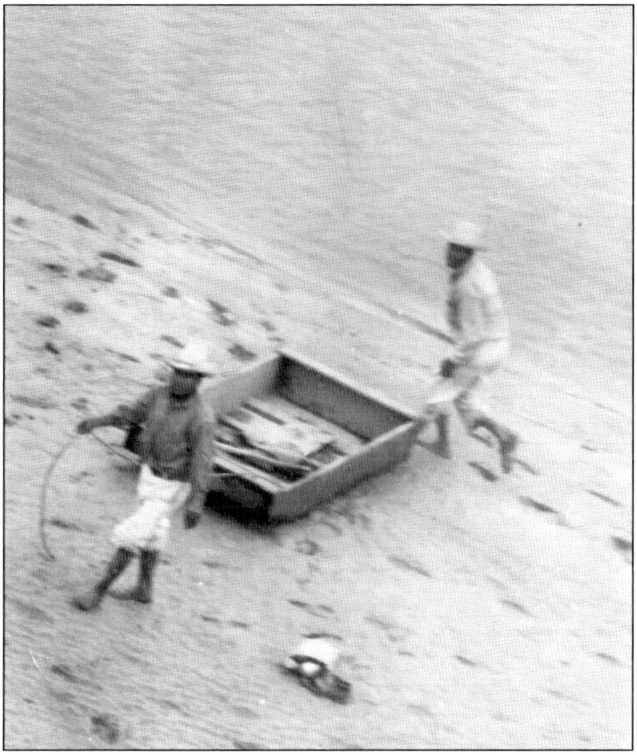

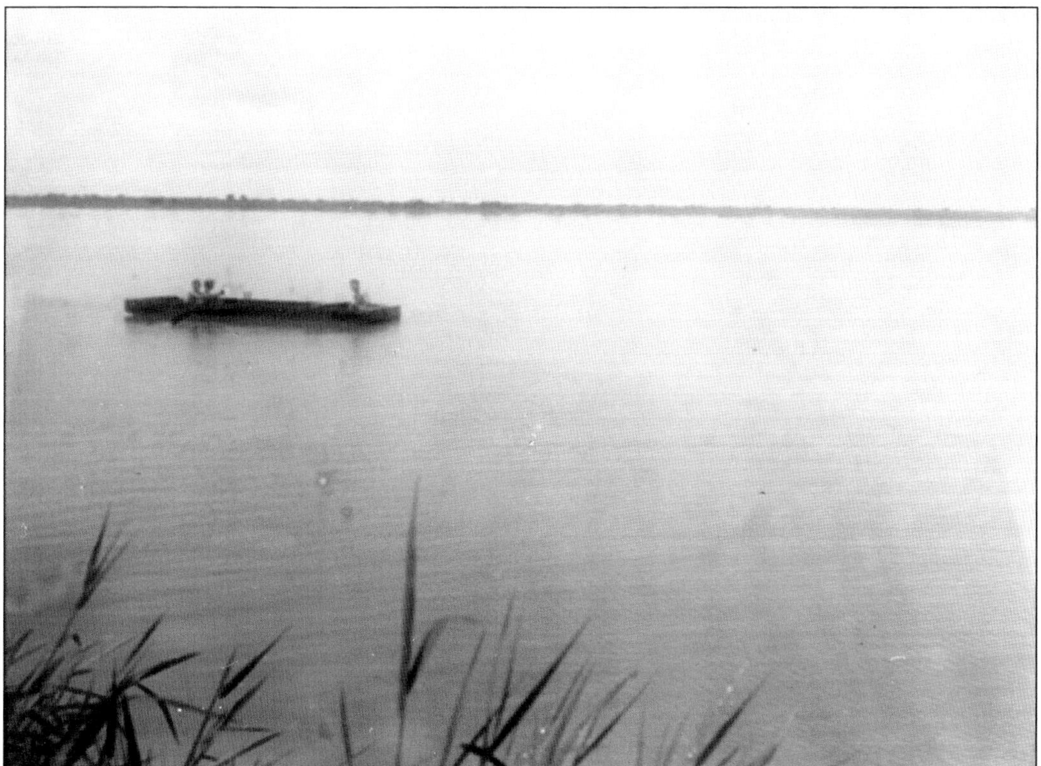

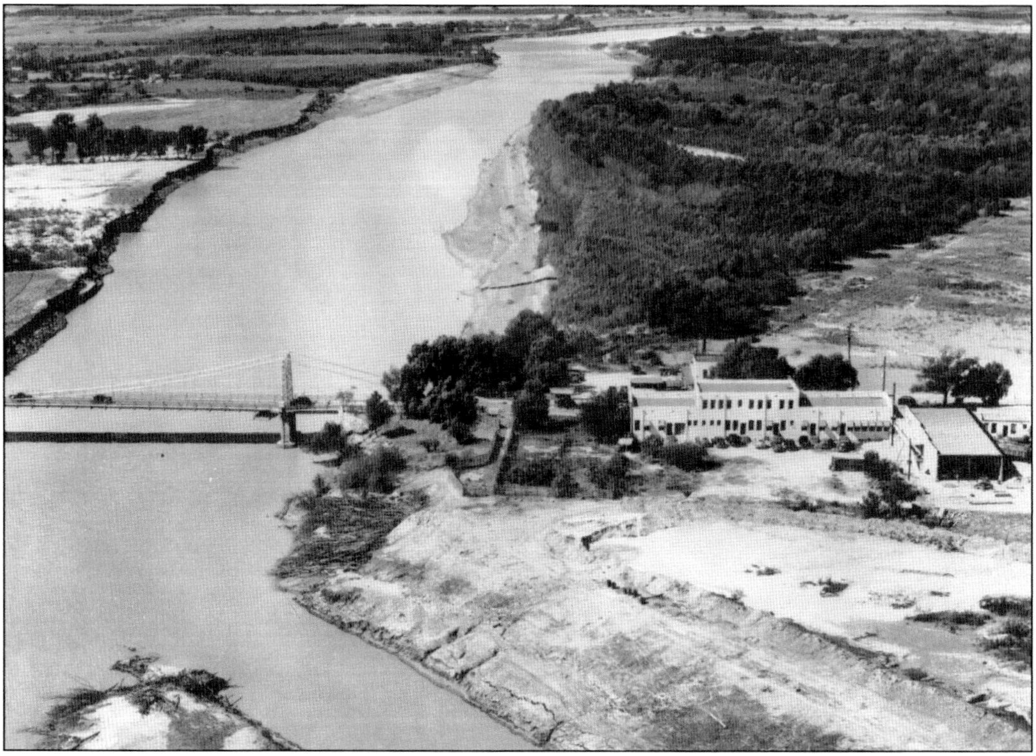

Travel between Hidalgo and Reynosa was a common and casual event before increased border security in the mid 1900s. For the first 150 years of settlement in the Valley, roads and train tracks on the southern side of the river were much better than those to the north. People wishing to travel from the town of Hidalgo to Brownsville often crossed the river via ferry to Reynosa, took the train to Matamoros, then crossed the river again to Brownsville. It wasn't until 1904 that a railroad was built in southern Texas and 1926 that an international toll suspension bridge was constructed between Hidalgo and Reynosa, as shown above. The bridge was destroyed by a hurricane in 1933 as shown below. (Courtesy of The University of Texas–Pan American Library.)

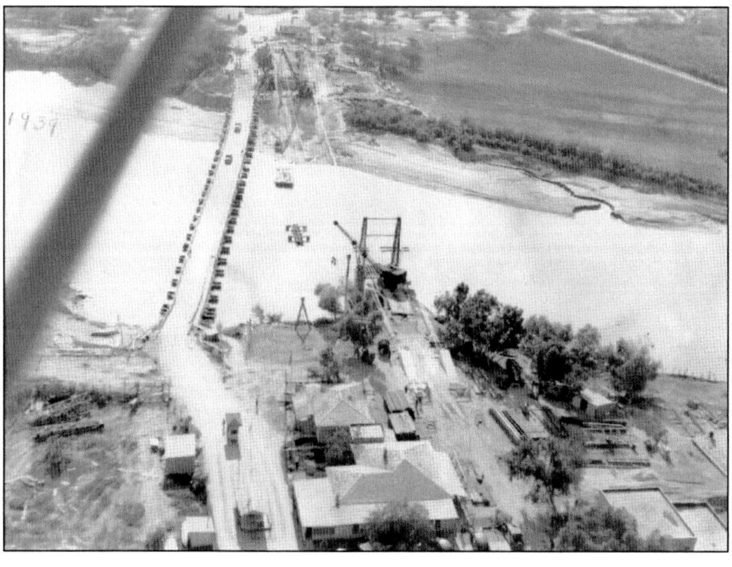

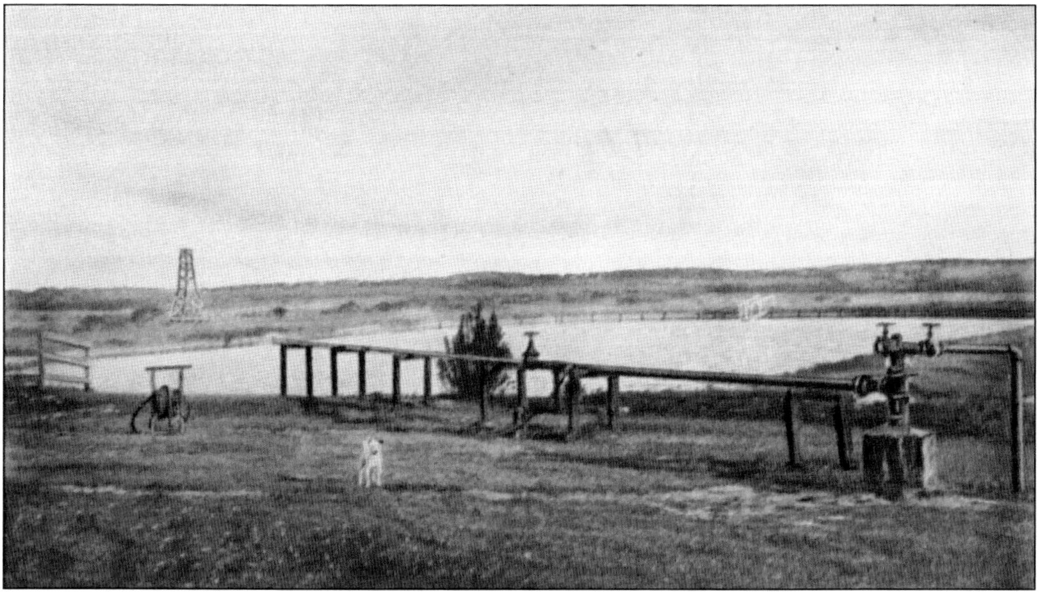

Two major events changed this region from ranching to farming country—the development of ways to bring water to crops and the building of the railroad. Artesian wells were one method used to bring water to crops, as shown above. The advantage of artesian wells is that the water is pushed up under natural pressure and does not require a mechanical pump. The other, more popular method of bringing water to the farms in South Texas was the building of canals, as shown below in a photograph of the Valley Reservoir Canal Company with, from left to right, surveyor Henry P. Griffen, chief engineer Colonel Warren, sponsor and manager D.B. Chapin, director W.F. Sprague, and four laborers. (Above, courtesy of The University of Texas–Pan American Library; below, courtesy of the Museum of South Texas History.)

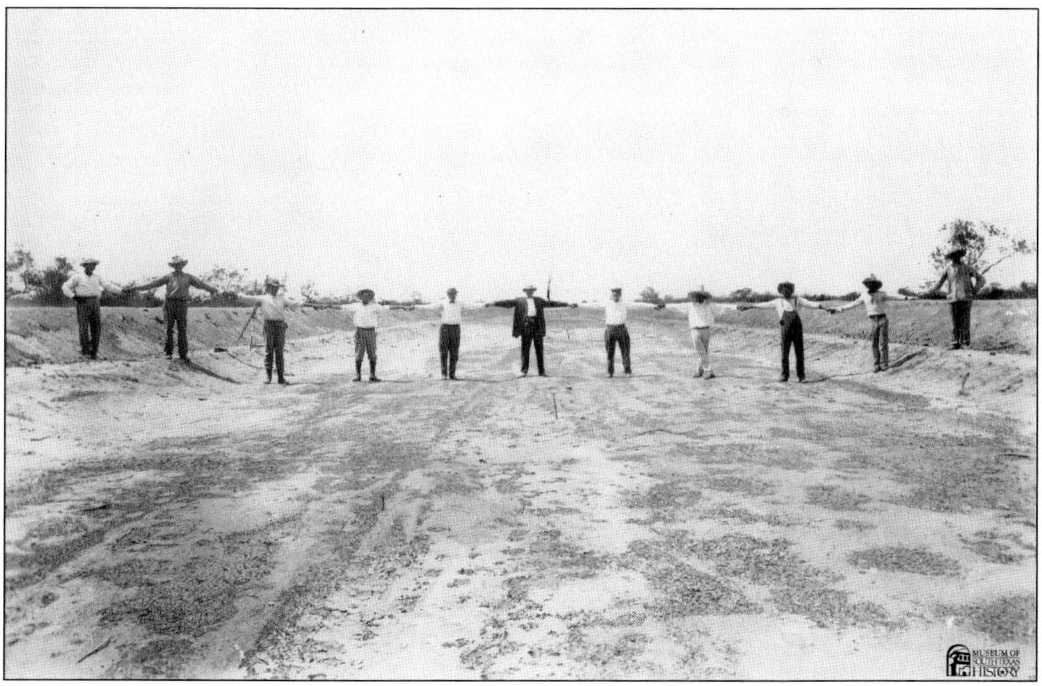

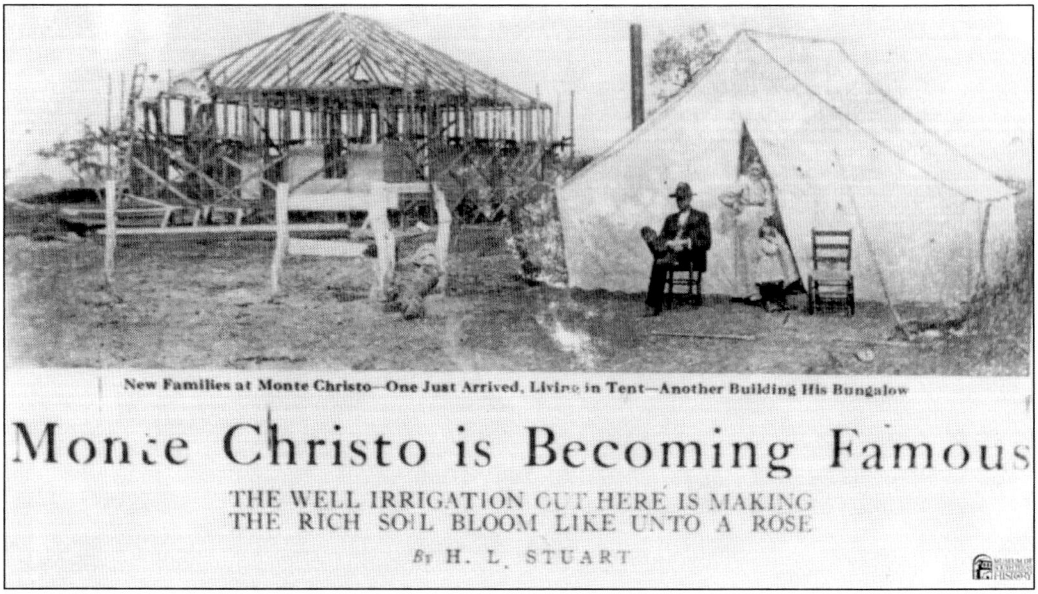
New Families at Monte Christo—One Just Arrived, Living in Tent—Another Building His Bungalow

Monte Christo is Becoming Famous

THE WELL IRRIGATION OUT HERE IS MAKING
THE RICH SOIL BLOOM LIKE UNTO A ROSE

By H. L. STUART

The first large scale attempt in the Valley of using water from wells for irrigation occurred in Monte Christo, "Christ in the Brush." Monte Christo was north of Mission and west of Edinburg and today is no more than a ghost town. The founders of Monte Christo, the Melado Land Company, began promoting it as "The Garden Spot of the United States" in 1910. They hired Otto Woods to manage the town site, dig four artesian wells and the reservoir, and build concrete irrigation pipes. Within a few years, the town had grown to support a train station, a school, a church with a visiting preacher, a post office, and nine businesses including two hotels. The photograph below shows Otto Woods's home in Monte Christo. (Courtesy of the Museum of South Texas History.)

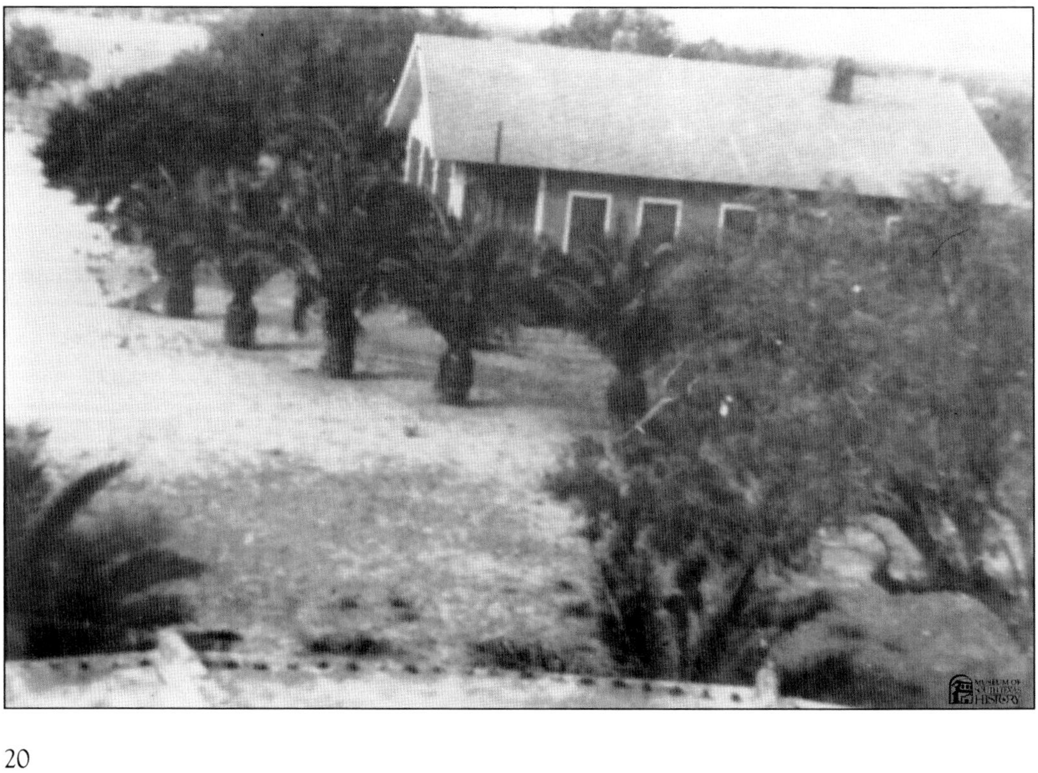

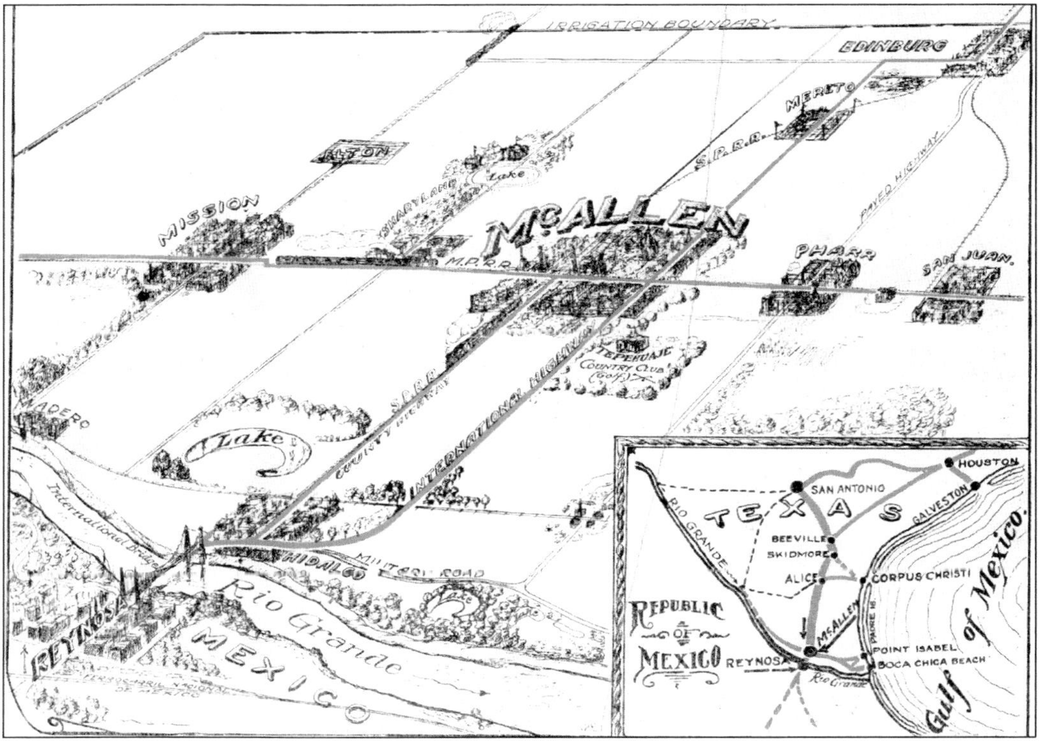

Monte Christo's heyday lasted only a few years. By 1934, the town had disappeared to be covered with sage, cactus, and mesquite. The town's relative isolation is apparent on the map above and is the major reason it became a ghost town. The wells began drying up, and with its location above the "irrigation boundary," it was difficult to get enough water to irrigate the crops. In addition, during the border raids of 1915–1916, there were increasing threats of bandits. Although there were no actual bandit raids in Monte Christo itself, bandits, similar to those in the photograph below, often rode past. The distance between Monte Christo and neighboring towns left its inhabitants feeling isolated enough to scare many of them away. (Courtesy of The University of Texas–Pan American Library.)

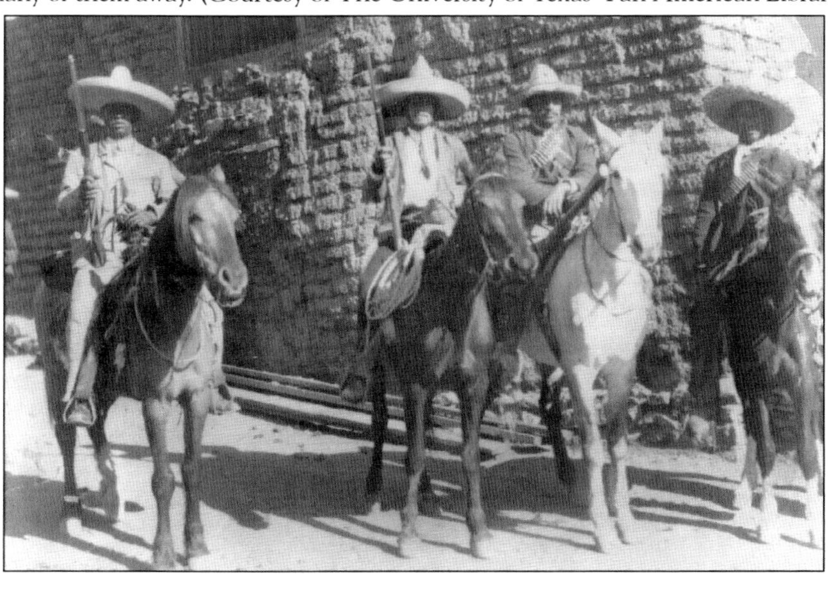

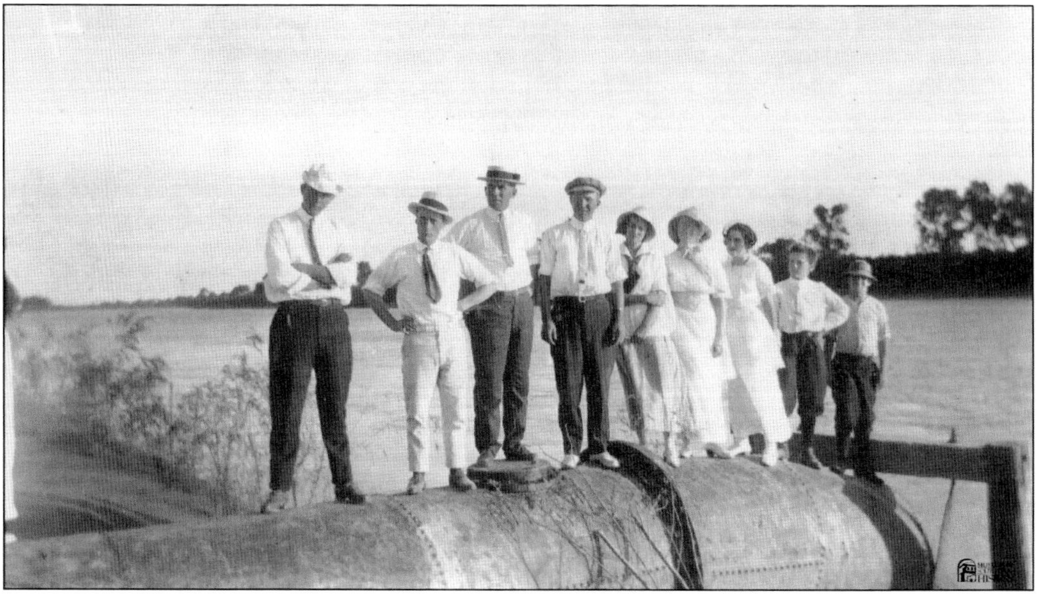

The construction of canals and irrigation systems was second only to the coming of the railroad in changing the face of the Valley. Canals had advantages over wells—they did not dry up, nor did the water turn salty. As long as the pumps were working and there was water in the river, they could supply water to the farms. In 1907, the Valley Reservoir and Canal Co., represented by John Closner and W.S. Dougherty, filed an application to supply water to the Edinburg area. As the company grew it was eventually able to supply water to 30,000 acres. Fred Warren, chief engineer, oversaw the filling of this main lateral canal in 1913. (Courtesy of the Museum of South Texas History.)

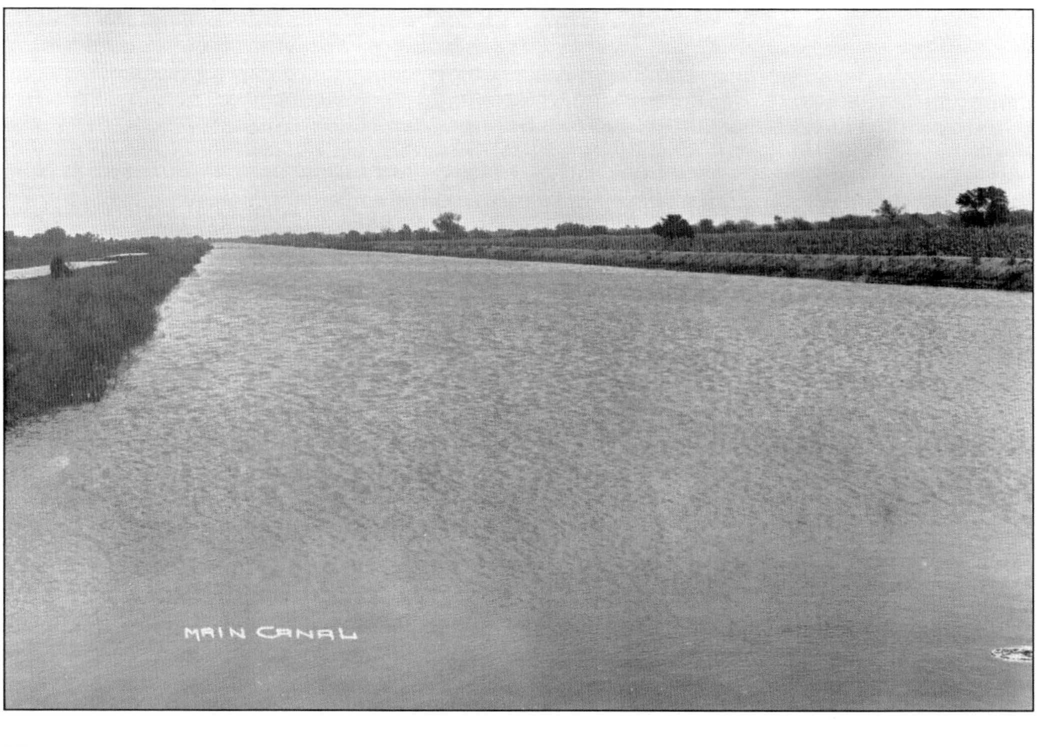

It is hardly surprising that this region became known as the "Magic Valley." The Rio Grande Delta sits on top of rich alluvial soil, is supplied with water by the Rio Grande via irrigation canals, and has a year-round growing season. The lands around Edinburg were typical of the region, and could support a large and rich variety of agricultural products including citrus, wheat and corn, vegetables, and fruits as well as livestock such as cattle, hogs, and poultry. The photographs on this page are typical agricultural shots designed to show prospective landowners the abundance and potential success of farmland. (Courtesy of The University of Texas–Pan American Library.)

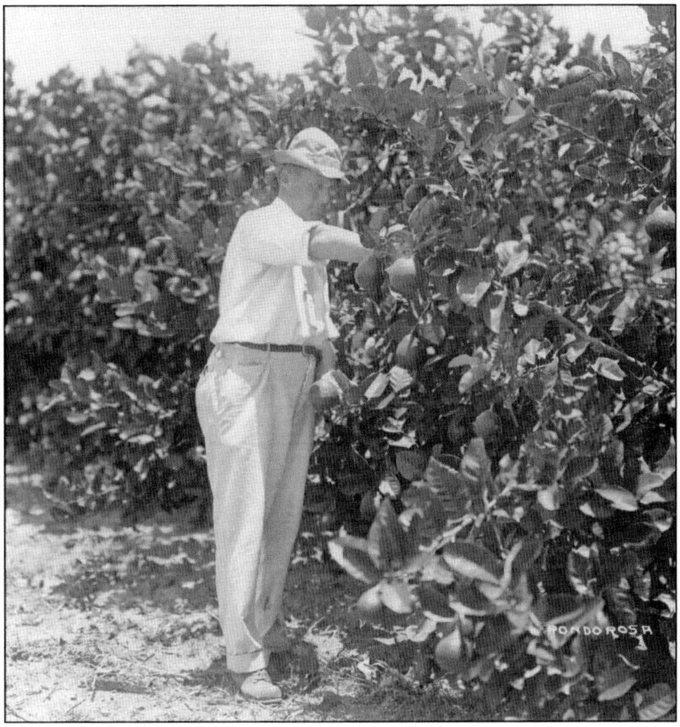

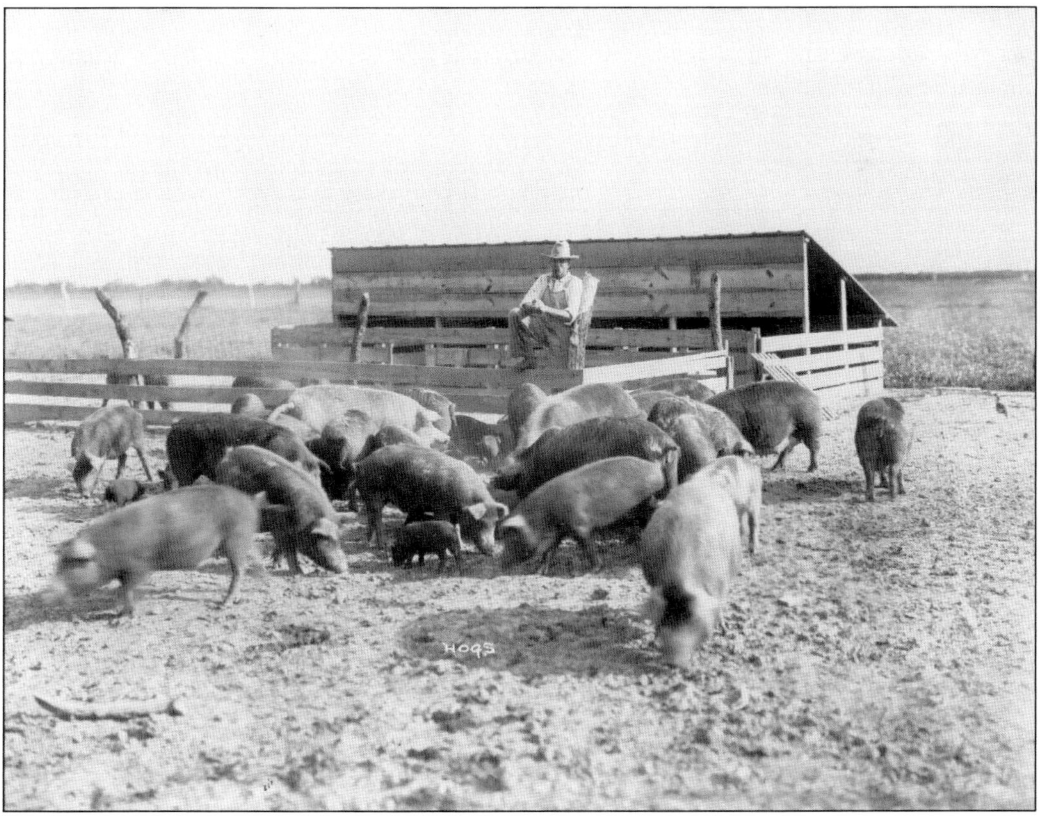

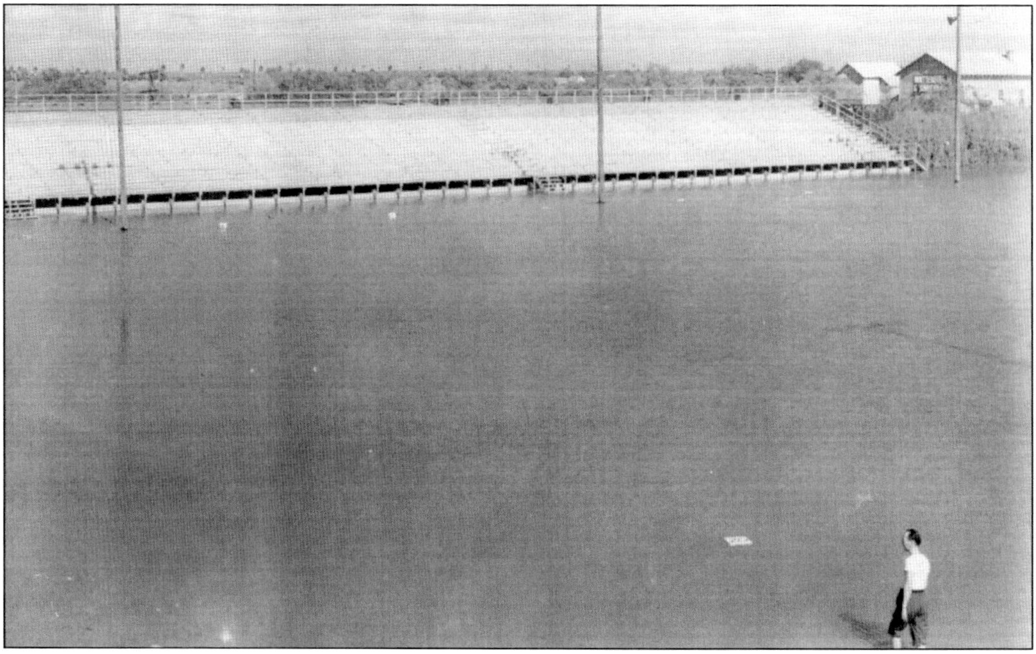

Despite its distance from the river, Edinburg still flooded. March is historically the driest month of the year for the Lower Rio Grande Valley. March 1941 defied the odds, however, and delivered a flood. The picture above shows a young man walking in water up to his shins on the Edinburg High School football field. A 20-yard-line marker is floating on the water in front of him. The photograph below shows the courthouse looking southeast from Sam Houston School. The sign of the Edinburg Hotel is just visible above the brick building on the right. (Courtesy of the Edinburg Consolidated Independent School District.)

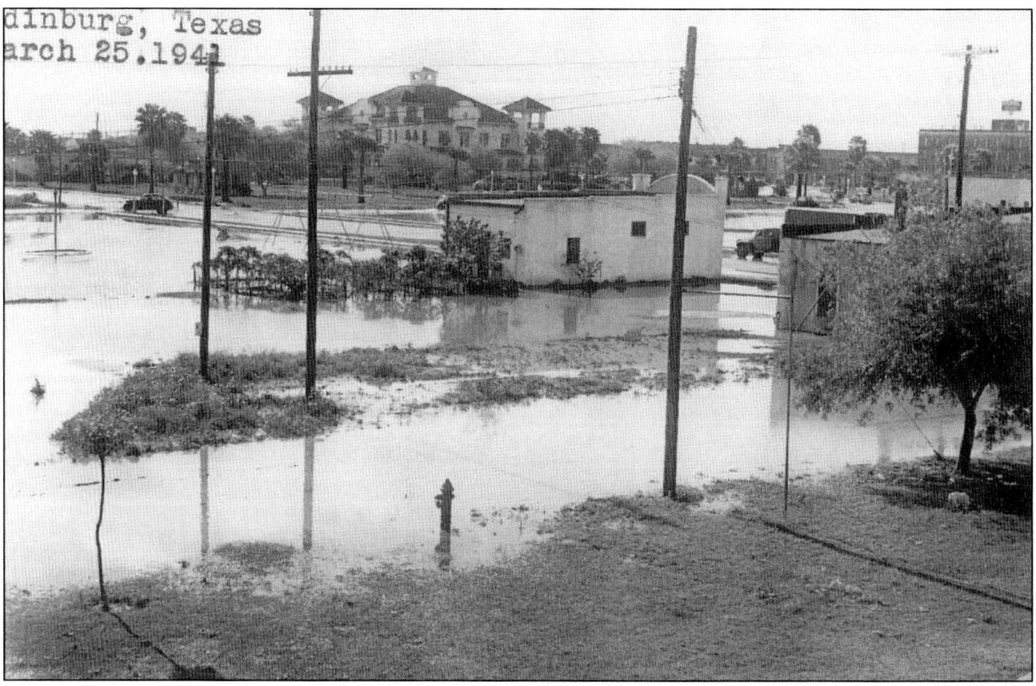

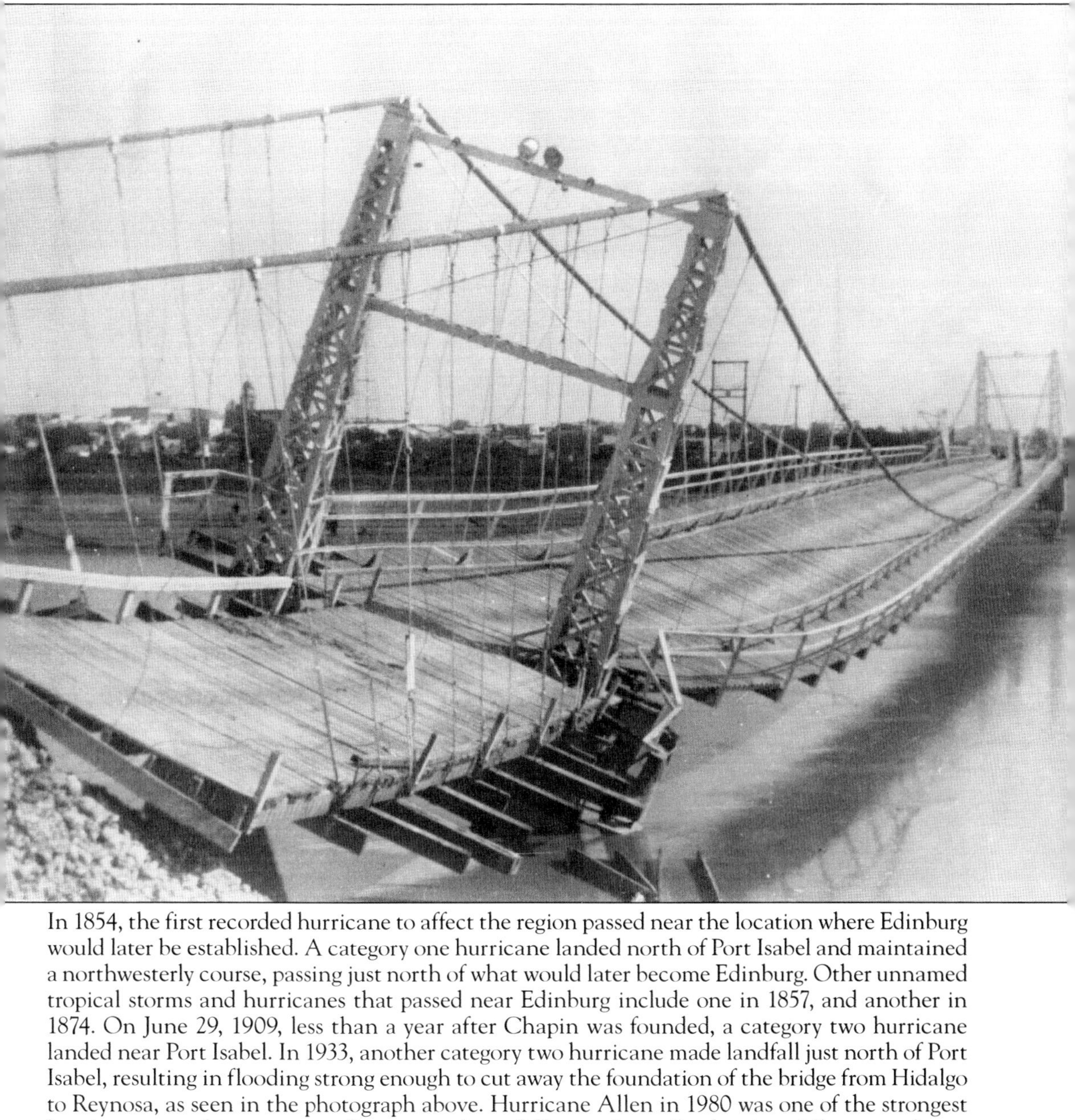

In 1854, the first recorded hurricane to affect the region passed near the location where Edinburg would later be established. A category one hurricane landed north of Port Isabel and maintained a northwesterly course, passing just north of what would later become Edinburg. Other unnamed tropical storms and hurricanes that passed near Edinburg include one in 1857, and another in 1874. On June 29, 1909, less than a year after Chapin was founded, a category two hurricane landed near Port Isabel. In 1933, another category two hurricane made landfall just north of Port Isabel, resulting in flooding strong enough to cut away the foundation of the bridge from Hidalgo to Reynosa, as seen in the photograph above. Hurricane Allen in 1980 was one of the strongest hurricanes, reaching category five status three different times. By the time Allen passed over Port Isabel, it had weakened to a category three, still a very strong storm. The latest storm was Hurricane Dolly in 2008, which made landfall north of Port Isabel as a category one hurricane. (Courtesy of The University of Texas–Pan American.)

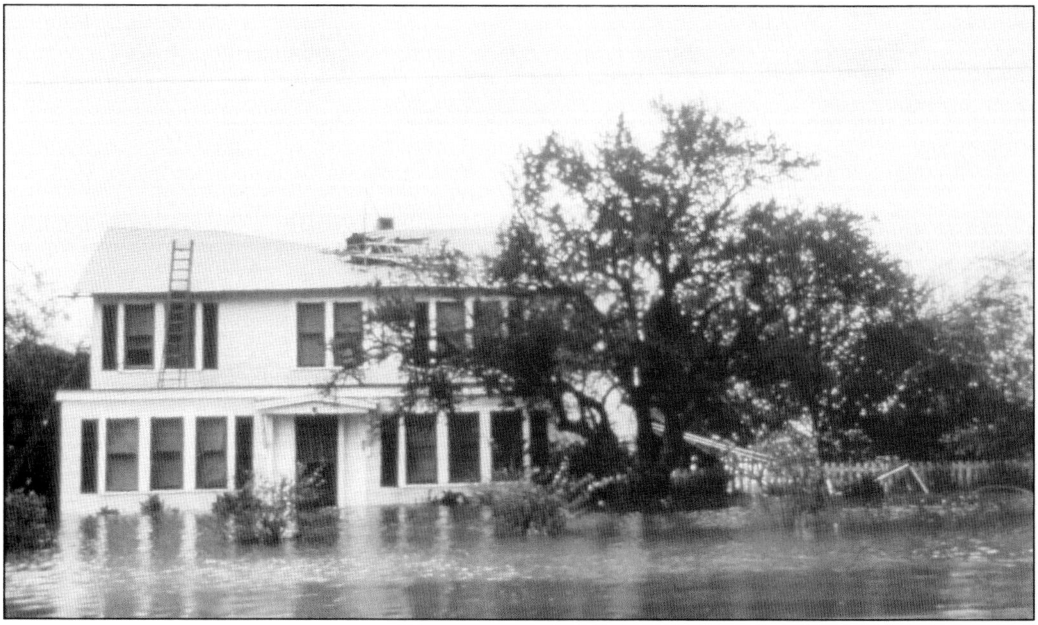

Hurricane Beulah is the most famous hurricane of the Valley and the third largest hurricane of the 1900s. Beulah made landfall early on the morning of September 20, 1967. Its name has been retired and will never be used for another hurricane. Over the Gulf of Mexico, it reached category five, although by the time it made landfall it had weakened to a category three with winds of 136 miles per hour. The storm traveled north to Duval County, where it turned around and headed south again, crossing the Rio Grande a day later. The photographs on this page show a house on Highway 281 between Edinburg and Pharr. (Courtesy of The University of Texas–Pan American Library.)

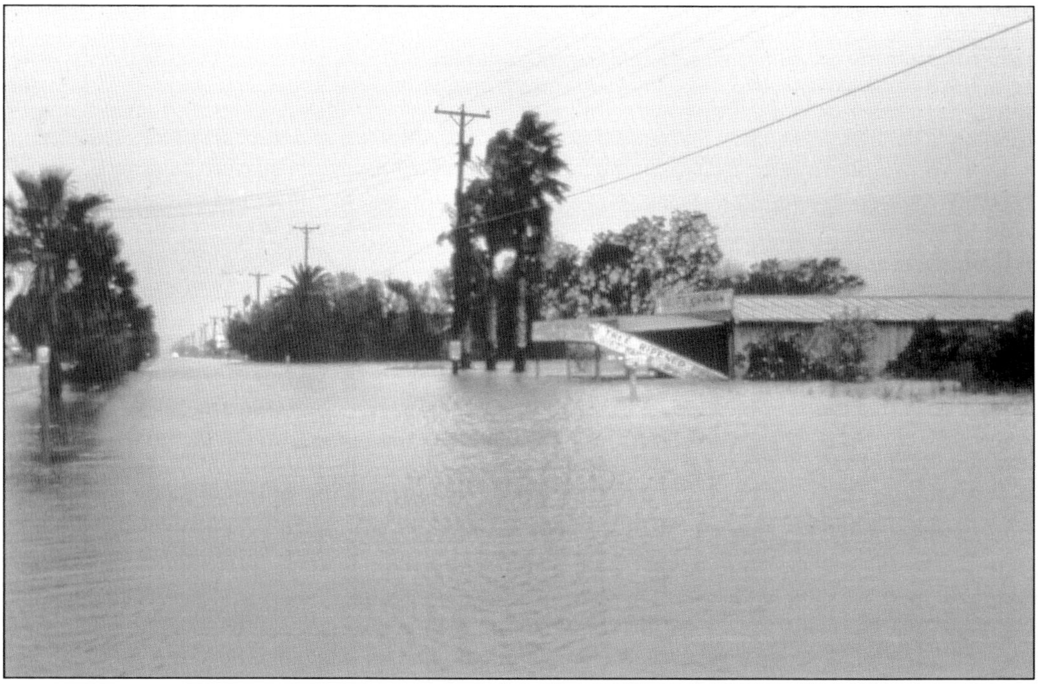

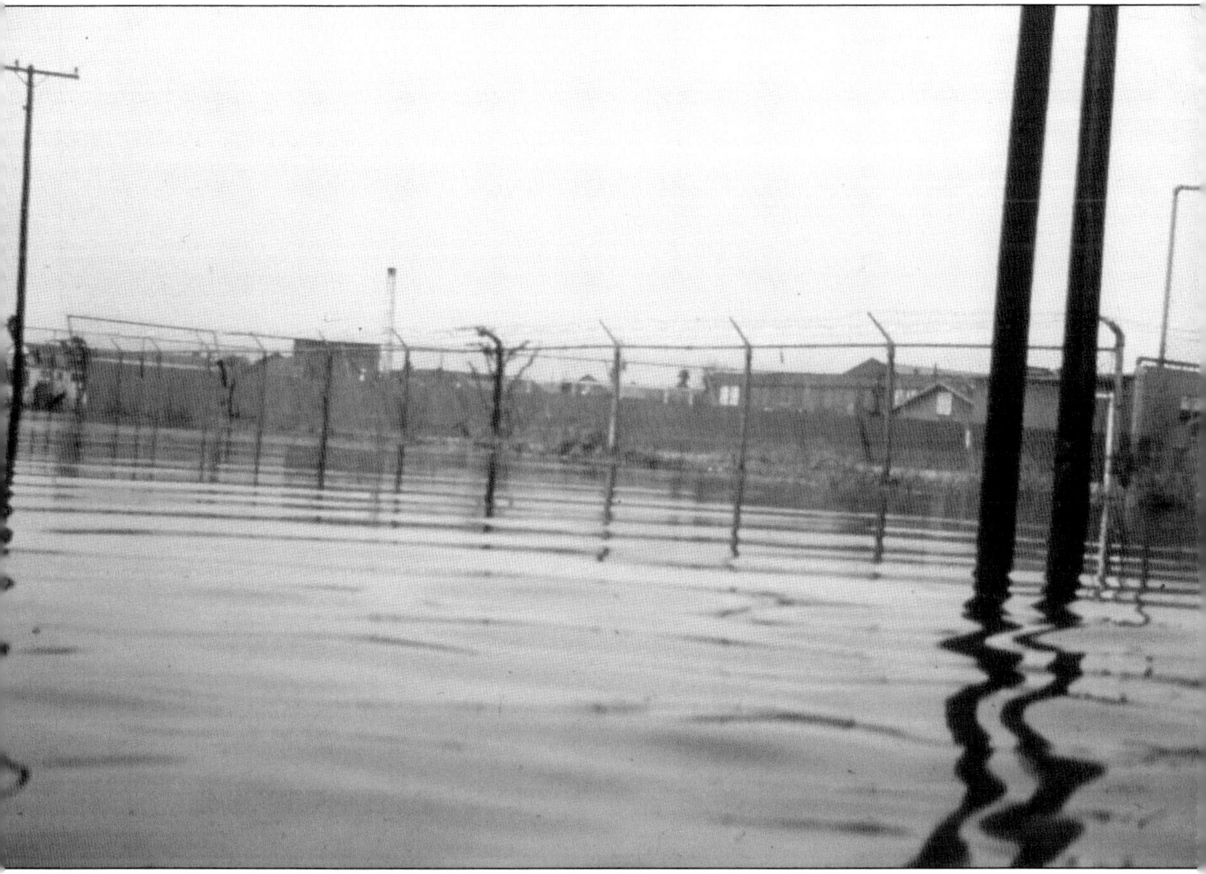

Winds, tornadoes, and, most significantly, flooding from Hurricane Beulah and the resulting loss of power made this hurricane the most damaging of the region. Beulah spawned a record number of 115 tornadoes. The slow moving storm dumped over 25 inches of water in the area, causing the most damage. Although other communities closer to the river were hit worse than Edinburg, there was still considerable flooding. On September 28, 1967, Pres. Lyndon B. Johnson declared 24 counties in South Texas disaster areas. The photographs on this and the subsequent page show the North Junior High School on Lovett Street. (Courtesy of The University of Texas–Pan American Library.)

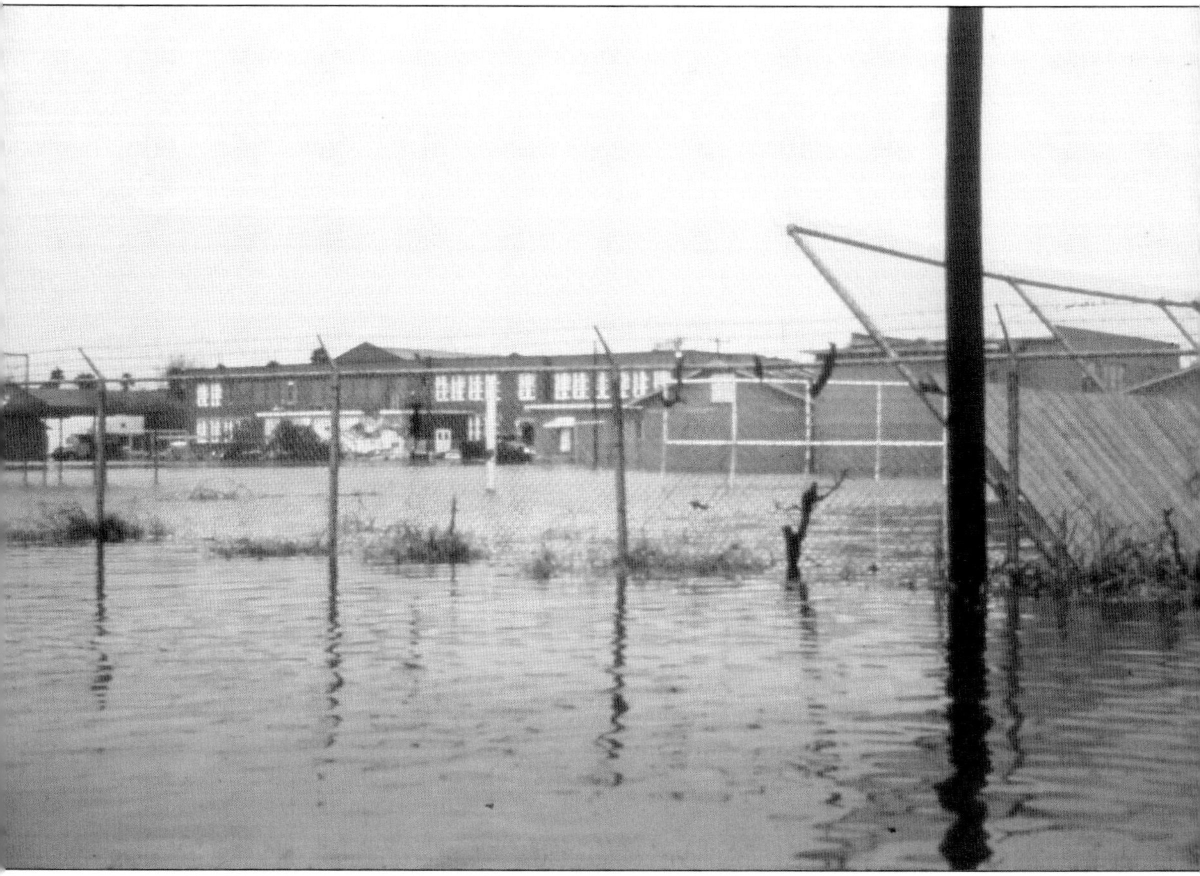

This image shows flooding at the North Junior High School on Lovett Street. (Courtesy of The University of Texas–Pan American Library.)

Two

The County Seat
Three Locations, Four Names, Five Courthouses

In 1852, 2,343 square miles were taken out of Starr and Cameron Counties to create the county of Hidalgo, the seventh-largest county in Texas. "Hidalgo" was chosen as the county name to honor Miguel Hidalgo y Castillo, the Father of Mexican Independence. A town on the river by the name of Edinburgh, Texas was selected as the county seat. In 1885, the name of the county seat was changed to Hidalgo to match the name of the county. The original county seat only existed 34 years before it was washed away by floods in 1886, prompting a move to its second location on higher ground two miles north of the river. There a second courthouse was constructed, an impressive two story brick building. By 1908, the riverbed had again changed its course closer to the courthouse, prompting another move. This time, the county leaders scouted for lands far away from the danger of floods. They found a place north of McAllen, a site in the brush, a town with no buildings named Chapin after county judge D.B. Chapin. An election was held in 1908 to select Chapin as the next county seat. Records were transported overnight to the new location and were stored in tents until a brick vault and the county's third courthouse, a quickly constructed wooden building, was built. The voters quickly approved a new permanent courthouse in Chapin, and two years later in 1910, courthouse number four was completed. One year later, D.B. Chapin, for whom the town was named, found himself on trial for murder, and the people of Hidalgo County decided to change the name of the county seat yet again. In 1911, the town's name reverted to its former name of Edinburg, this time minus the final h. In 1954, the county had grown so fast that the 1910 courthouse was no longer large enough to conduct business. The voters once again approved another building, and thus courthouse number five was constructed next to the 1910 courthouse.

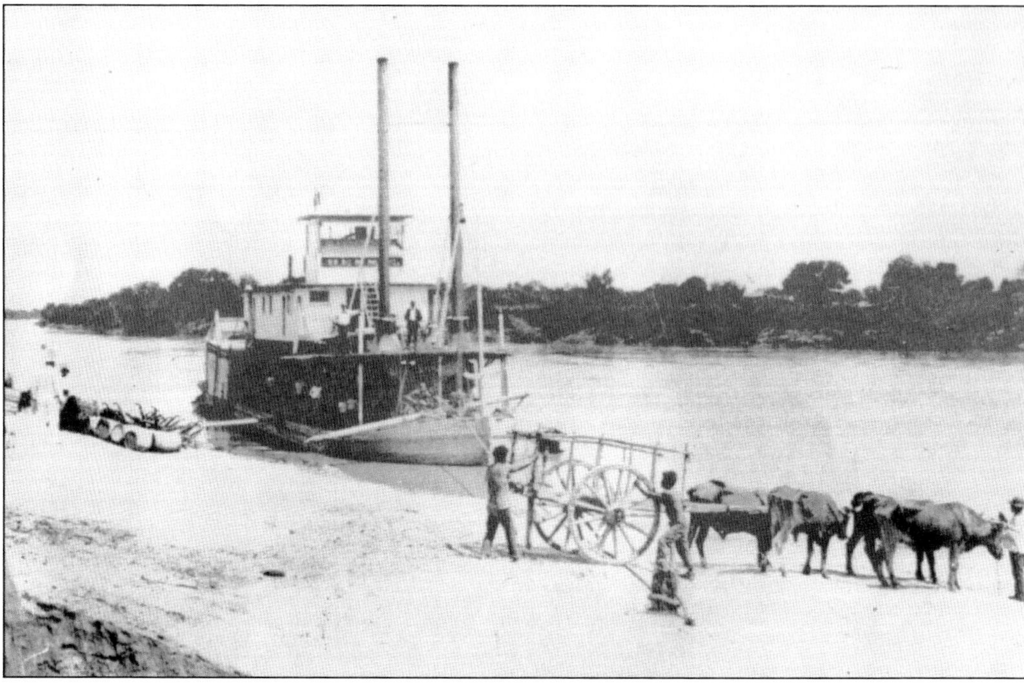

E.D. Smith named Edinburgh, Texas, (later renamed Hidalgo) after the Scottish birthplace of John Young, his business partner. Young, Smith, and a third partner, James McAllen, operated a trading store in Edinburgh, and would have relied heavily upon the Steamboat *Bessie* to transport goods to and from the settlements along the Rio Grande. The steamboats transported products from the ranches and the salt from Sal del Rey to Matamoros where they would be picked up by ocean-going clipper and shipped on to Europe. The steamboats would have brought hardware, guns, and foodstuffs to the ranchers and townspeople, and in return would have taken hides, bones, wild mustangs, cotton, sugar, and salt. The steamboats would stop once or twice a week to unload and load their freight.

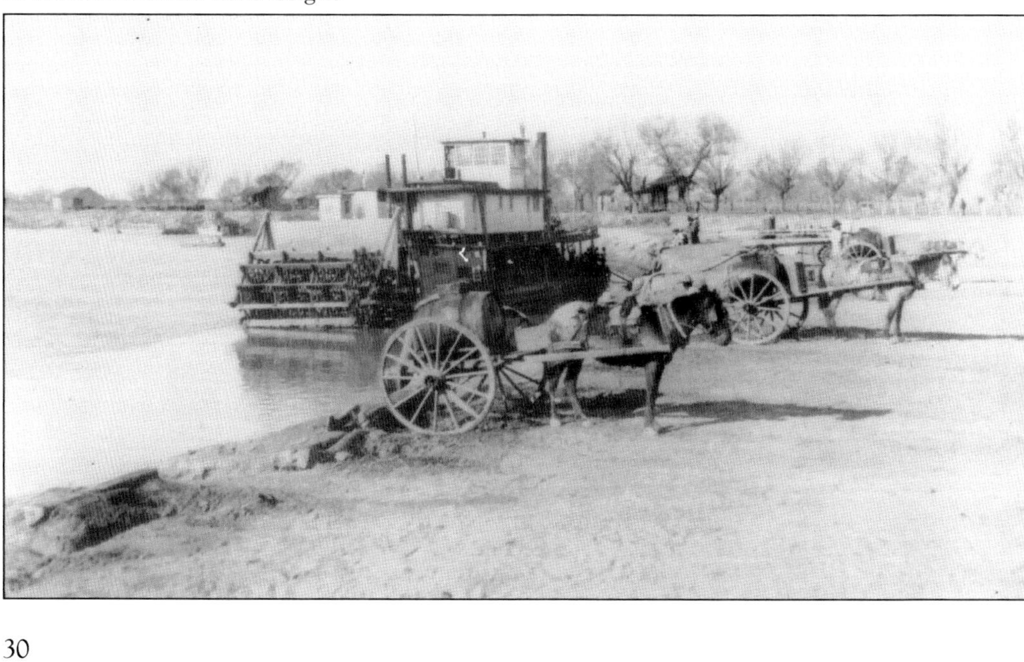

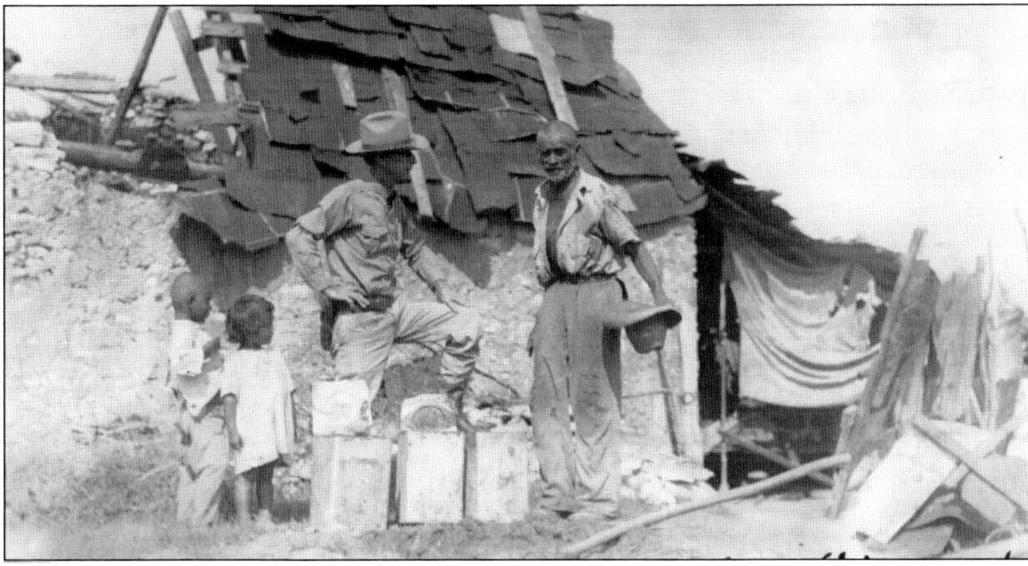

The original town of Edinburgh would have had several jacals serving as homes for the town's residents. Jacals were built from readily available materials and could be found all along the Valley. In fact, the lack of numerous jacals in the new town of Hidalgo was remarked upon in the book *Twin Cities of the Border*, written in 1893. The book attributes the flood, which had washed away the original town, to have also washed away "unsightly buildings of all descriptions." *Jacal* was the Mexican word for hut, borrowed from the Nahuatl word *xacalli*. (Courtesy of The University of Texas–Pan American Library.)

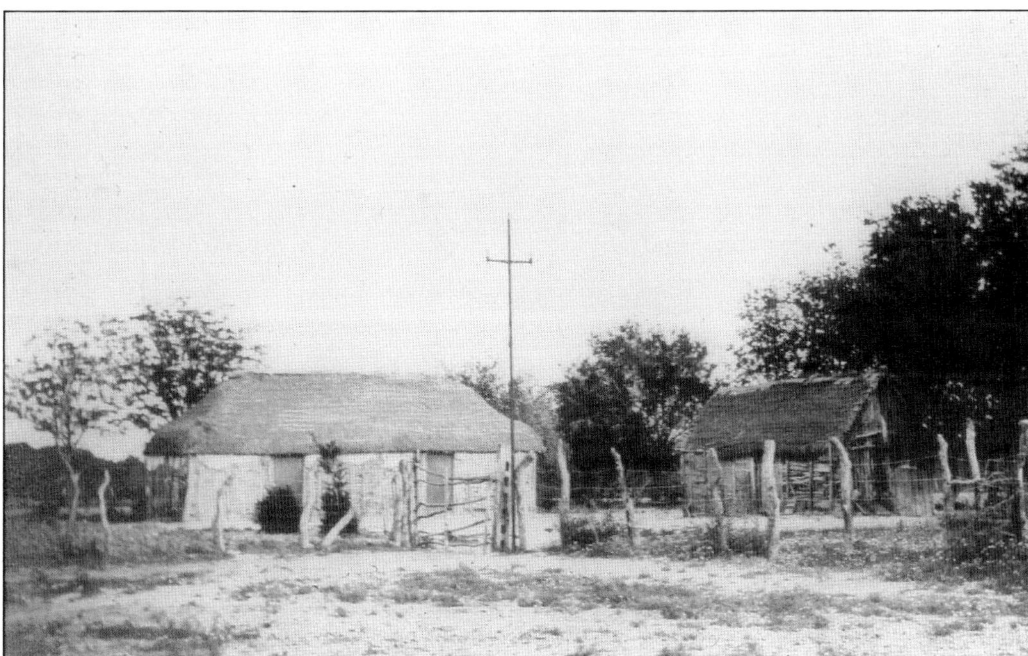

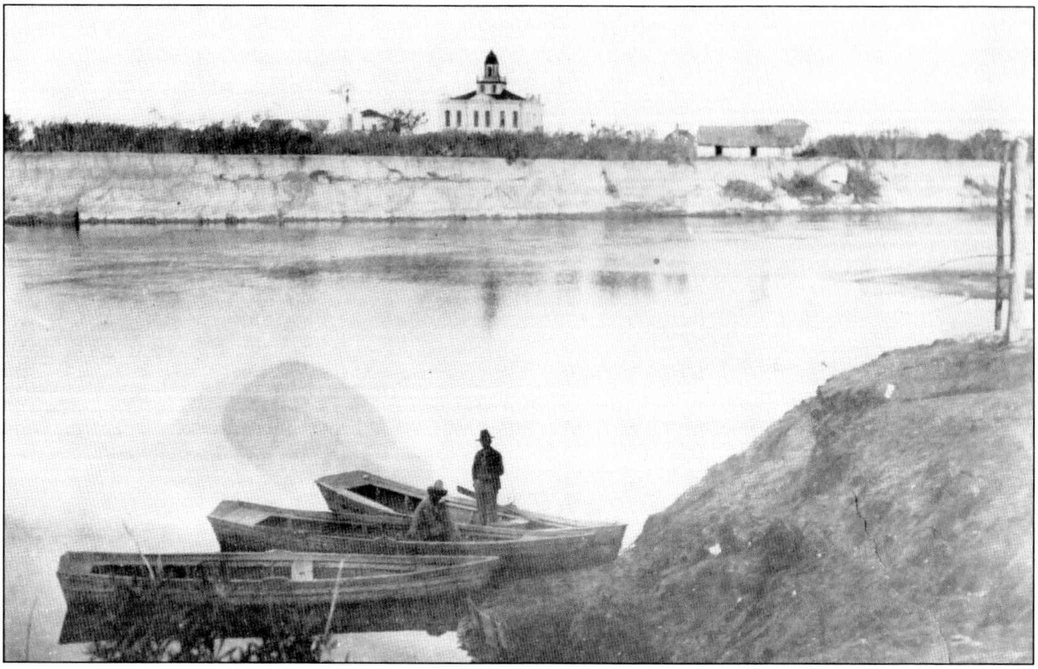

When the second Hidalgo Courthouse was built in the new town of Hidalgo, the largest town nearby was Reynosa. In 1893, Hidalgo's population numbered 389 according to *Twin Cities of the Border.* The photographs on this page were both taken from the southern bank by Reynosa in the early 1900s. Boats such as the ones in the photograph above were still the only way to get from Hidalgo to Reynosa. In both photographs the courthouse dominates the landscape even from a distance. The town site was selected specifically to reduce the risk of flooding; nevertheless, on August 10, 1887, the court ordered a levee to be erected to protect the courthouse from encroachment of the river. (Above, courtesy of The University of Texas–Pan American Library; below, courtesy of the Museum of South Texas History.)

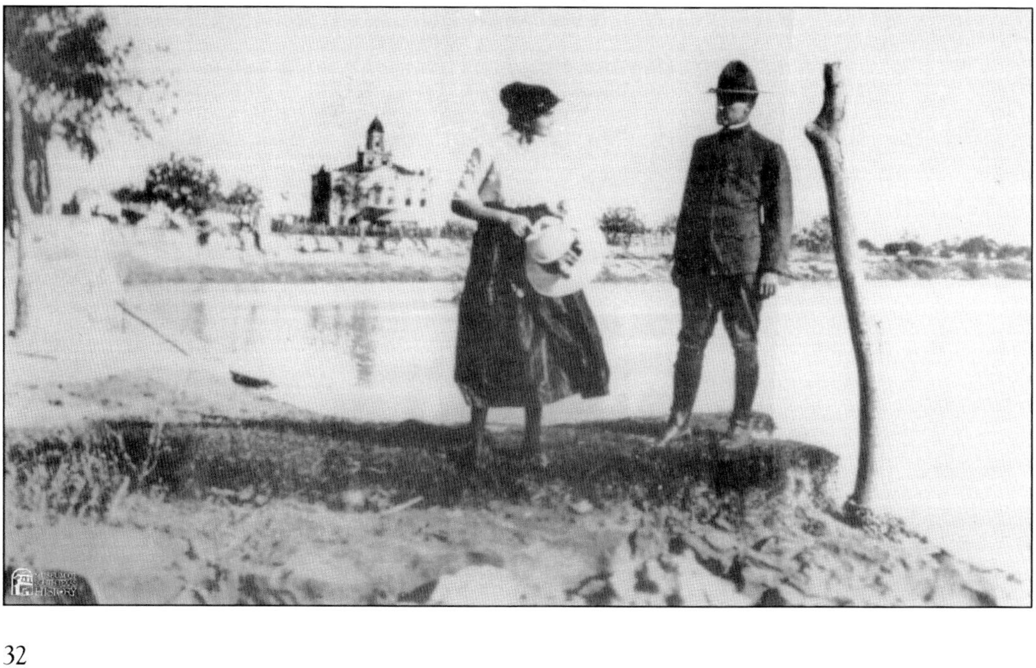

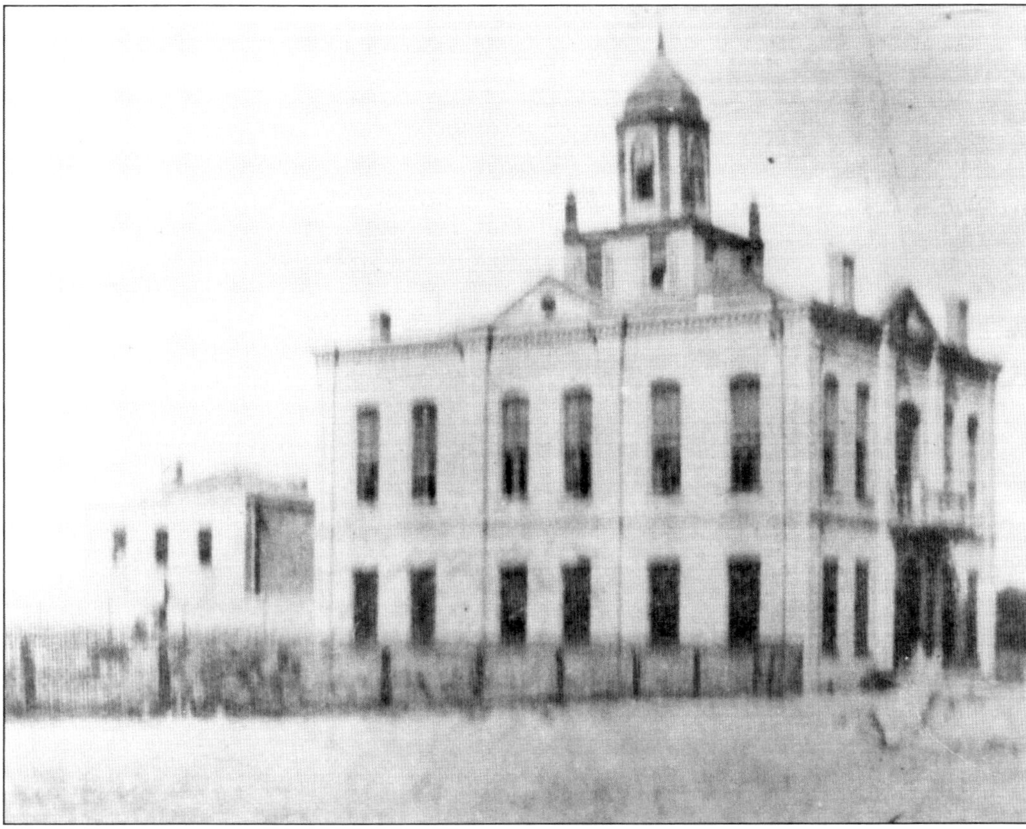

The second courthouse constructed in 1886 was a two-story brick building with a cupola, large windows and doors, and large interior rooms finished with hard wood floors. The ground floor held the offices of the sheriff, the county judge, the tax collector, and the county clerk. The second floor held the district court room and court offices. The one story jail was built to the west and was large enough to hold 25 prisoners. The courthouse was built for $14,000 and the jail was built for $6,000 in 1886. Around 1918 the courthouse building burned down and was later renovated as a one-story building.

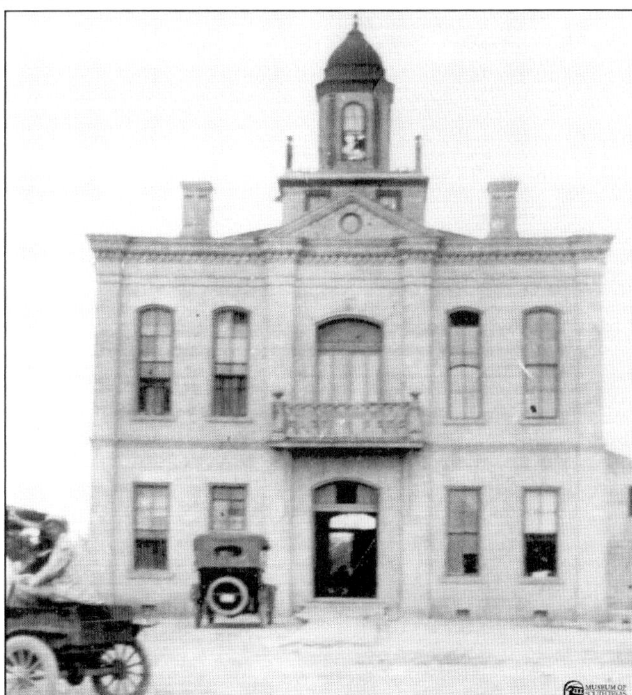

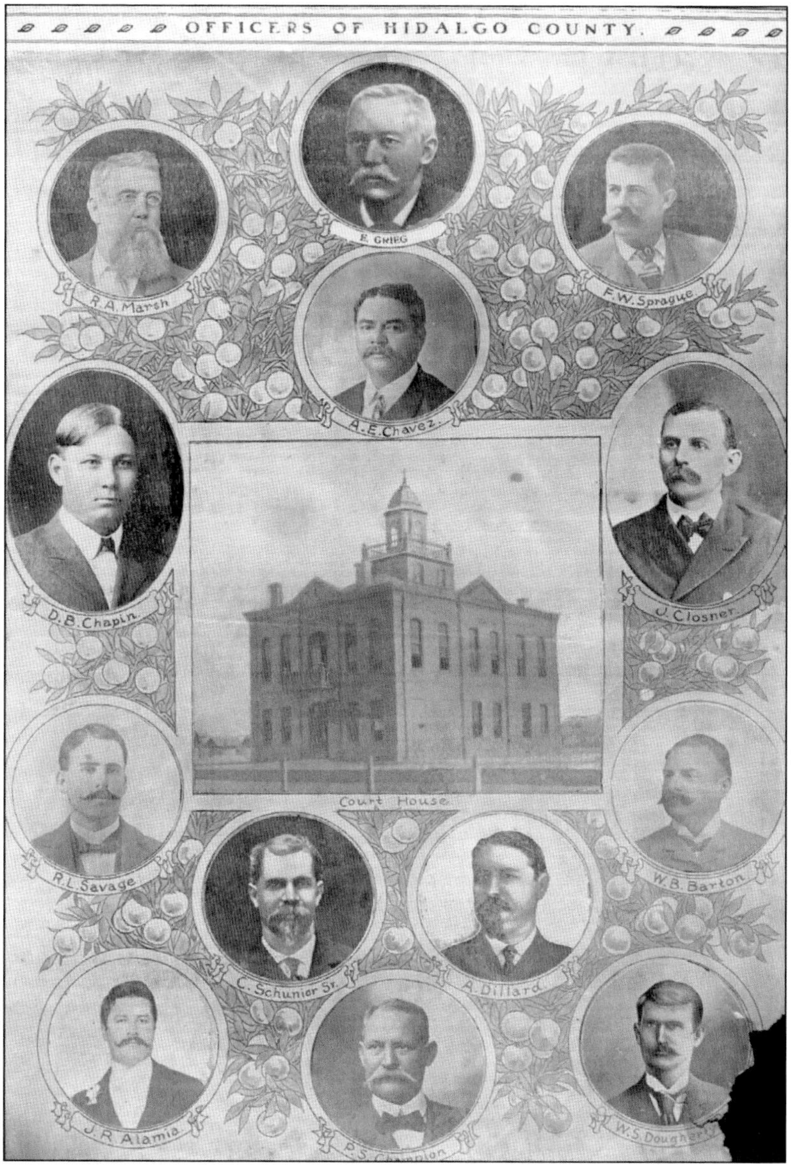

Early county officers are shown around the 1886 courthouse on this sheet held by the University of Texas–Pan American Library. Among those pictured are Richard Alvis Marsh, who was a judge and superintendent of the school; E. Grieg; William F. Sprague, county commissioner and one of the original founders of Chapin/Edinburg; Andres. E. Chavez, county clerk; Dennis Bangs Chapin, judge and the man for whom the town of Chapin (later Edinburg) was named; John Closner, county sheriff; R.L. Savage, county commissioner; Charles Schunior Sr., county commissioner; A. Dillard; Joe R. Alamia, tax assessor and collector; Peter. S. Champion; and William S. Dougherty, Hidalgo county judge. These men and others remained influential, such as Alex Champion, who was also a county commissioner, and the Dougherty family, including James, Edward, and Marcellus. The town founders also honored these names as they named their streets. Several of the east-west streets were named after local people, including (from north to south) Chapin, Chavez, Schunior, Champion, and Sprague. Closner Boulevard is the main north-south street that runs through the courthouse square.

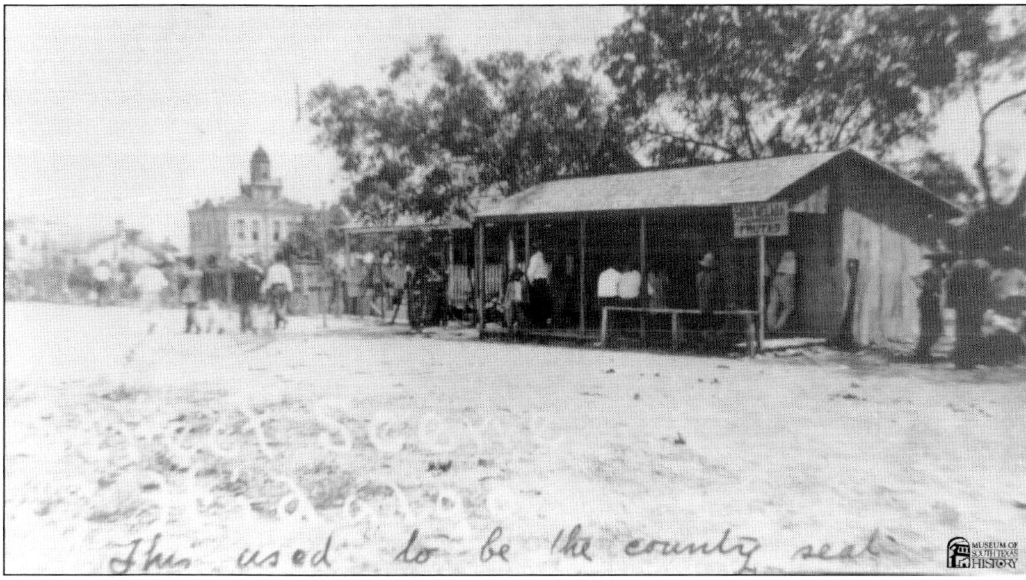

Why and where to move the county seat was debated in the early 1900s. County leaders argued that the risk of damage to the courthouse and fear of losing records due to flooding was a real and constant threat. In addition, the railroad refused to build tracks to Hidalgo because of issues of flooding. The final argument was that the county seat should be near the geographic center of the county. McAllen was approached, but would not donate land. Mercedes, already a successful and growing town near the eastern border of the county, sponsored vocal supporters but their opponents felt they were too far from the center. The photograph above shows the town of Hidalgo after the county seat was moved. The photograph below shows the children of John Closner, Mamie and John, in the town of Hidalgo. (Above, courtesy of the Museum of South Texas History; below, courtesy of The University of Texas–Pan American Library.)

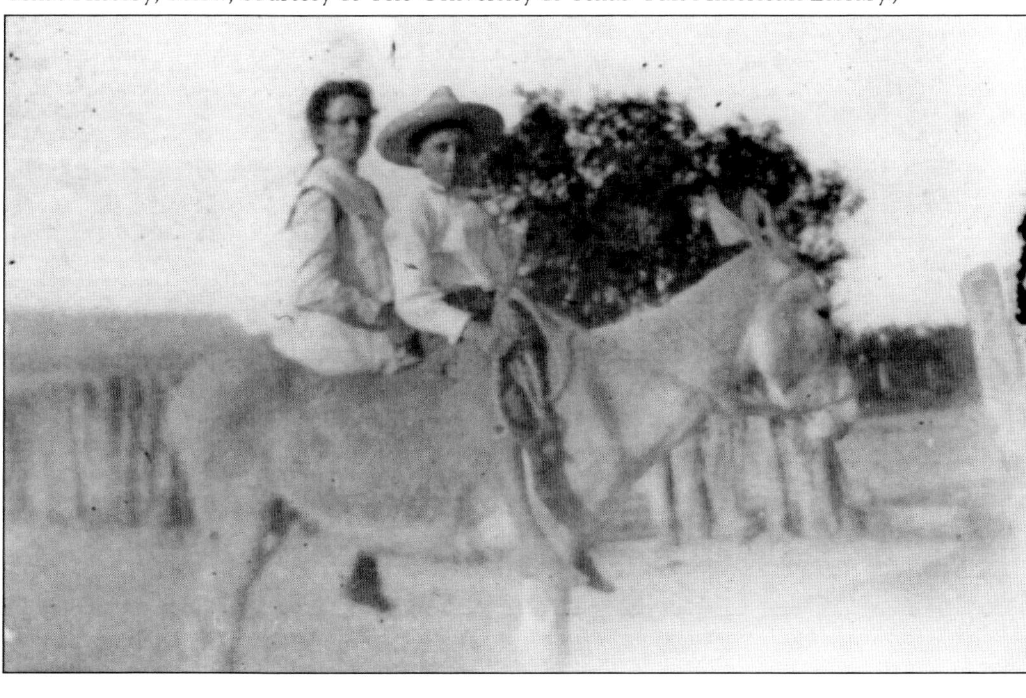

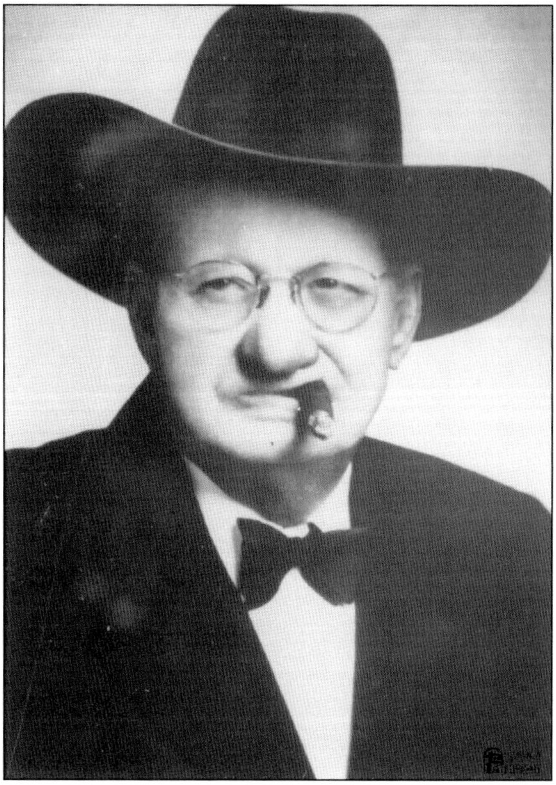

John Closner, Dennis B. Chapin (at left), and William F. Sprague (below) had acquired a tract of land north of McAllen. The land was near the geographic center of the county, and land for a town was identified, although by 1908 not a single building had been erected. Judge Chapin ordered a countywide election to move the county seat to Chapin, a town named after himself. After having ordered the election, Chapin then resigned to prevent accusations of outright fraud, and Judge S.P. Silver from Mercedes was selected as his replacement. The election was held October 10, 1908. By October 12, the votes had been counted with 420 votes for moving the county seat to Chapin and 90 against. (Left, courtesy of the Museum of South Texas History; below, courtesy of The University of Texas–Pan American Library.)

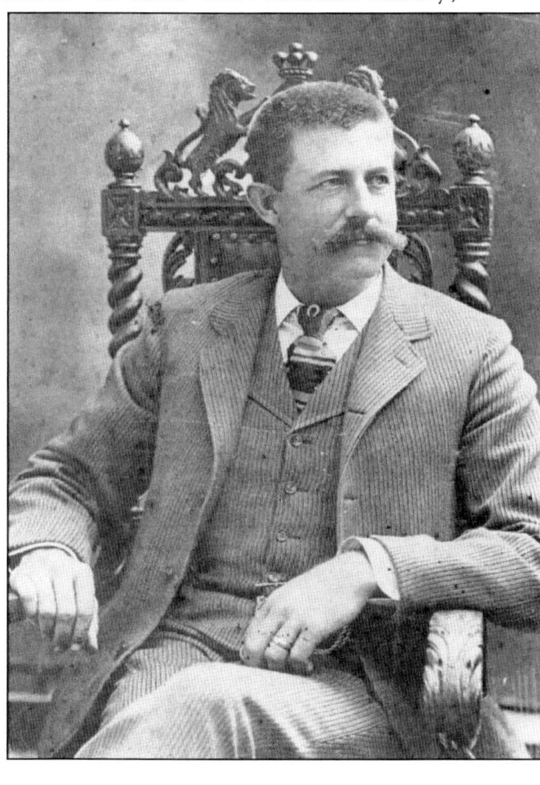

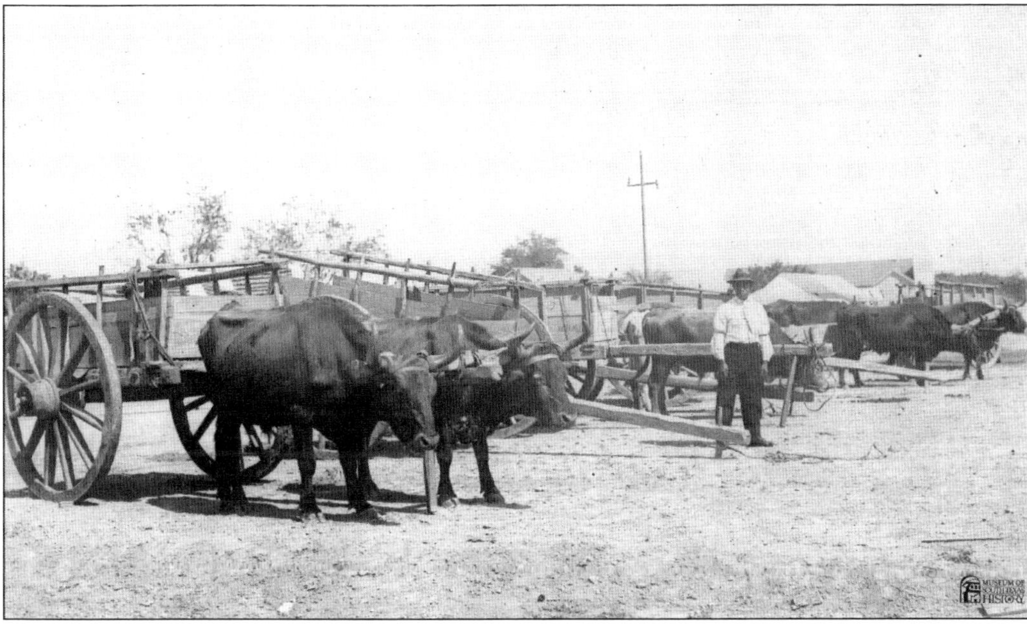

On October 12, 1908, the same day the votes were counted, those who opposed the move to Chapin sent a telegram to the Corpus Christi District Court requesting an injunction against the move. Fearing a positive response, the proponents of the move met early the next morning. On October 13, 1908, they packed up everything they could carry from the old courthouse into ox carts and transported it to Chapin. They arrived after midnight at the new town site, which at that time had four tents, 10 engineers, and 400 Mexican workers. The man in the picture above was the owner and manager of the Ox Cart Dray Service in Hidalgo. The photograph below shows another example of an oxcart. (Above, courtesy of the Museum of South Texas History; below, courtesy of The University of Texas–Pan American Library.)

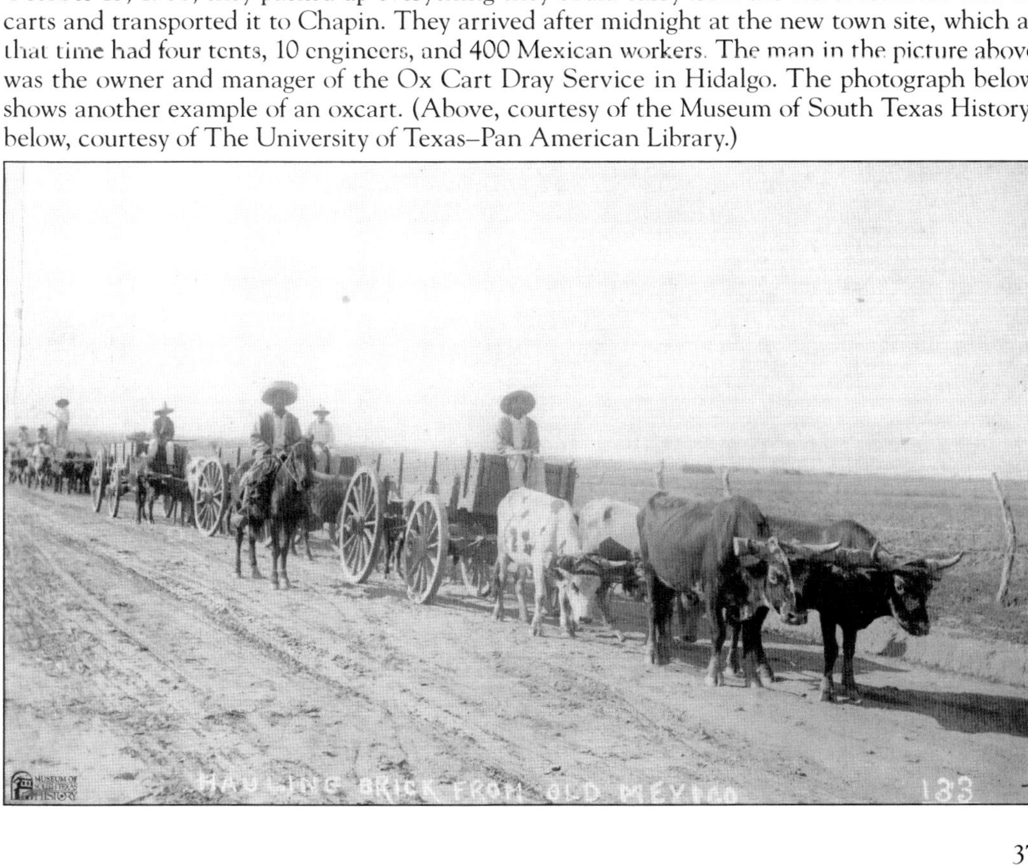

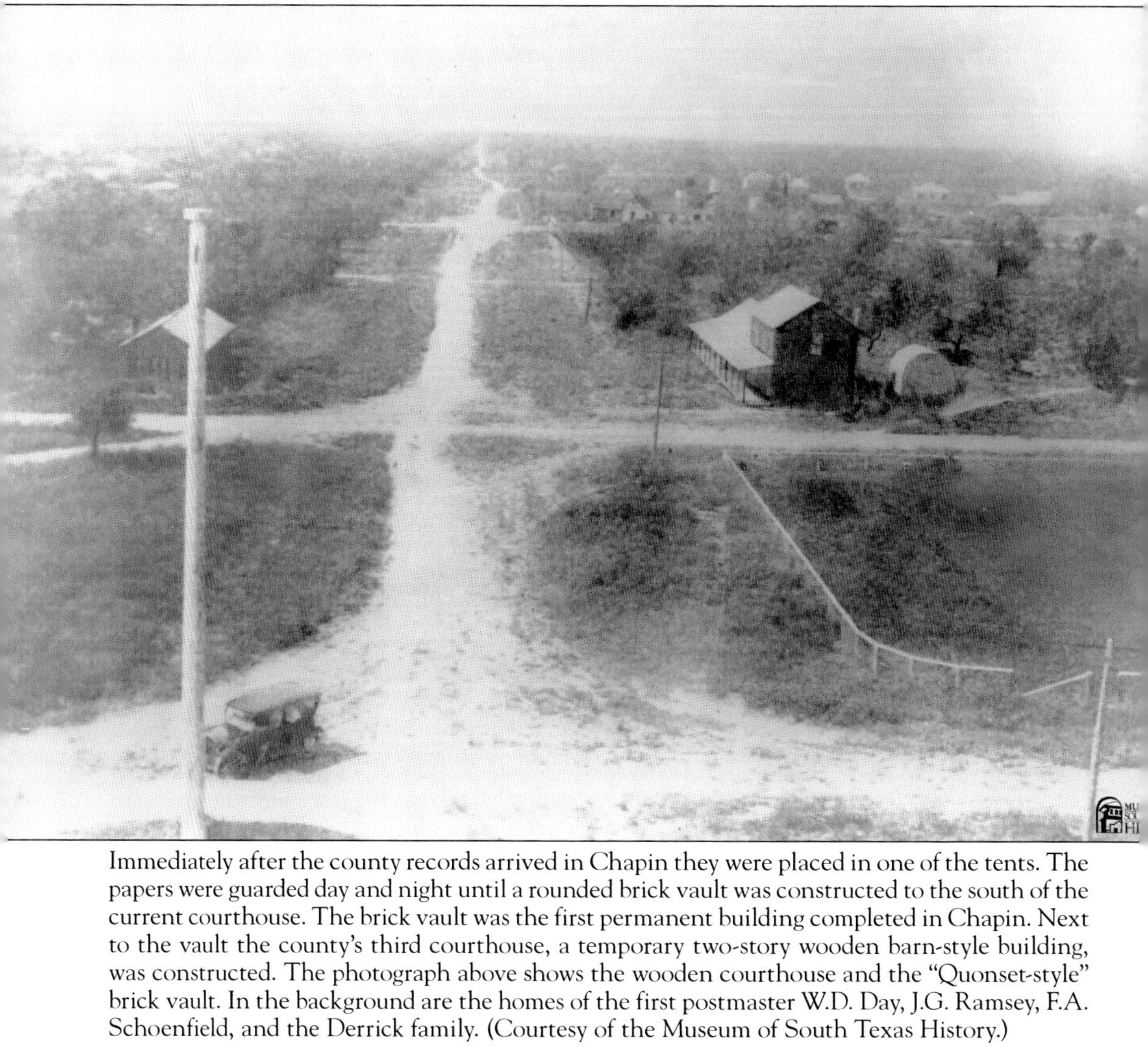

Immediately after the county records arrived in Chapin they were placed in one of the tents. The papers were guarded day and night until a rounded brick vault was constructed to the south of the current courthouse. The brick vault was the first permanent building completed in Chapin. Next to the vault the county's third courthouse, a temporary two-story wooden barn-style building, was constructed. The photograph above shows the wooden courthouse and the "Quonset-style" brick vault. In the background are the homes of the first postmaster W.D. Day, J.G. Ramsey, F.A. Schoenfield, and the Derrick family. (Courtesy of the Museum of South Texas History.)

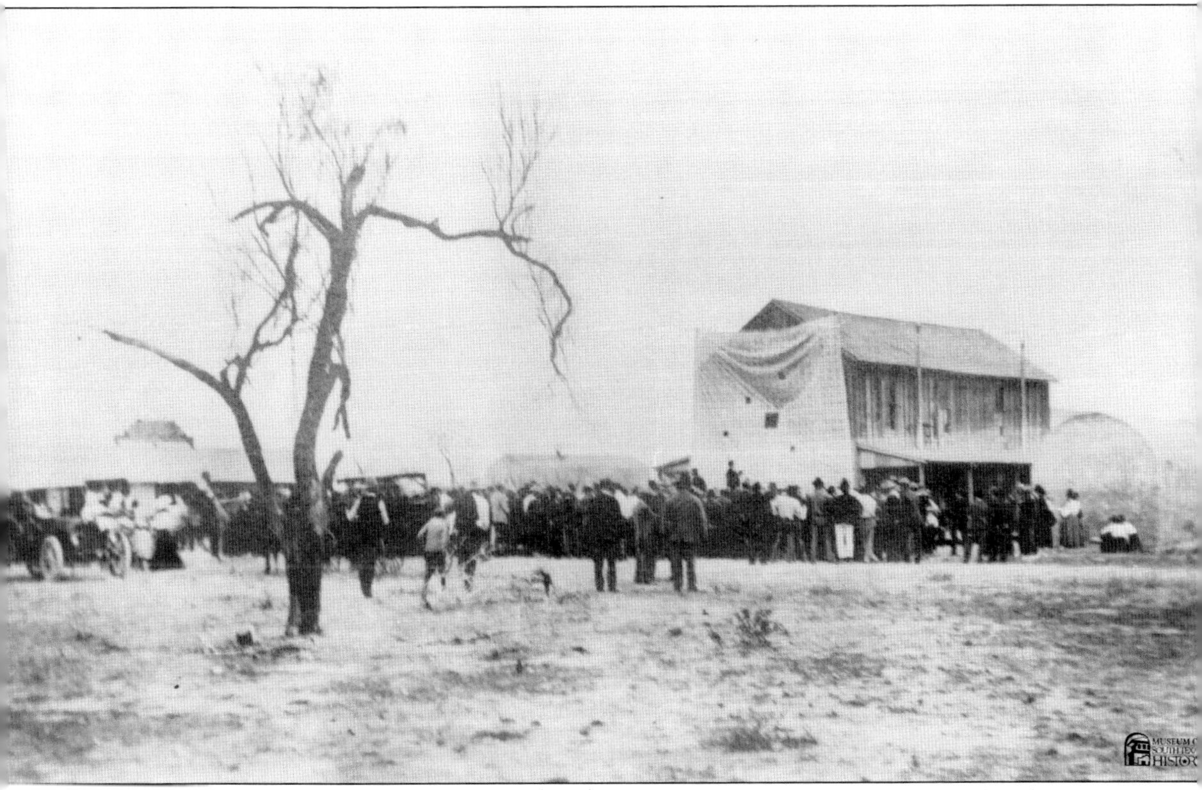

The town site was soon surveyed and platted with streets, the courthouse square, and parks. A huge map of the town was made and hung in front of the two story courthouse, seen here. An event was held inviting potential residents to come and choose a city lot for their new homes. The courthouse was always considered to be a temporary building and was never painted. Besides the county offices, the courthouse also housed a bank. After the permanent courthouse was erected, the building was converted into a boarding house for young men. (Courtesy of the Museum of South Texas History.)

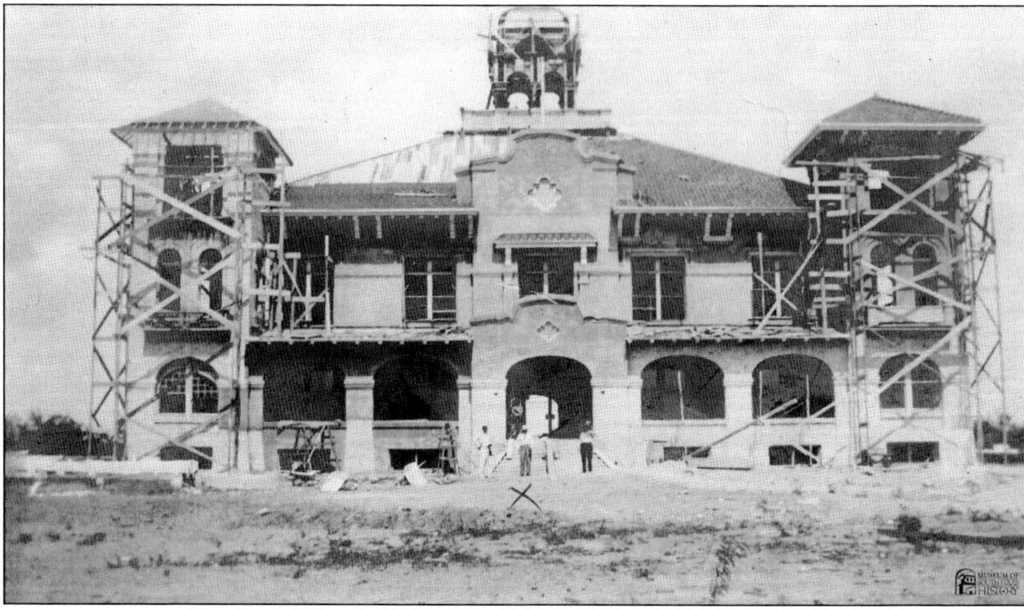

In December 1908, an election was held and voters overwhelmingly approved a bond to replace the wooden courthouse with courthouse number four. John Closner donated four blocks in the center of Chapin, and Felix A. Schoenfield was hired as a building contractor. A special railroad spur was built directly to the building site to bring the necessary supplies for the construction of the new courthouse. Inspecting the construction in the photograph above are, from left to right, county commissioner William L. Lipscomb, county sheriff John Closner, and county commissioner W.F. Sprague. The photograph below shows the courthouse construction crews. (Above, courtesy of the Museum of South Texas History; below, courtesy of The University of Texas–Pan American Library.)

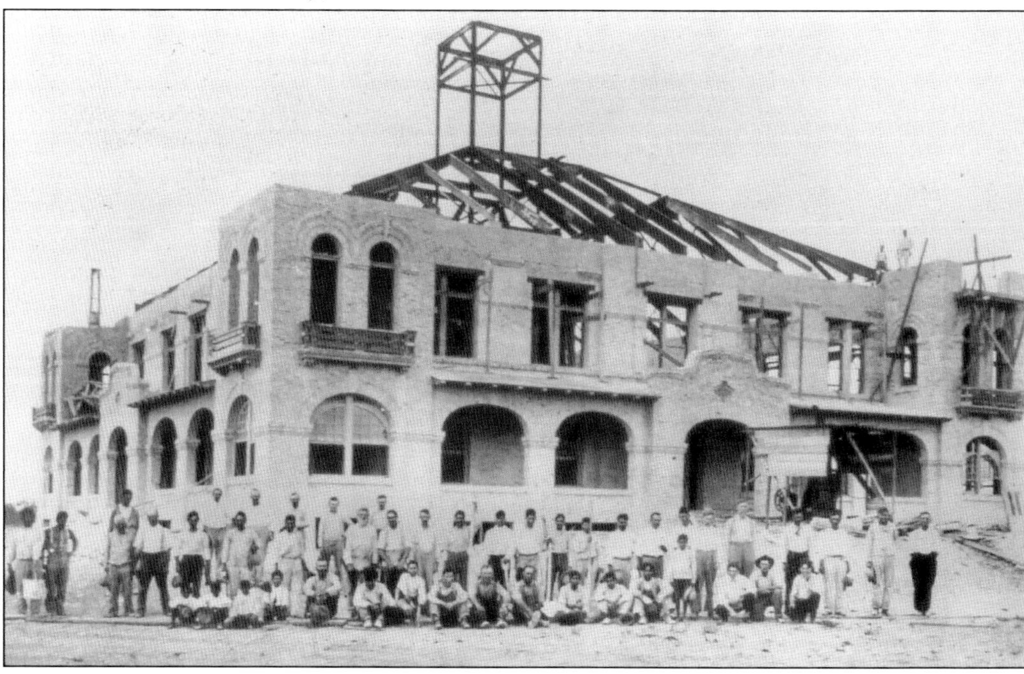

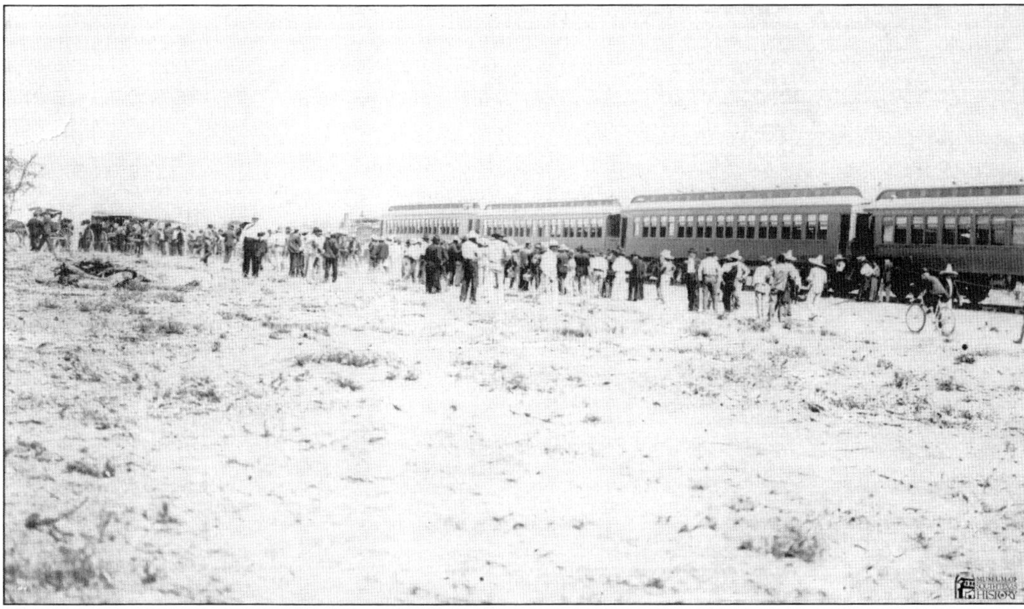

On June 24, 1910, a dedication celebration was held for the laying of the cornerstone. Visitors came from all along the Lower Rio Grande Valley for the event. A special train with 13 passenger cars was required to bring people from Brownsville and the other towns that lay along the tracks. The round trip fare from Brownsville was $1 per person. The photograph above shows the special train and the crowd walking to the courthouse. After the ceremony, the people of Chapin sponsored a barbecue, feeding 700 people, as can be seen in the photograph below. After the courthouse construction was completed, the tracks leading to the courthouse were torn up. (Above, courtesy of the Museum of South Texas History; below, courtesy of The University of Texas–Pan American Library.)

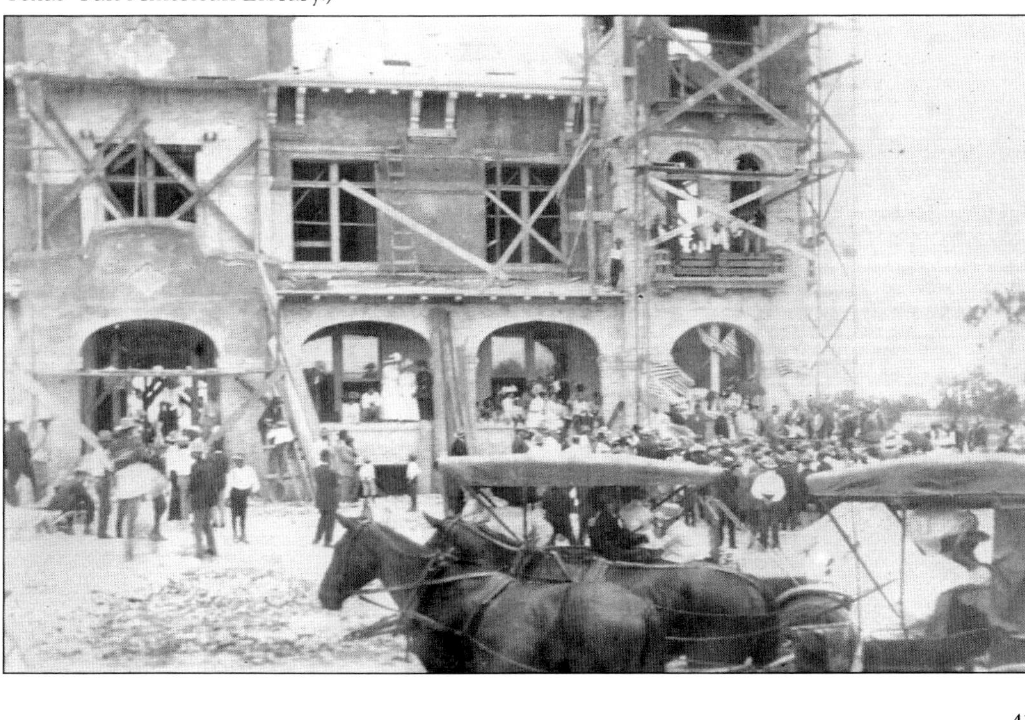

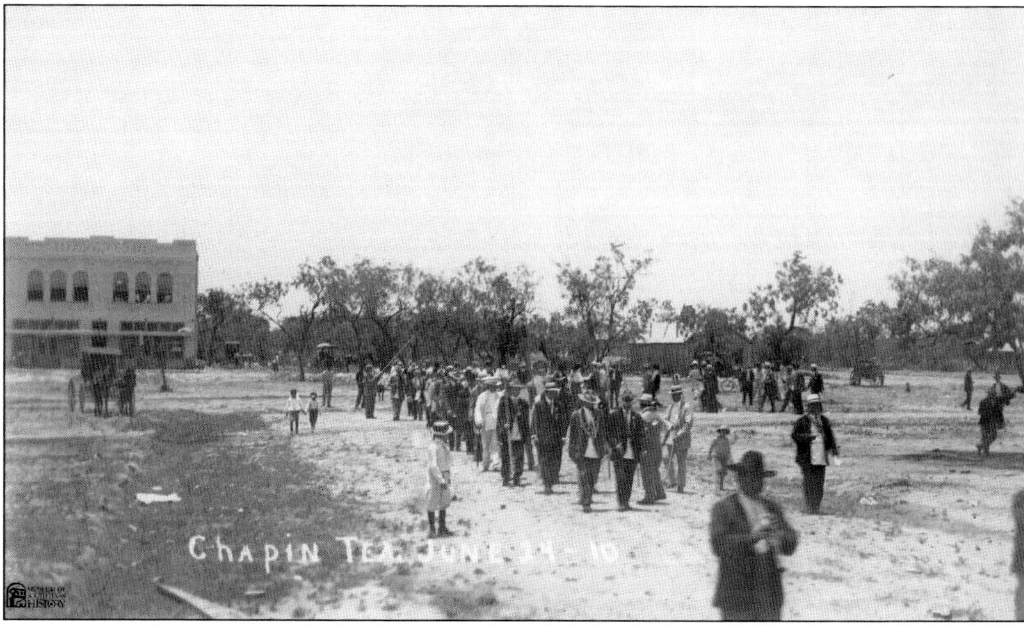

Members of the Mercedes Masonic Lodge participated in the courthouse dedication ceremony. Mercedes had been the location of most of the opposition when the election was held two years earlier in 1908. When the election was held, Mercedes had a population of 1,000, a school, a newspaper, a bank, and stores. Chapin, in contrast, besides having the potential of being a good town, had the advantage of its centralized location within the county. Both photographs on this page show the members of the Mercedes Masonic Lodge as they gather in front of the Lipscomb building and in front of the courthouse. (Courtesy of the Museum of South Texas History.)

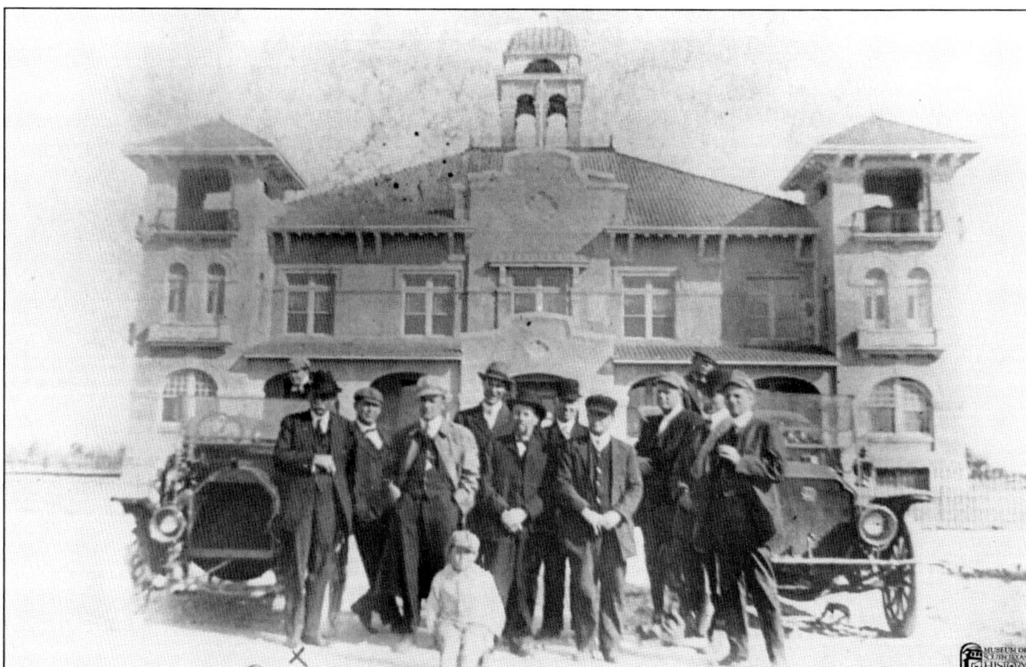

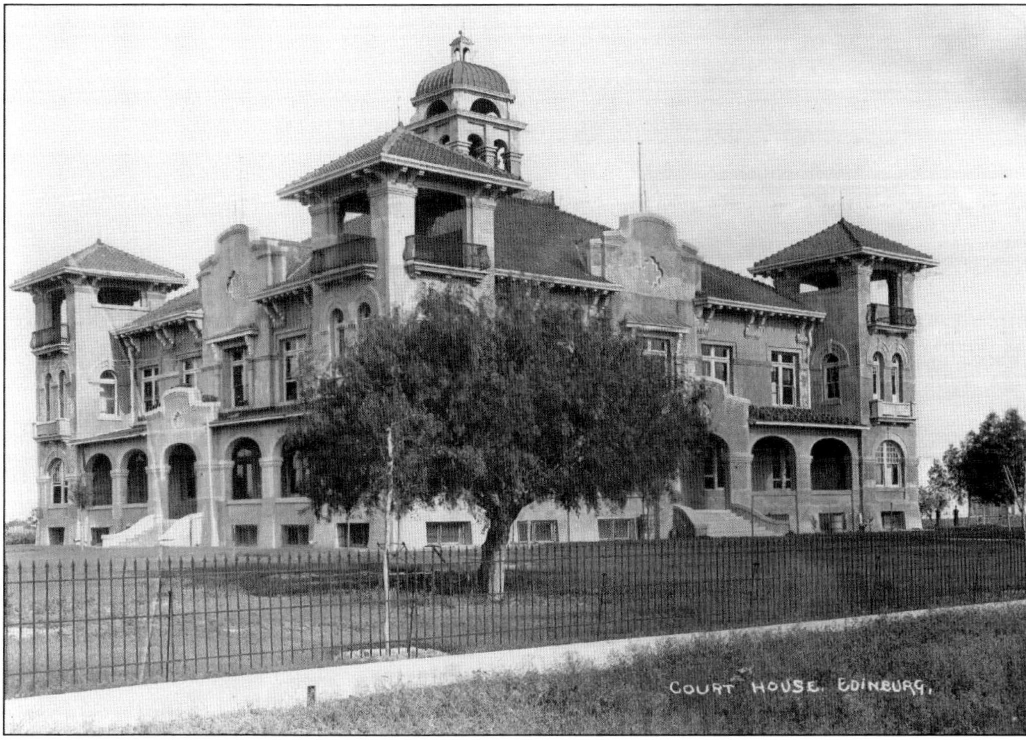

The 1910 courthouse was an elegant building with rounded cupolas and a red tile roof. Throughout the years the landscaping around the courthouse has changed. When the records were moved from the courthouse in the town of Hidalgo, the men also transported the iron fence from Hidalgo to Chapin. Later, citrus trees were planted around the courthouse. The county officers at the time were county judge W.M. Dougherty; commissioners Alex Champion, W.L. Lipscomb, Charles Schunior, and W.F. Sprague; county treasurer A.Y. Baker, county and district clerk A.E. Chavez; Sheriff John Closner; county assessor W.B. Barton; and county school superintendent R.A. Marsh. In 1940, the corner cupolas became too heavy for the aging building and were knocked down. (Courtesy of The University of Texas–Pan American Library.)

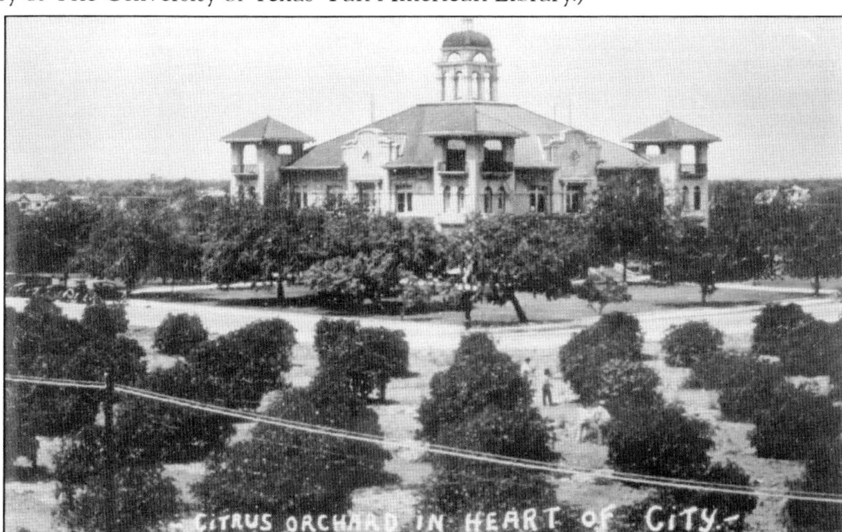

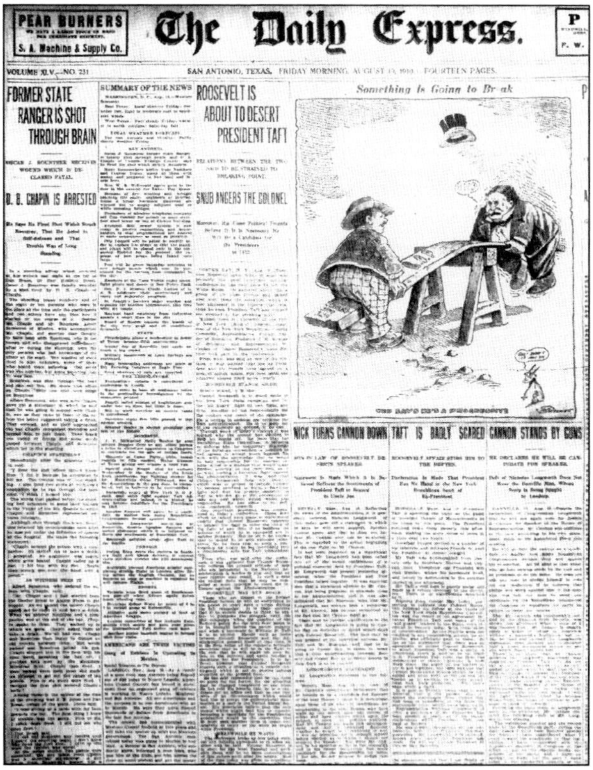

PEAR BURNERS

S. A. Machine & Supply Co.

The Daily Express.

VOLUME XLV—NO. 231 SAN ANTONIO, TEXAS, FRIDAY MORNING, AUGUST 19, 1910.—FOURTEEN PAGES.

FORMER STATE RANGER IS SHOT THROUGH BRAIN

D. B. CHAPIN IS ARRESTED

SUMMARY OF THE NEWS

ROOSEVELT IS ABOUT TO DESERT PRESIDENT TAFT

SNUB ANGERS THE COLONEL

Something Is Going to Break

NICK TURNS CANNON DOWN

TAFT IS BADLY SCARED

CANNON STANDS BY GUNS

A shooting in San Antonio on August 18, 1910, put D.B. Chapin in jail for murder, and was the reason why six months later the town's name was changed to Edinburg. Although Chapin had a lot of local support and a jury in Victoria found him not guilty by reason of self-defense, his reputation and name had already been damaged. The shooting occurred when D.B. Chapin and Oscar J. Rountree met in Dan Breem's saloon in San Antonio. Rountree was a former Arizona and Texas Ranger, and from a well-known family. He was representing one of Chapin's business partners from New York. During the trial the defense showed that the business partner had hired Rountree to kill Chapin. Simultaneously with Chapin's trial, the residents of the town changed its name from Chapin to Edinburg.

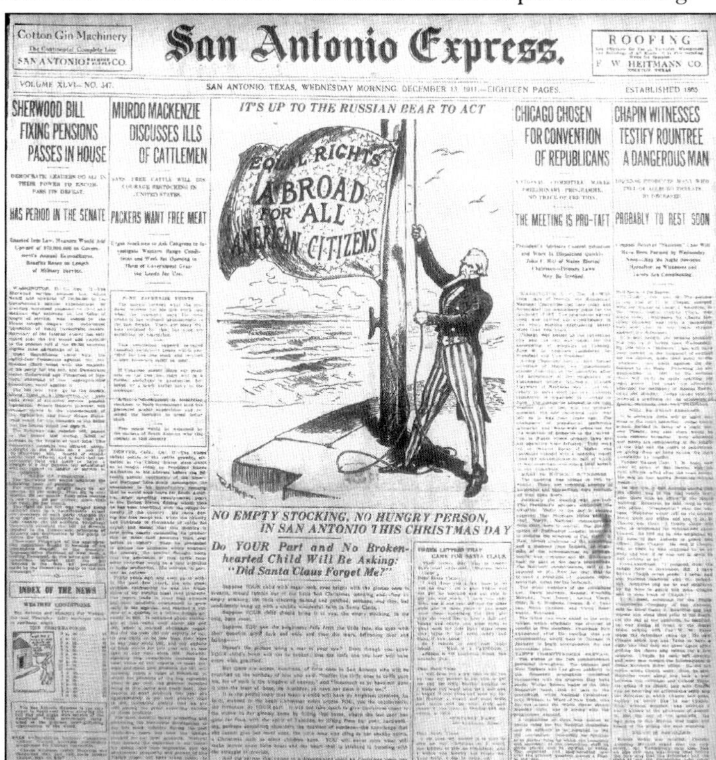

Cotton Gin Machinery

SAN ANTONIO

San Antonio Express.

ROOFING

F. W. HEITMANN CO.

VOLUME XLVI—NO. 347. SAN ANTONIO, TEXAS, WEDNESDAY MORNING, DECEMBER 13, 1911.—EIGHTEEN PAGES. ESTABLISHED 1865

SHERWOOD BILL FIXING PENSIONS PASSES IN HOUSE

HAS PERIOD IN THE SENATE

MURDO MACKENZIE DISCUSSES ILLS OF CATTLEMEN

PACKERS WANT FREE MEAT

IT'S UP TO THE RUSSIAN BEAR TO ACT

NO EMPTY STOCKING, NO HUNGRY PERSON, IN SAN ANTONIO THIS CHRISTMAS DAY

Do YOUR Part and No Broken-hearted Child Will Be Asking: "Did Santa Claus Forget Me?"

INDEX OF THE NEWS

CHICAGO CHOSEN FOR CONVENTION OF REPUBLICANS

THE MEETING IS PRO-TAFT

CHAPIN WITNESSES TESTIFY ROUNTREE A DANGEROUS MAN

PROBABLY TO REST SOON

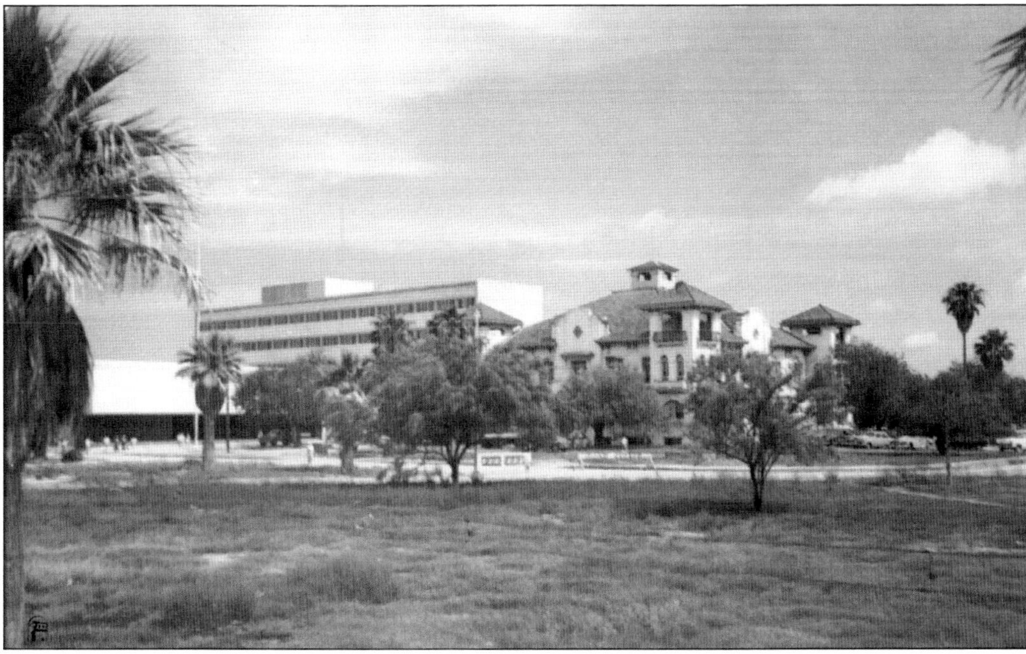

After just 41 years of service, the 1910 courthouse was deemed too small for the county's growing needs. During those years, both the city and the county had seen an enormous population growth, and there was no longer any room in the 1910 courthouse to accommodate all the courts and offices required to transact business. Voters once again elected to finance the construction of a new courthouse, and three years later, in 1954, the fifth courthouse, a $1.5 million, five-story building was completed. For a short time, both the new and the old courthouses coexisted, as can be seen above. In 1955, the old courthouse was demolished. (Courtesy of the Museum of South Texas History.)

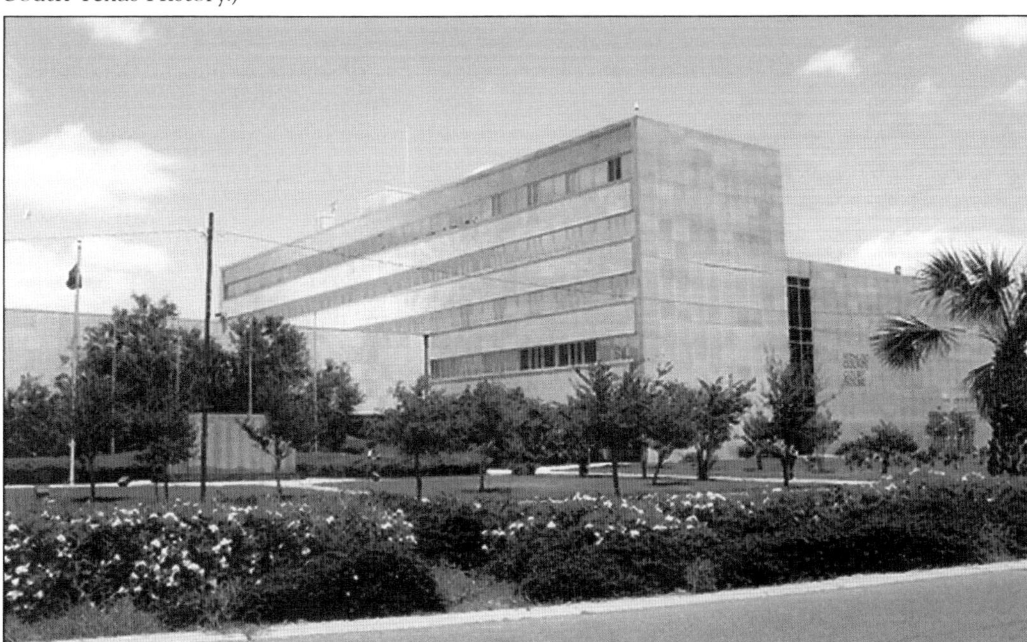

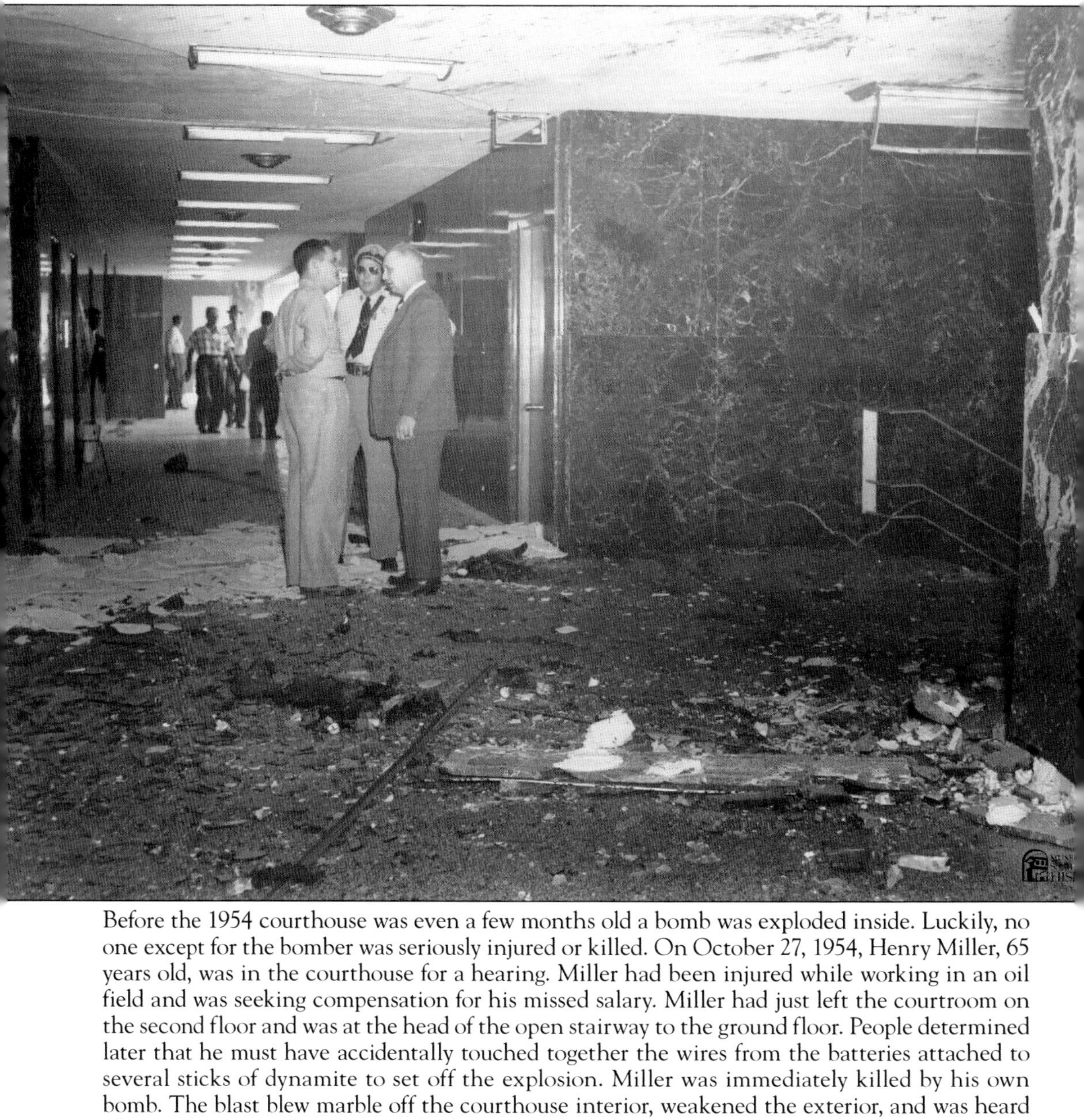

Before the 1954 courthouse was even a few months old a bomb was exploded inside. Luckily, no one except for the bomber was seriously injured or killed. On October 27, 1954, Henry Miller, 65 years old, was in the courthouse for a hearing. Miller had been injured while working in an oil field and was seeking compensation for his missed salary. Miller had just left the courtroom on the second floor and was at the head of the open stairway to the ground floor. People determined later that he must have accidentally touched together the wires from the batteries attached to several sticks of dynamite to set off the explosion. Miller was immediately killed by his own bomb. The blast blew marble off the courthouse interior, weakened the exterior, and was heard all over the town. The photograph above was taken shortly after the explosion. (Courtesy of the Museum of South Texas History.)

Three

A Town Grows Up
From a Ranch to a Branch Line

On May 3, 1914, an article in the *San Antonio Express* described Edinburg and the surrounding lands. The article was written just six years after Chapin/Edinburg became the county seat and discussed its modest beginnings, continuing to its tremendous growth, and speculating on its potential future:

> Less than six years ago the town was first platted. The country was a primeval wilderness of mesquite and cactus for the most part, but the soil was as rich as the world afforded. On the entire tract of some 40,000 acres, there was no human habitation more pretentious than a jacal or a goat herder's shanty of protecting boughs and bark. The whole prospect was altogether desolate and just about as forbidding as a man of progressive agricultural ideas could have found in travels extending over several days. The town was originally named Chapin as all the old timers in the Lower Rio Grande country know. For three or four years the town remained on the map only. There was no development, no progress no interest to speak of. The people knew there was such a place as Chapin, but very few ever went there. To attract them thither there was nothing.

The article also discussed the tremendous growth that Edinburg had seen to date: "It is not every town that springs over the starting tape at a given signal and boasts a population of several thousand in a few weeks that continues in the race and wins greatness in the end." Finally, the article ends with a prediction for the future:

> There is a firm belief that Edinburg will have another railroad within a year. The importance of the Valley has become so widespread and the tonnage of its products so great that railroad men are becoming more than alive to the fact that additional transportation facilities are demanded. It is admittedly time that the railroad company which first builds a line into the wonderful Valley from the north to the south will bountifully share in the tonnage.

Turn the page to learn more about what this newspaper article described and prophesied.

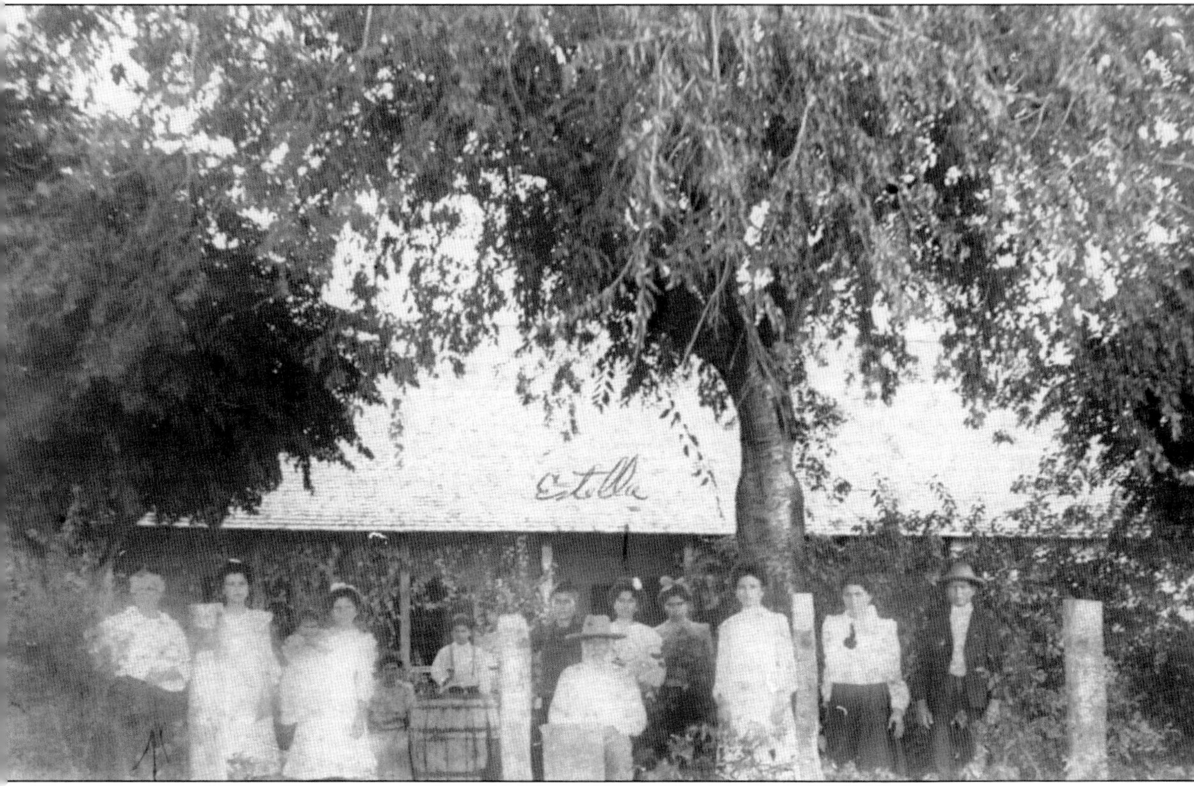

In the 1800s, ranches were the most important communities north of the river. One of the biggest ranches was the Laguna Seca Ranch, located 12 miles north of Edinburg. In 1857, just five years after Hidalgo County was formed, Macedonio Vela and his wife, Mercedes Chapa, both from well-known Reynosa families, moved to the area. The story was told that Macedonio had been caught in the middle between two rival groups in Mexico, the Crinolines and the Rojos. Macedonio was captured and ordered to be executed unless he left the country. He and his wife immediately moved across the river to Texas. There they founded the Laguna Seca Ranch. Many of the Vela descendents have had great influence on the town of Edinburg and the university. The photograph above, courtesy of Carola Chapa, was taken at the Laguna Seca Ranch and shows the first generation of Velas who grew up in Hidalgo County, including Delfina (for whom the post office was later named), Maria, Estella, Joaquin, Cedova, and unidentified.

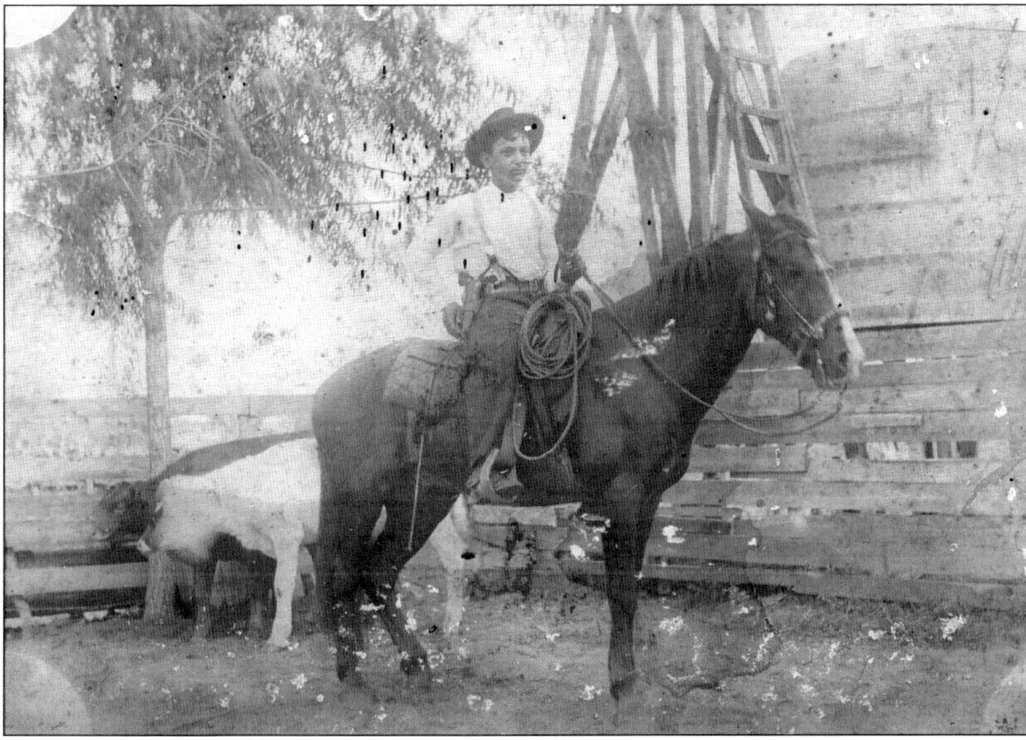

When Macedonio Vela first arrived in Texas he obtained a position as a foreman at the El Tule Ranch. In 1867, he made a deal with Salome Balli and John McAllen to work 4,428 acres of brush land. If he could pay off the land within seven years, they would grant him the land. Vela worked so hard, he was able to pay off the land and the improvements within just three years. This land was just the first in several thousands of acres that Macedonio acquired for himself and his family. The photograph above shows Ramon Vela Vega, son of Macedonio and Mercedes, and the photograph below shows Miguel Raul Chapa and Jose Enerardo Chapa, sons of Miguel Chapa Montalva and Adelina Vela de Chapa, grandchildren of Macedonio and Mercedes. (Courtesy of Carola Chapa.)

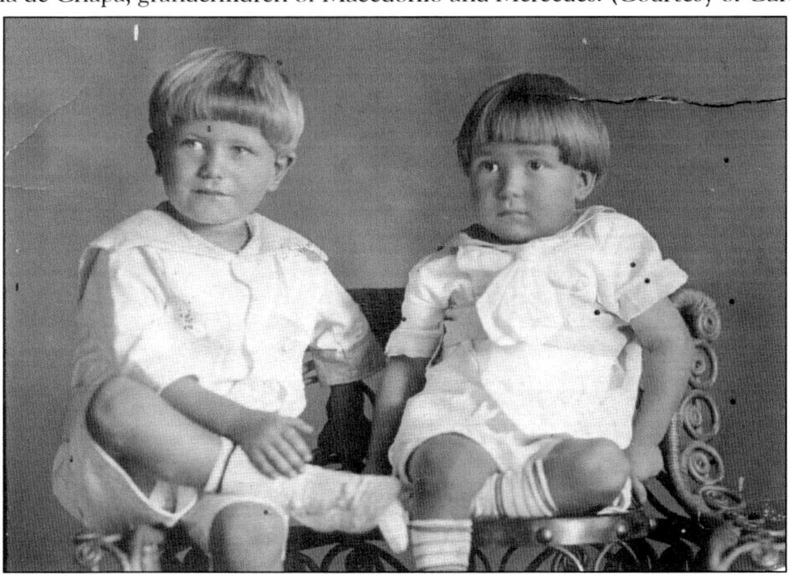

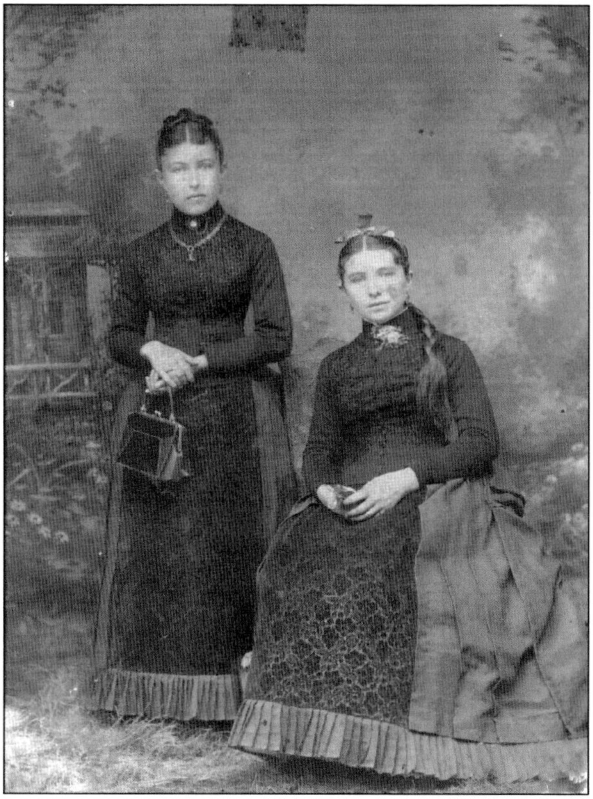

Laguna Seca, or "dry lake" was named after a watering hole or lake that was more dry or muddy than wet. The ranch flourished, and in 1876, the first cattle drive occurred in which longhorns were driven north from Laguna Seca to Kansas. By 1892, through continued hard work and good business sense, Vela had accumulated over 75,000 acres. The ranch was so large it had its own Catholic Church, school, and post office. Macedonio and Mercedes had seven children who lived to maturity: Ramon, Jesus, Macedonio Vela Chapa, Carlota, Delfina, Eloisa, and Alberto. The post office was named after his daughter, Delfina. Delfina and Eloisa Vela are posing in this portrait. The photograph below shows Joaquina Chapa, a granddaughter of Macedonio and Mercedes. (Courtesy of Carola Chapa.)

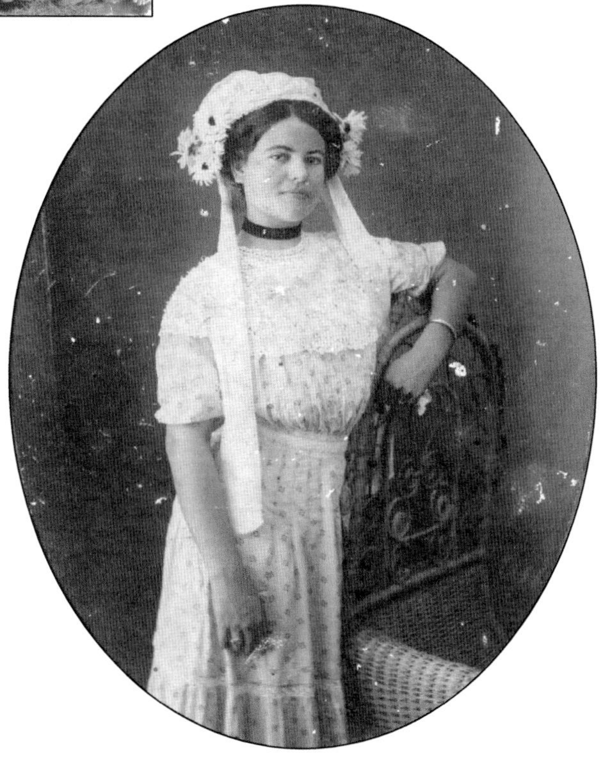

The Vela family is credited with planting the first orange trees in Hidalgo County, an act that would eventually flourish into a prosperous industry. One day in 1871, one of the fathers from the Oblate of Mary Immaculate made one of his regular trips from Brownsville to visit ranches in South Texas, including the Laguna Seca Ranch. He had brought with him oranges as gifts for the Vela children. The seeds were planted and grew into trees. The seed planted by Carlota is credited with growing into the tree that flourished into the 1950s. The photograph at right shows Carlota Vela on February 28, 1866 at El Tule Ranch. The photograph below shows the first orange tree planted in Hidalgo County. (Right, courtesy of Carola Chapa; below, courtesy of The University of Texas–Pan American Library).

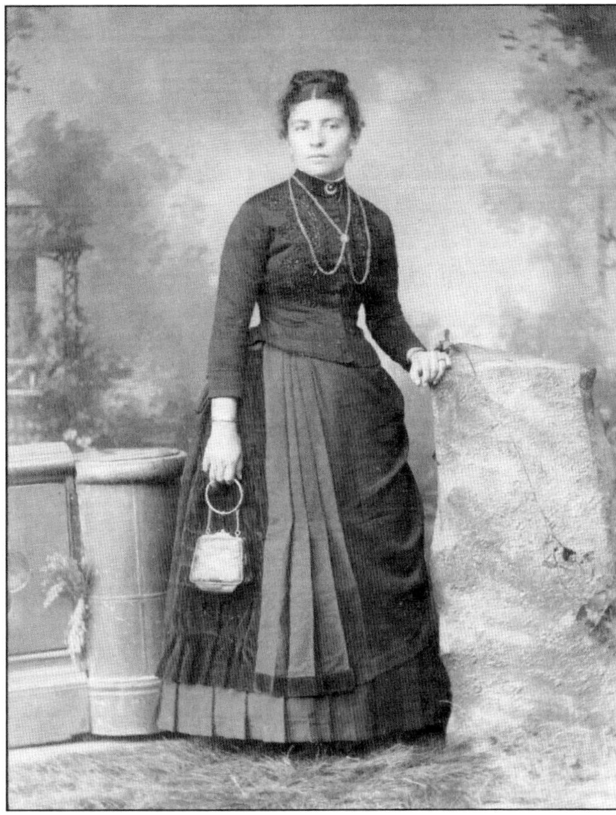

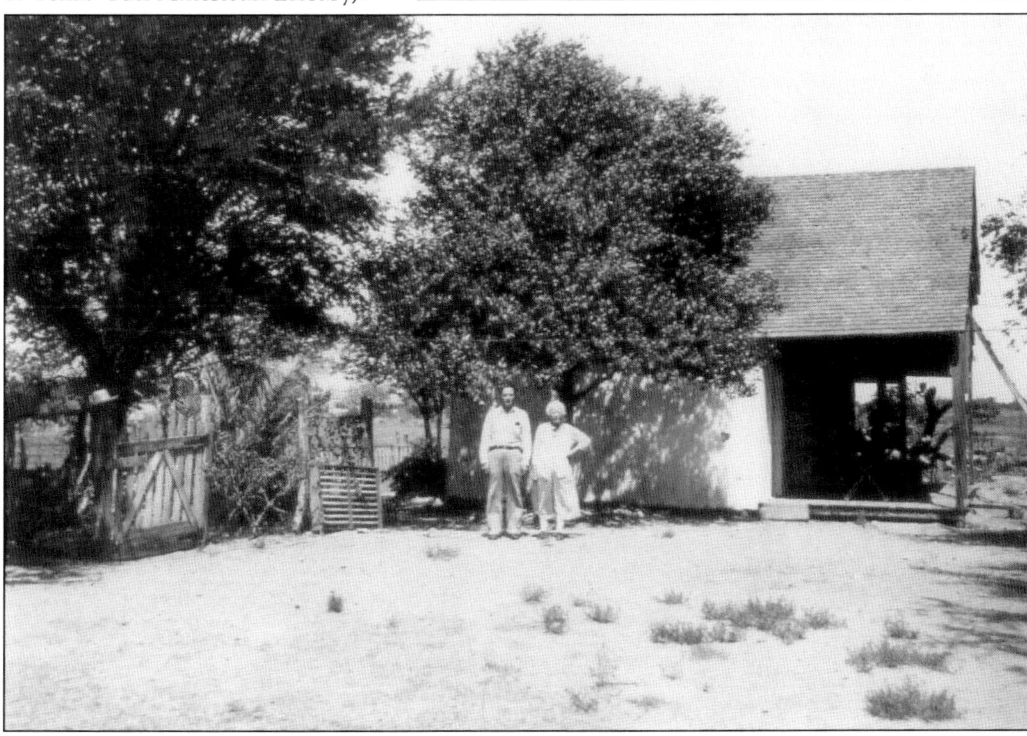

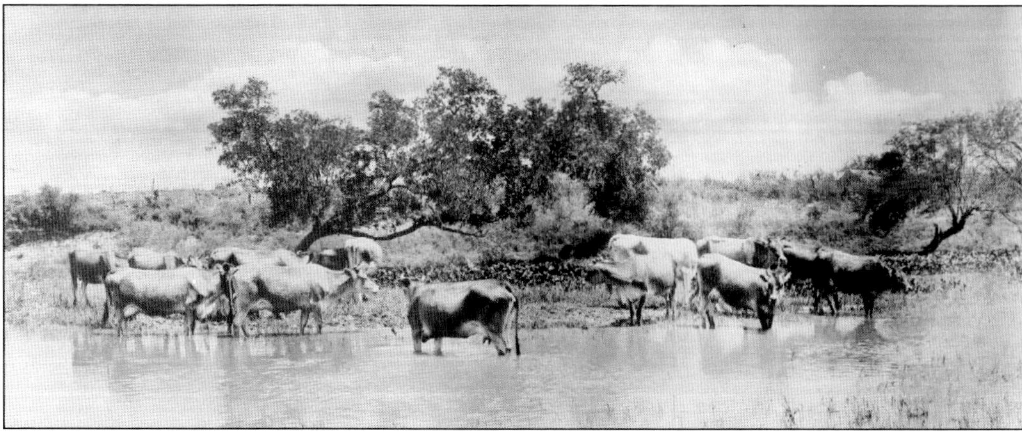

The Laguna Seca Ranch was just one of many ranches in Hidalgo County. In the 1900s, the county experienced a population explosion spawned by the building of the railroads and the development of irrigation canals, which encouraged the growth of farms and towns all along its tracks. Prior to 1900, however, livestock far outnumbered people. In 1870, there were 18,141 cattle, 11,270 sheep, and only 2,387 people. Cattle represented 57 percent, sheep 35 percent, and humans only 8 percent of those counted. By 1890, the numbers had increased to 71,176 cattle (72 percent) and 20,906 sheep (21 percent), but only 6,534 people (7 percent). When Chapin was chosen as the county seat in 1908, the only "residents" would have been cattle and sheep, as there were no humans yet residing there. (Courtesy of The University of Texas–Pan American Library.)

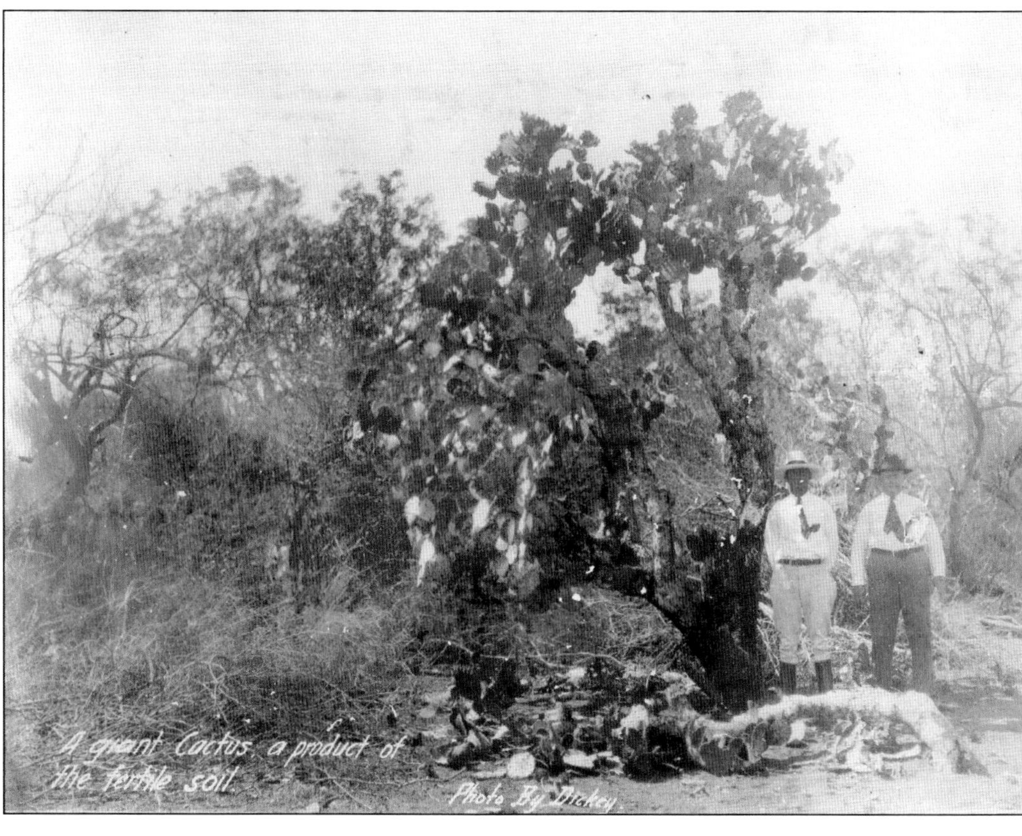

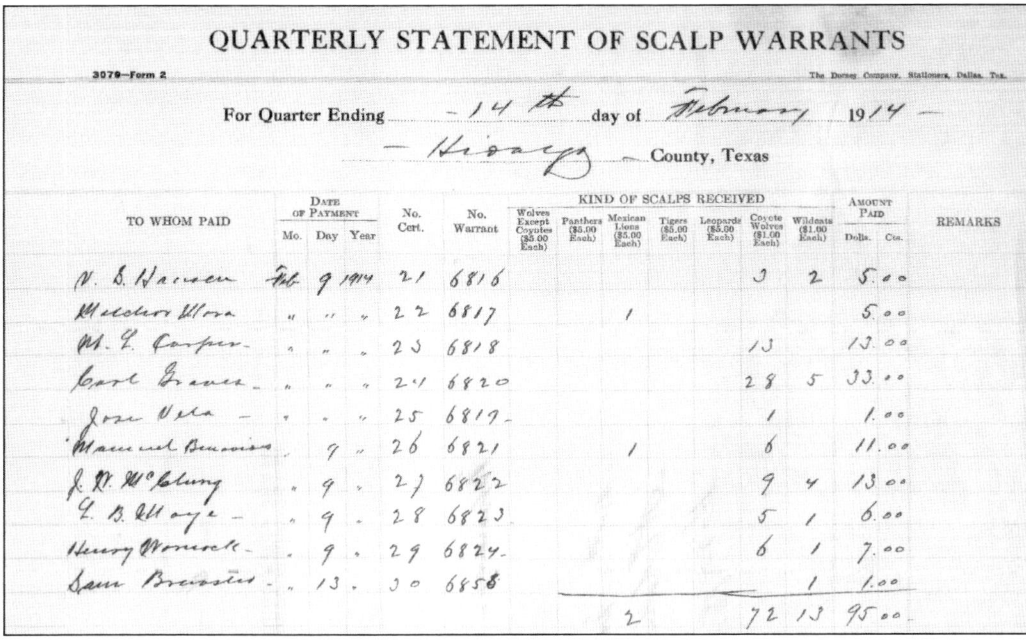

QUARTERLY STATEMENT OF SCALP WARRANTS

3079—Form 2 The Dorsey Company, Stationers, Dallas, Tex.

For Quarter Ending – 14th day of February 1914 –

– Hidalgo – County, Texas

TO WHOM PAID	Date of Payment Mo.	Day	Year	No. Cert.	No. Warrant	Wolves Except Coyotes ($5.00 Each)	Panthers ($5.00 Each)	Mexican Lions ($5.00 Each)	Tigers ($5.00 Each)	Leopards ($5.00 Each)	Coyote Wolves ($1.00 Each)	Wildcats ($1.00 Each)	Amount Paid Dolls.	Cts.	REMARKS
N. S. Hansen	Feb	9	1914	21	6816						3	2	5	00	
Melchor Mora	"	"	"	22	6817			1					5	00	
M. L. Cooper	"	"	"	23	6818						13		13	00	
Carl Graves	"	"	"	24	6820						28	5	33	00	
Jose Vela	"	"	"	25	6819						1		1	00	
Manuel [illegible]		9	"	26	6821			1			6		11	00	
J. W. McClung	"	9	"	27	6822						9	4	13	00	
L. B. [illegible]	"	9	"	28	6823						5	1	6	00	
Henry Womack	"	9	"	29	6824						6	1	7	00	
Sam Brewster	"	13	"	30	6858							1	1	00	
								2			72	13	95	00	

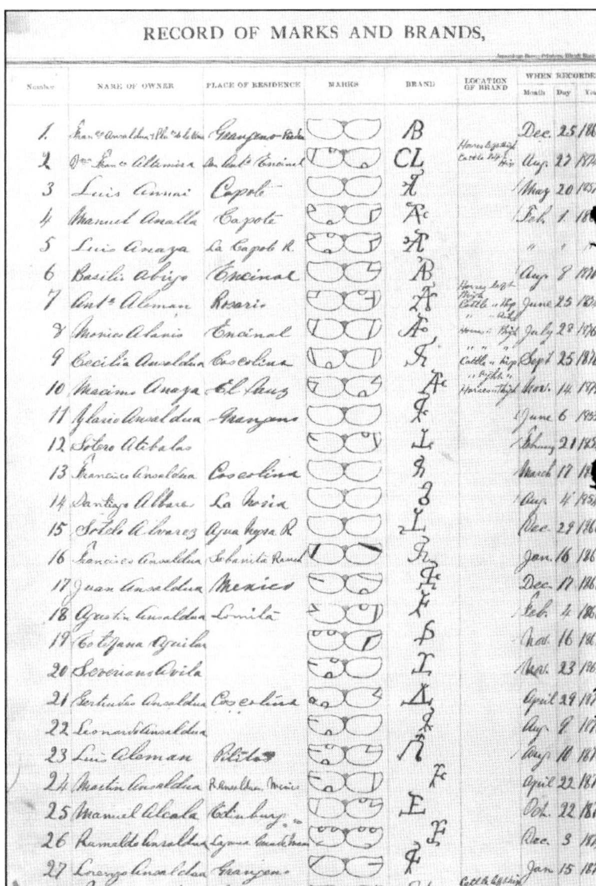

RECORD OF MARKS AND BRANDS,

Number	Name of Owner	Place of Residence	Marks	Brand	Location of Brand	When Recorded Month	Day	Year
1.	[illegible]	Granjeno [illegible]				Dec.	25	1868
2	[illegible] Altamirano	[illegible] Encinal		CL		Aug.	27	1874
3	Luis [illegible]	Capote				May	20	1857
4	Manuel Anaya	Capote				Feb.	1	[illegible]
5	Luis Anaya	La Capote R.				"	"	"
6	Basilio Abrego	Encinal				Aug.	8	1870
7	Ant. Aleman	Rosario				June	25	18[illegible]
8	Monica Alanis	Encinal				July	28	1876
9	Cecilia Anaya	Coscolina				Sept.	25	1876
10	Maximo Anaya	El Sauz				Nov.	14	1879
11	[illegible]	Granjeno				June	6	1853
12	Sotero Atibalas					February	21	1854
13	Francisco [illegible]	Coscolina				March	17	[illegible]
14	Santiago Albarez	La Rosia				Aug.	4	1858
15	Sotelo Alvarez	Agua Negra R.				Dec.	29	1866
16	Francisco [illegible]	[illegible] Ranch				Jan.	16	1867
17	Juan [illegible]	Mexico				Dec.	17	1867
18	Agustin [illegible]	Lomita				Feb.	4	1867
19	[illegible] Aguilar					Nov.	16	1869
20	Severiano Avila					Nov.	23	1869
21	[illegible]	Coscolina				April	29	1870
22	Leonardo [illegible]					Aug.	9	1870
23	Luis Aleman	[illegible]				Aug.	10	1870
24	Martin [illegible]	[illegible]				April	22	1871
25	Manuel Alcala	Edinburg		E		Oct.	22	187[illegible]
26	[illegible]	[illegible]				Dec.	3	187[illegible]
27	Lorenzo [illegible]	Granjeno				Jan.	15	1876

Ranchers dislike wild animals that can kill their livestock. Because the county was so dependent upon ranching, the needs of the ranchers were reflected in county regulations. This included the payment of scalps, as can be seen in the page from the scalp book above. Each time a wild animal was killed; the hunter would scalp it and take it to the courthouse and get paid up to $5 per scalp. Wolves, panthers, Mexican lions, tigers, and leopards were worth $5 each. Coyotes and wildcats, which at that time were much more numerous, were worth $1 each. The county was also responsible for keeping the records of the earmarks and brands used on cattle and other livestock. (Courtesy of The University of Texas–Pan American Library.)

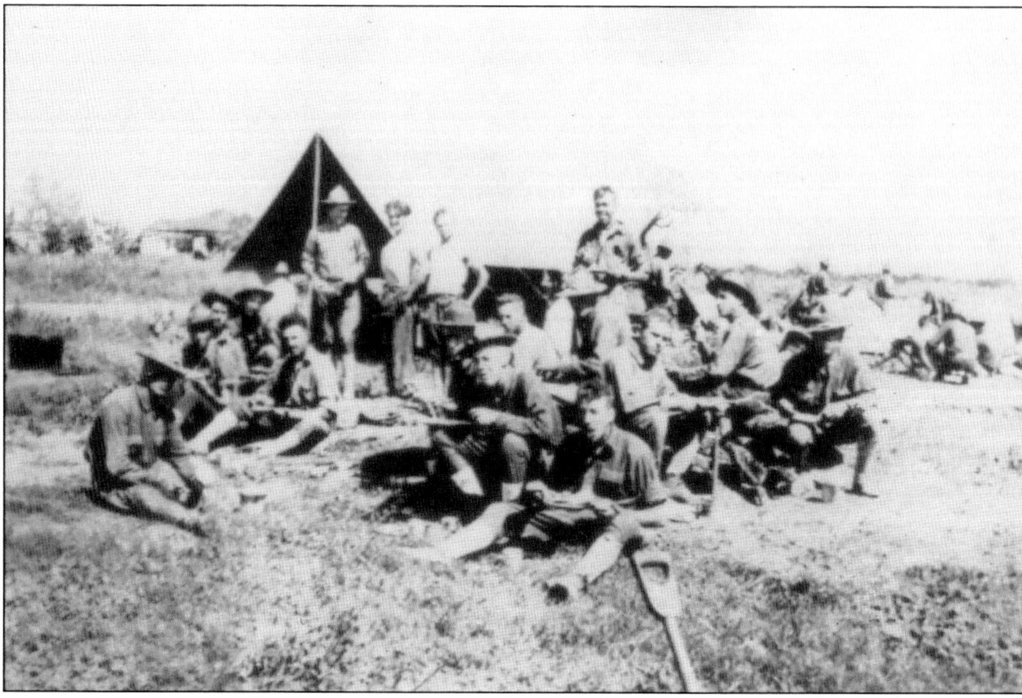

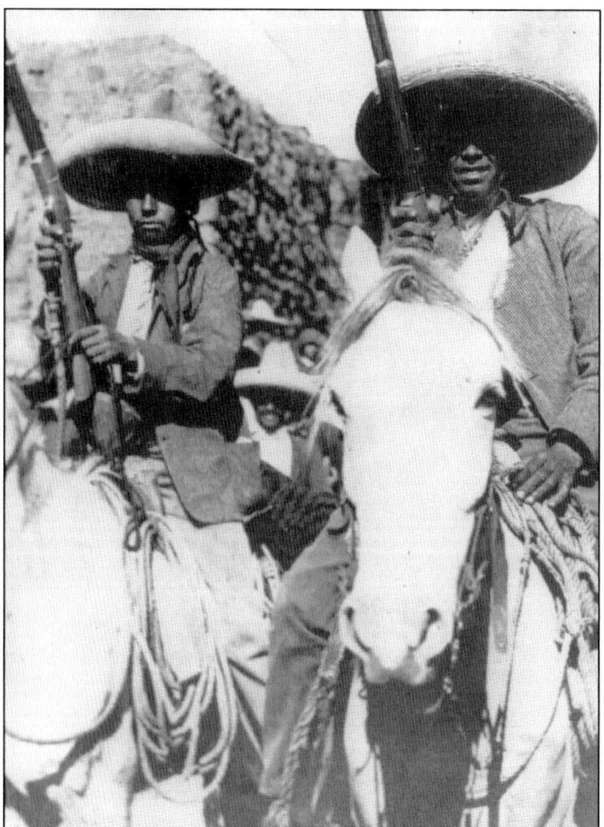

This land, empty of people and full of cattle, created an opportune environment for cattle rustlers. In addition, during the Mexican Revolution, bandits would cross the river, spreading fear and gun fights. As a result, both Texas Rangers and US Army troops were dispatched to the Lower Rio Grande Valley to protect its citizens. There were fights and scares around Edinburg, but little was reported in the city itself. The photograph above shows US Army soldiers stationed in Edinburg in 1915. The photograph on the left shows two typical bandits. John Peavey was a border patrolman during the border troubles. (Above, courtesy of the Museum of South Texas History; left, courtesy of the Peavey Collection, The University of Texas–Pan American Library.)

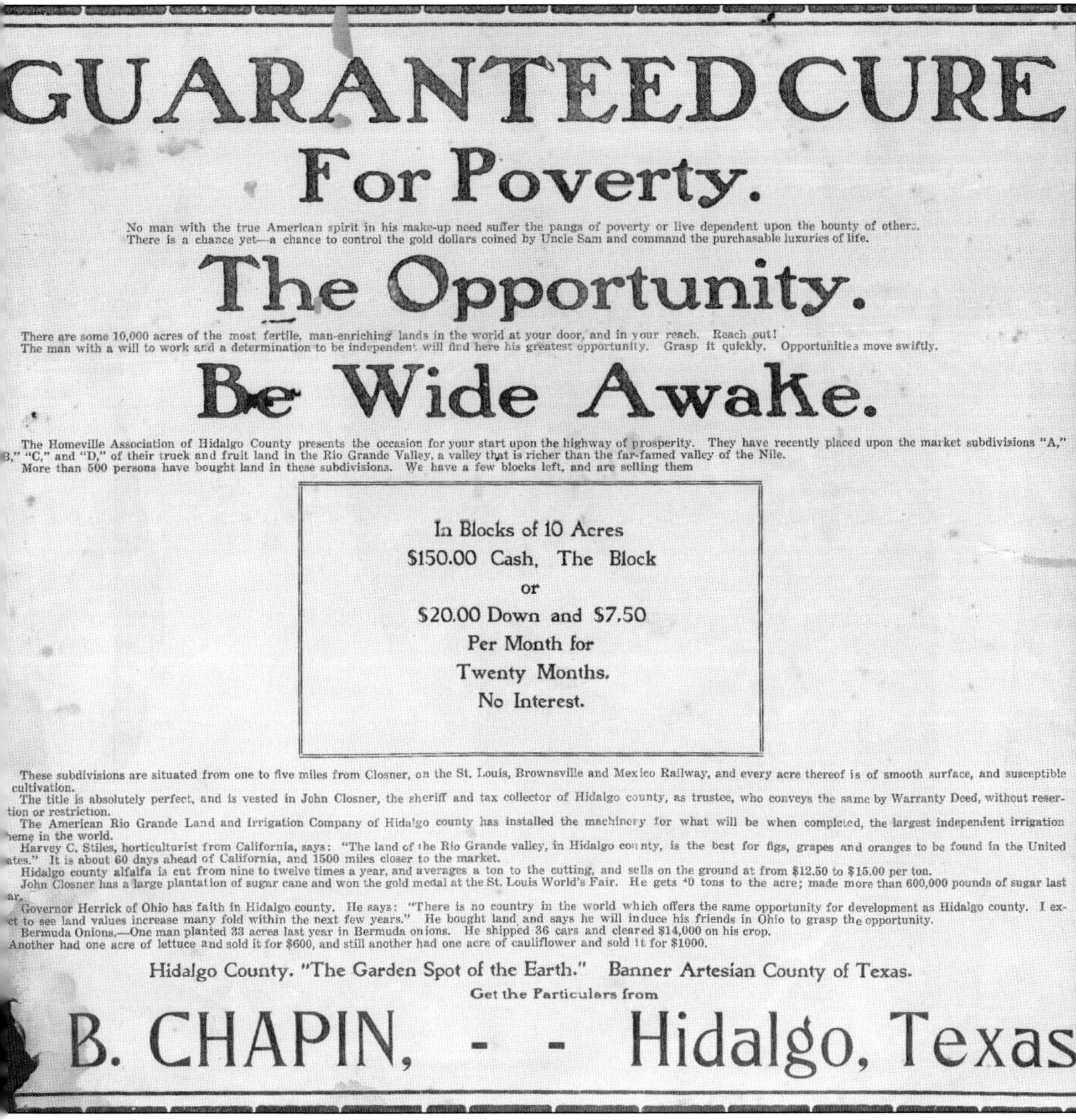

GUARANTEED CURE

For Poverty.

No man with the true American spirit in his make-up need suffer the pangs of poverty or live dependent upon the bounty of others. There is a chance yet—a chance to control the gold dollars coined by Uncle Sam and command the purchasable luxuries of life.

The Opportunity.

There are some 10,000 acres of the most fertile, man-enriching lands in the world at your door, and in your reach. Reach out! The man with a will to work and a determination to be independent will find here his greatest opportunity. Grasp it quickly. Opportunities move swiftly.

Be Wide Awake.

The Homeville Association of Hidalgo County presents the occasion for your start upon the highway of prosperity. They have recently placed upon the market subdivisions "A," 3," "C," and "D," of their truck and fruit land in the Rio Grande Valley, a valley that is richer than the far-famed valley of the Nile. More than 500 persons have bought land in these subdivisions. We have a few blocks left, and are selling them

In Blocks of 10 Acres
$150.00 Cash, The Block
or
$20.00 Down and $7.50
Per Month for
Twenty Months.
No Interest.

These subdivisions are situated from one to five miles from Closner, on the St. Louis, Brownsville and Mexico Railway, and every acre thereof is of smooth surface, and susceptible cultivation.

The title is absolutely perfect, and is vested in John Closner, the sheriff and tax collector of Hidalgo county, as trustee, who conveys the same by Warranty Deed, without reser-tion or restriction.

The American Rio Grande Land and Irrigation Company of Hidalgo county has installed the machinery for what will be when completed, the largest independent irrigation heme in the world.

Harvey C. Stiles, horticulturist from California, says: "The land of the Rio Grande valley, in Hidalgo county, is the best for figs, grapes and oranges to be found in the United ates." It is about 60 days ahead of California, and 1500 miles closer to the market.

Hidalgo county alfalfa is cut from nine to twelve times a year, and averages a ton to the cutting, and sells on the ground at from $12.50 to $15.00 per ton.

John Closner has a large plantation of sugar cane and won the gold medal at the St. Louis World's Fair. He gets 40 tons to the acre; made more than 600,000 pounds of sugar last ar.

Governor Herrick of Ohio has faith in Hidalgo county. He says: "There is no country in the world which offers the same opportunity for development as Hidalgo county. I ex-ct to see land values increase many fold within the next few years." He bought land and says he will induce his friends in Ohio to grasp the opportunity.

Bermuda Onions.—One man planted 33 acres last year in Bermuda onions. He shipped 36 cars and cleared $14,000 on his crop. Another had one acre of lettuce and sold it for $600, and still another had one acre of cauliflower and sold it for $1000.

Hidalgo County. "The Garden Spot of the Earth." Banner Artesian County of Texas.

Get the Particulars from

B. CHAPIN, - - Hidalgo, Texas

This "Guaranteed cure for poverty" advertisement was typical of the advertisements used by the early land developers. The prospective land purchaser is told of the "garden spot of the earth" and great riches to come if one were to purchase land from D.B. Chapin of Hidalgo, Texas. John Closner and D.B. Chapin were partners in the Homeville Association. John Closner's name and position as the sheriff and tax collector of Hidalgo County were given as reasons land buyers could trust the company. The land's "smooth surface and susceptible of cultivation" and nearness to the St. Louis, Brownsville, and Mexico Railway were highlighted. Examples of crops grown, including 'figs, grapes, and oranges" and the tremendous success of other farmers and their testimonies, were all designed to make farmers want to move and buy their land. Advertisements similar to this appeared in newspapers and magazines throughout Texas and the Midwest (Courtesy of The University of Texas–Pan American Library.)

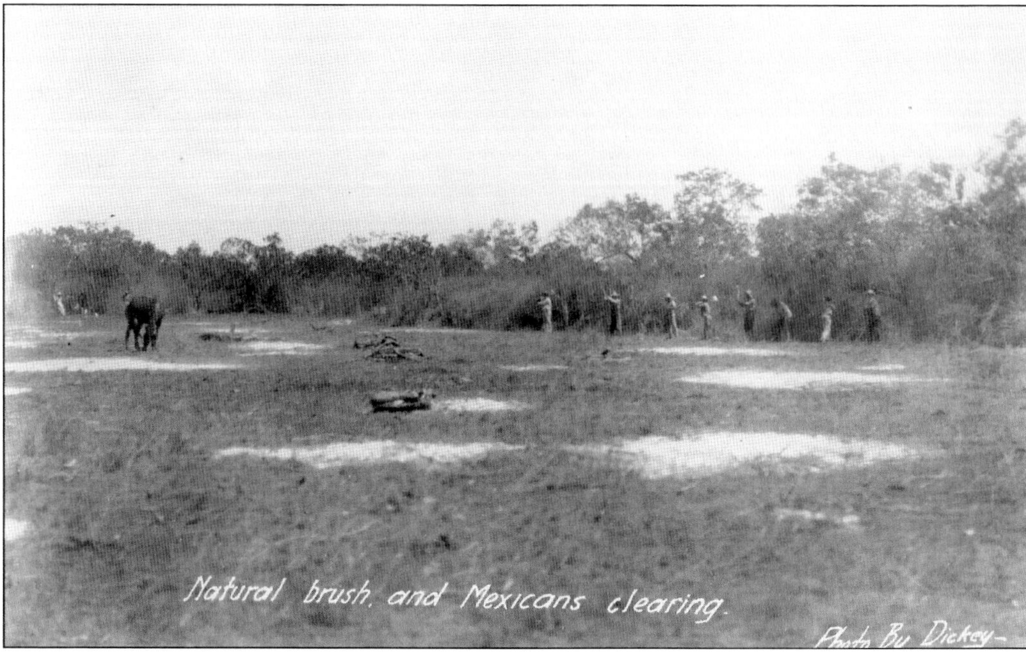

The future county seat had no buildings, no stores, and no homes. When the ox carts arrived, 10 engineers and about 400 Mexican workers were waiting, ready to clear the land and plan a new town. Early descriptions of the area describe a landscape full of brush and cactus, populated by rattlesnakes, quail, javelin, and deer. The photograph above shows a typical scene of clearing the land, in which the brush was cut, placed in large piles, and then burned. As the land was cleared, it was also surveyed to determine where streets, utilities, and buildings would be constructed. The photograph below shows D.B. Chapin, George Cleveland, and Henry Griffin at a surveyor's camp near McAllen around 1909. (Above, courtesy of The University of Texas–Pan American Library; below, courtesy of the Museum of South Texas History.)

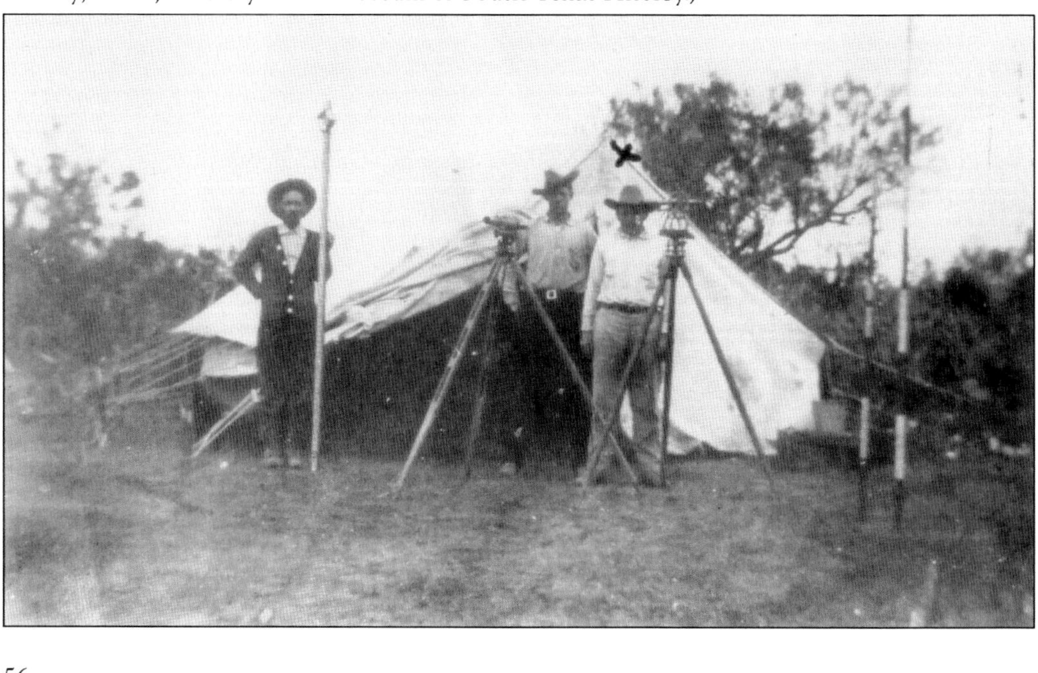

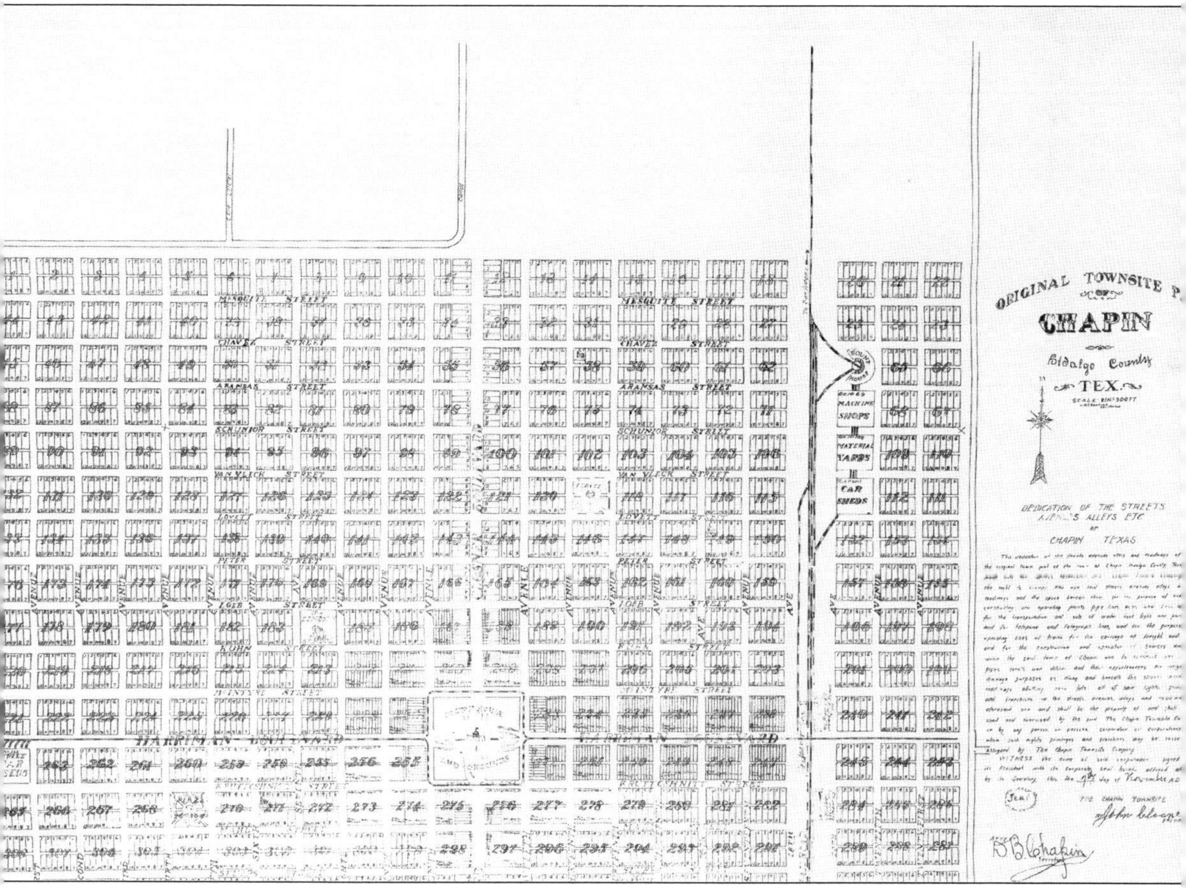

The advantage of planning a town from the beginning is that one may lay out straight streets, and designate from the beginning where parks and other community locations will be placed. The courthouse square took center stage in the middle of town, with parks located in each quadrant. Streets running north-south were numbered and were all called "Avenue." The only exception was Closner Boulevard, which ran right through the middle of the town to the courthouse square. Streets running east-west were named after railway executives and local leaders. The town founders sincerely wished that Edinburg would become the first stop on train tracks leading north to Falfurrias and eventually San Antonio. Streets named after railway executives include Harriman (later changed to University), McIntyre, Kruschnitt (later changed to Cano), Van Vleck (later changed to Van Week), Lovett, Peter, Loeb, Kuhn, Mahl, Stubbs, and Fay. Streets named after local leaders include Samano, Champion, Sprague, Closner, Chapin, Baker, and Chavez. (Courtesy of the Museum of South Texas History.)

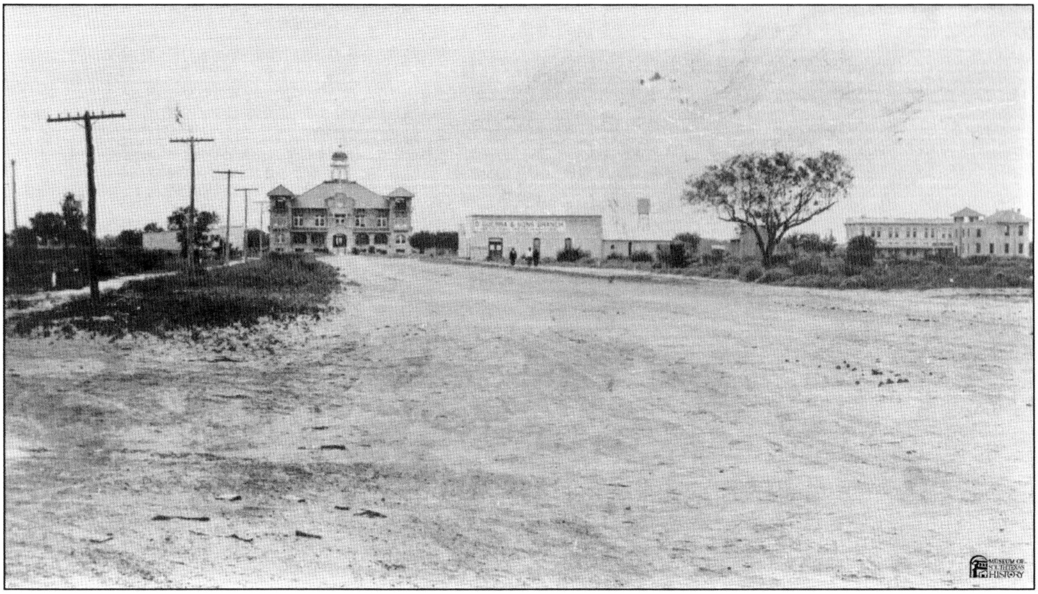

The founders of Chapin wished for and planned for a railroad from the very first days. To entice the Southern Pacific Railroad to come to town, the founders of Edinburg named east-west streets after railroad executives. E.H. Harriman, at that time president and chairman of the executive committee of the Southern Pacific Railroad, was honored with the main east-west street leading to the courthouse square. Harriman Street was changed in the early 1970s to University Boulevard. The photograph above shows a view of the courthouse looking west down Harriman Boulevard around 1912. (Courtesy of the Museum of South Texas History.)

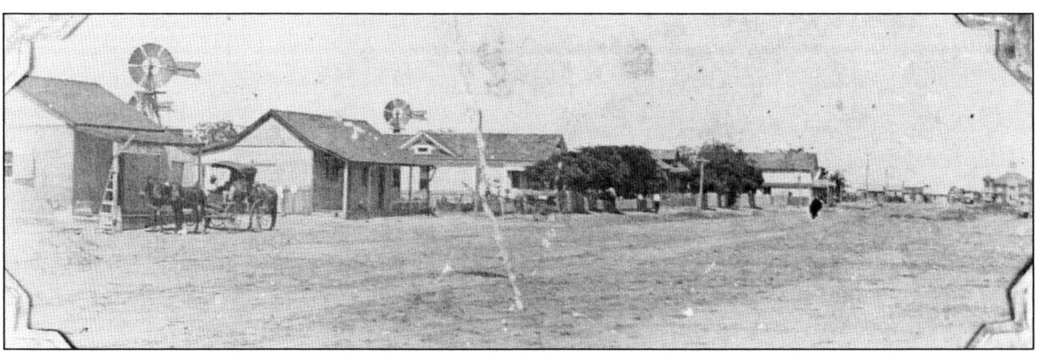

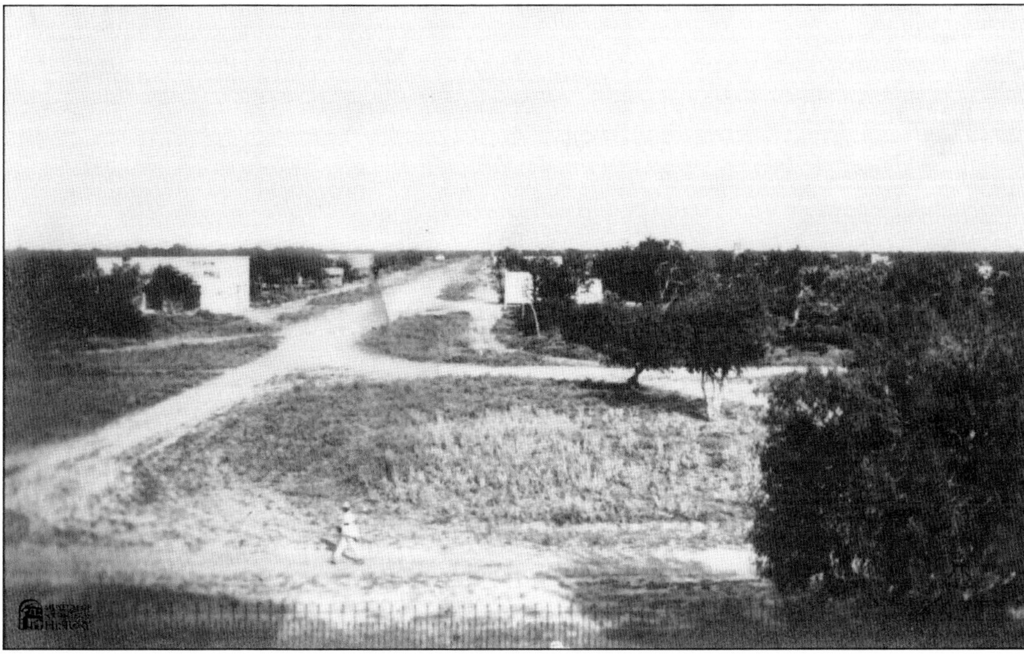

McIntyre Street, the street north of the courthouse, was named after W.H. McIntyre, president of the San Antonio & Aransas Pass. Both photographs on this page were taken from the cupola on top of the courthouse, looking north at the intersection of McIntyre and Closner. The photograph above shows the pool hall and saloon, one of the first buildings constructed in Chapin. The photograph below shows that same corner several years later. The two-story Edinburg State Bank and Trust Company is on the left hand corner. The jail and fire department is on the right hand corner. (Above, courtesy of the Museum of South Texas History; below, courtesy of the Edinburg Volunteer Fire Department Museum.)

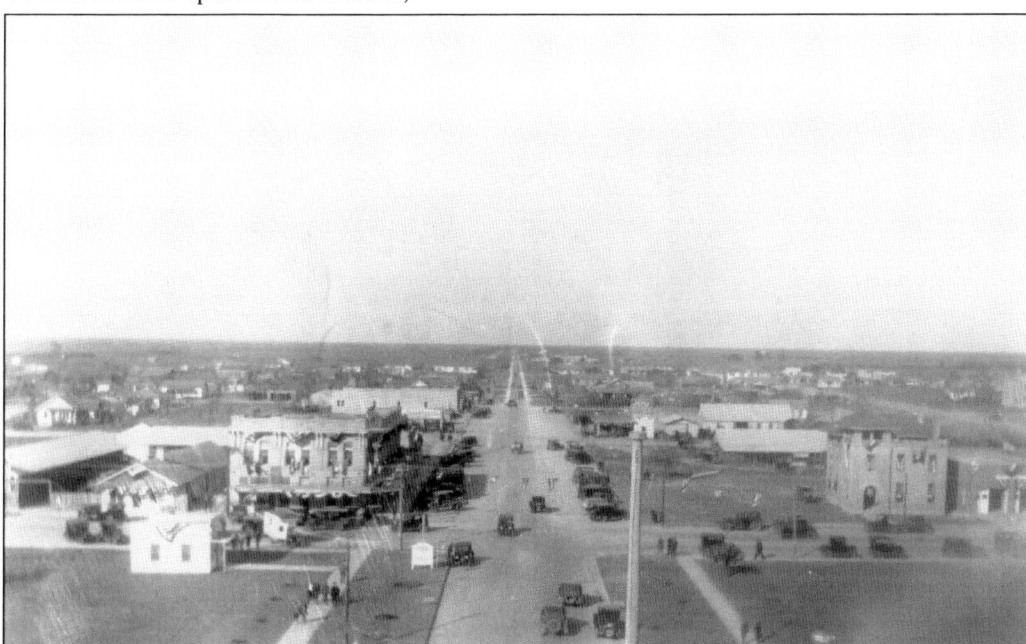

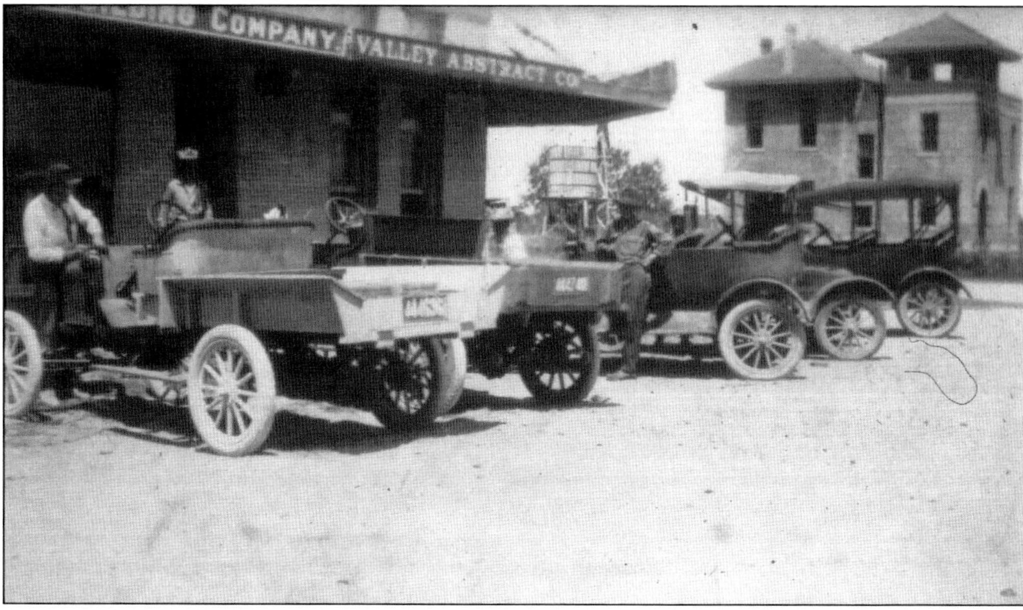

Looking north from the courthouse, the two buildings that dominated the scenery were the jail and the Edinburg State Bank and Trust Company. Both buildings were two story brick structures. The county jail was built in 1909 north of the courthouse on the eastern corner of Closner Boulevard and McIntyre Street and is easily recognizable by the third-floor hanging tower on the corner. The hanging tower had a trap door in the floor that would drop down. The photograph above shows the jail and a corner of the bank building. The Edinburg State Bank and Trust Company building was constructed in 1910 and is shown below. The bank building was badly damaged by Hurricane Beulah in 1933 and was torn down in 1937. (Above, courtesy of The University of Texas–Pan American Library; below, courtesy of the Museum of South Texas History.)

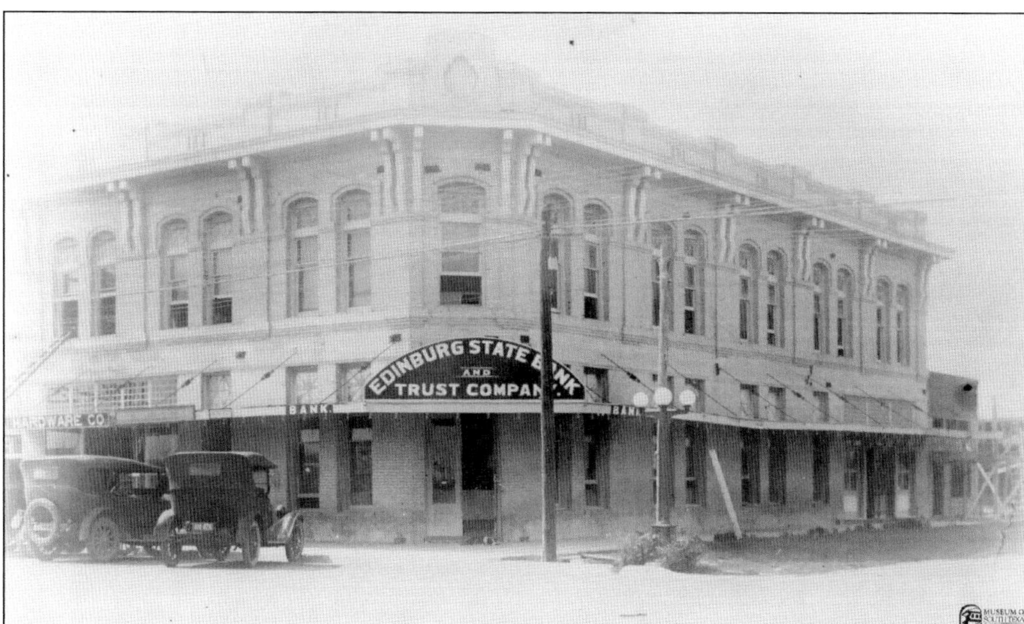

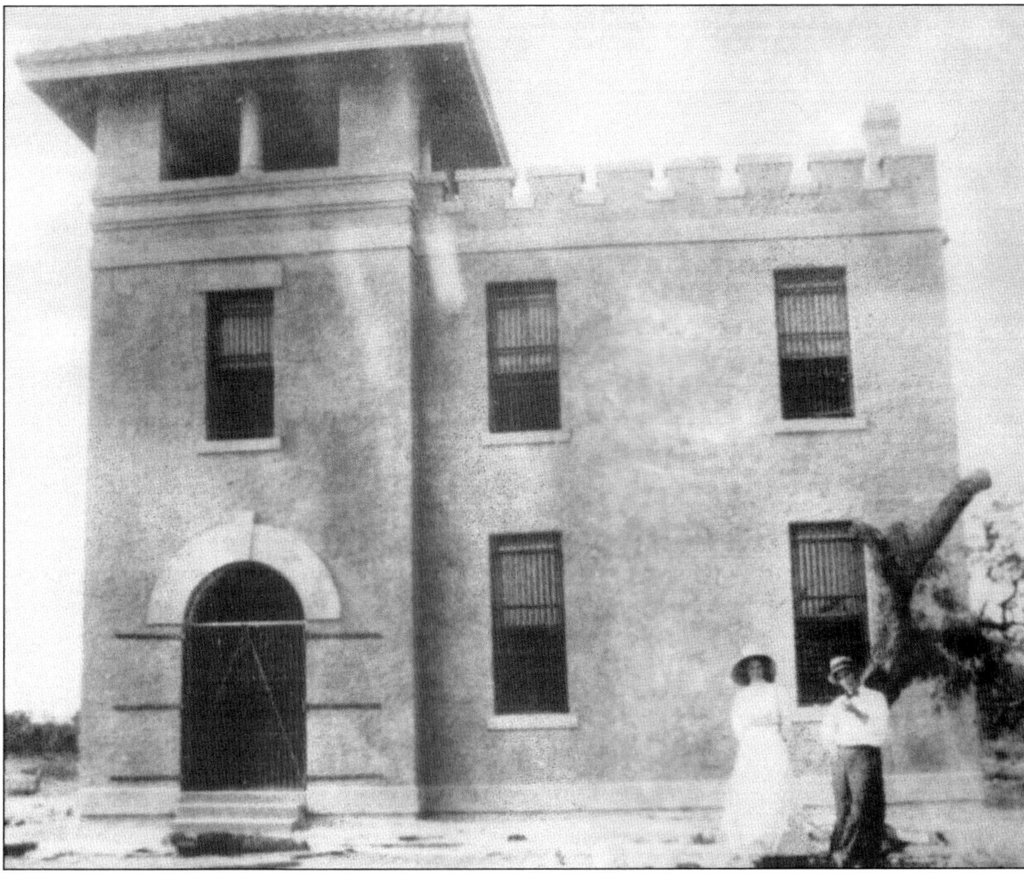

The photograph above of the newly completed county jail was taken looking north from the courthouse in 1910. Mabelle Umland and Gordon Schillings are posing in front of the jail. Mabelle Umland was a schoolteacher and school superintendent, and Gordon Schillings was a barber working in the J.B.F. McMillan barbershop. Only one person was ever given the death penalty during the time that the building served as a jail. According to the indictment documents on the right, in 1912, Abraham Ortiz and Domingo Gonzalez "did with malice aforethought kill Martin Martinez by beating and striking the said Martin Martinez with a stick of wood." Gonzalez escaped the law, leaving Ortiz alone to face punishment. Ortiz was hanged on Friday, May 2, 1913, in the hanging tower. (Courtesy of the Museum of South Texas History.)

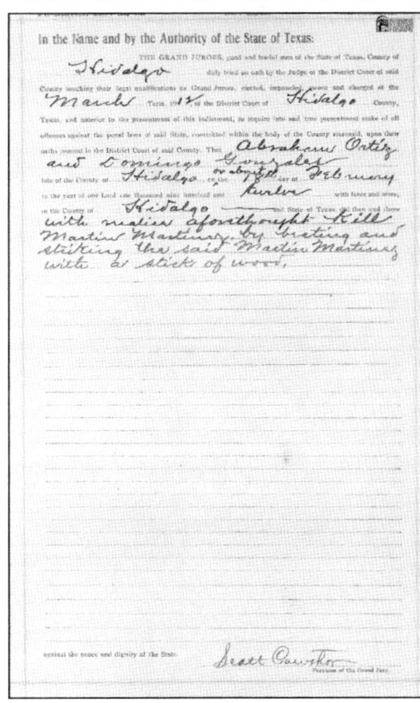

In the Name and by the Authority of the State of Texas:

THE GRAND JURORS, good and lawful men of the State of Texas, County of Hidalgo duly tried on oath by the Judge of the District Court of said County touching their legal qualifications as Grand Jurors, elected, impaneled, sworn and charged at the March Term, 1912, of the District Court of Hidalgo County, Texas, and ... to the presentment of this indictment, to inquire into and true presentment make of all offenses against the penal laws of said State, committed within the body of the County aforesaid, upon their oaths present in the District Court of said County, That Abraham Ortiz and Domingo Gonzalez late of the County of Hidalgo, on or about the 18th day of February in the year of our Lord one thousand nine hundred and twelve with force and arms, in the County of Hidalgo and State of Texas, did then and there with malice aforethought kill Martin Martinez by beating and striking the said Martin Martinez with a stick of wood,

against the peace and dignity of the State.

Scott Crawford
Foreman of the Grand Jury.

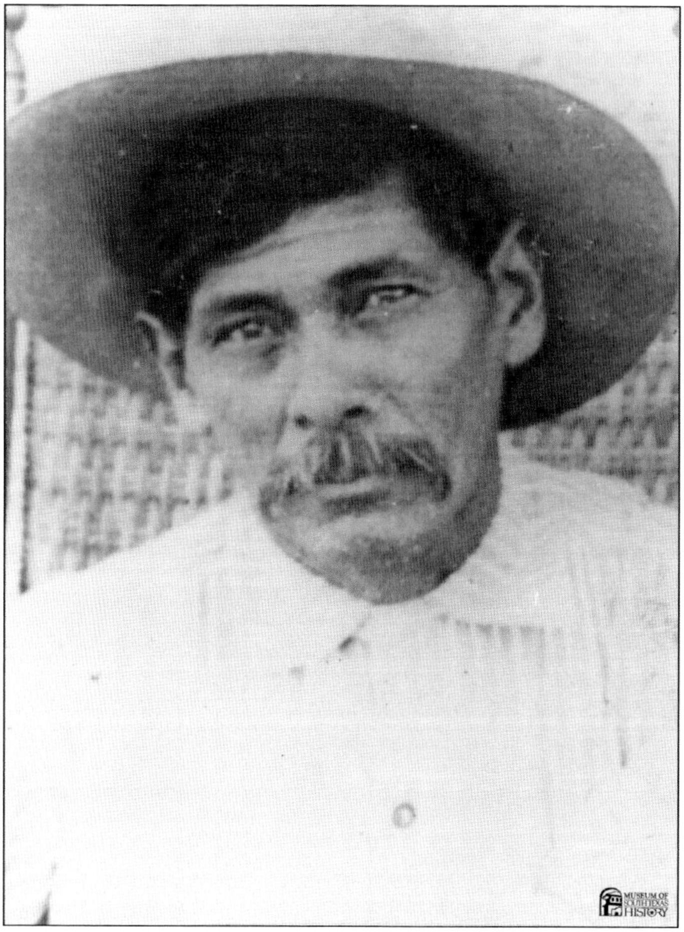

It is seldom that people think of a jail building with fondness, but that is how the jail on the courthouse corner is thought of today. Perhaps this positive aspect began with Nemencio Cortina, the first jailer who was hired and deputized by John Closner in 1910. Cortina (left) was reported to be a kind and caring jailer. The building was later converted to the city hall. The fire department was added on the side, the second floor converted to a dorm for the volunteer firefighters, and the ground floor housed the police department as shown below. The building was later converted to the Museum of South Texas History. (Left, courtesy of the Museum of South Texas History; below, courtesy of the Edinburg Volunteer Fire Department Museum).

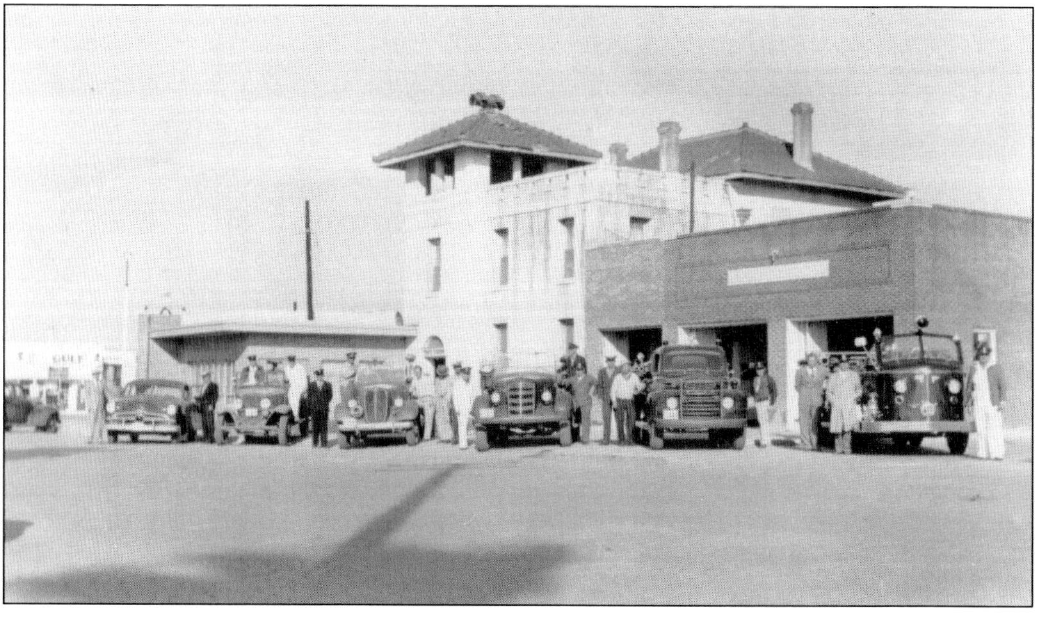

Besides filling the county jail, two of the most famous Hidalgo County sheriffs were also very influential in other respects. John Closner was one of the most noted sheriffs of Hidalgo County, and the one who is reported to have finally brought peace and order to a county where in previous years eight sheriffs had all resigned under threats of assassination. Closner was appointed deputy sheriff by James L. Dougherty in 1884 and county sheriff and tax collector in 1889. Closner survived two assassination attempts and a bounty placed on his head by Mexican bandits of 10,000 to 20,000 Mexican pesos. Below, the *San Antonio Express* dedicated a full page on September 7, 1911, honoring Closner's successes (Right, courtesy of the Museum of South Texas History; below, courtesy of The University of Texas–Pan American Library.)

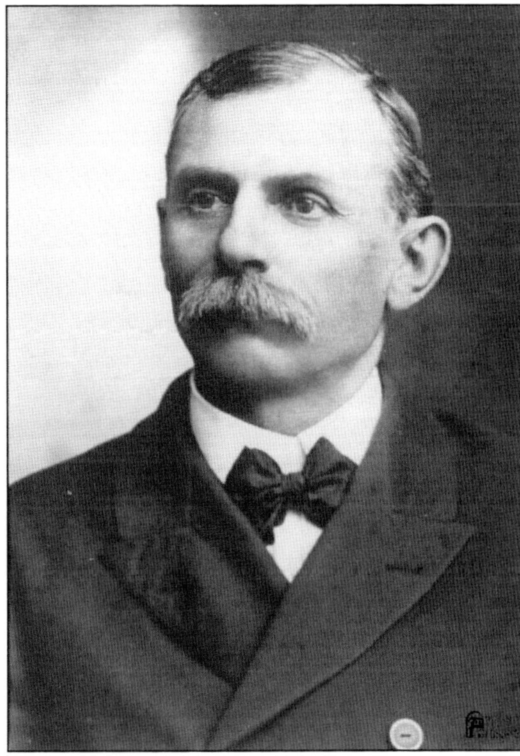

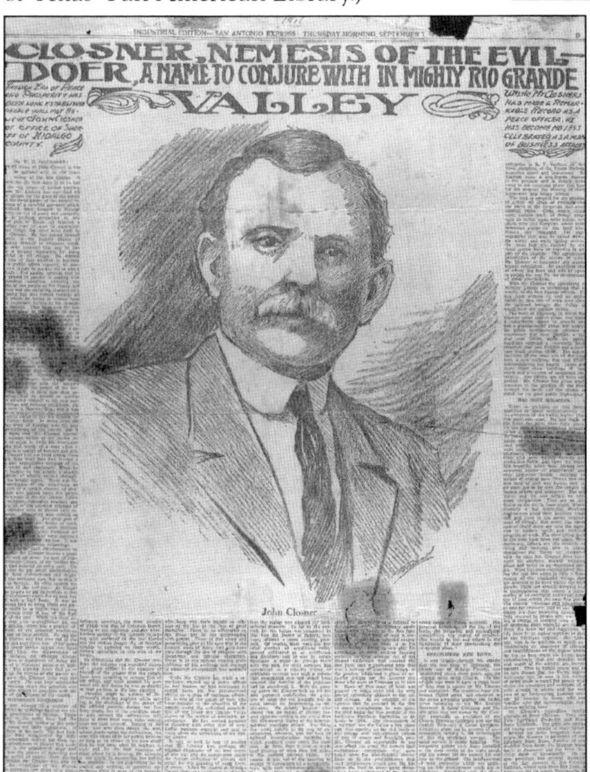

CLOSNER, NEMESIS OF THE EVIL-DOER, A NAME TO CONJURE WITH IN MIGHTY RIO GRANDE VALLEY

John Closner

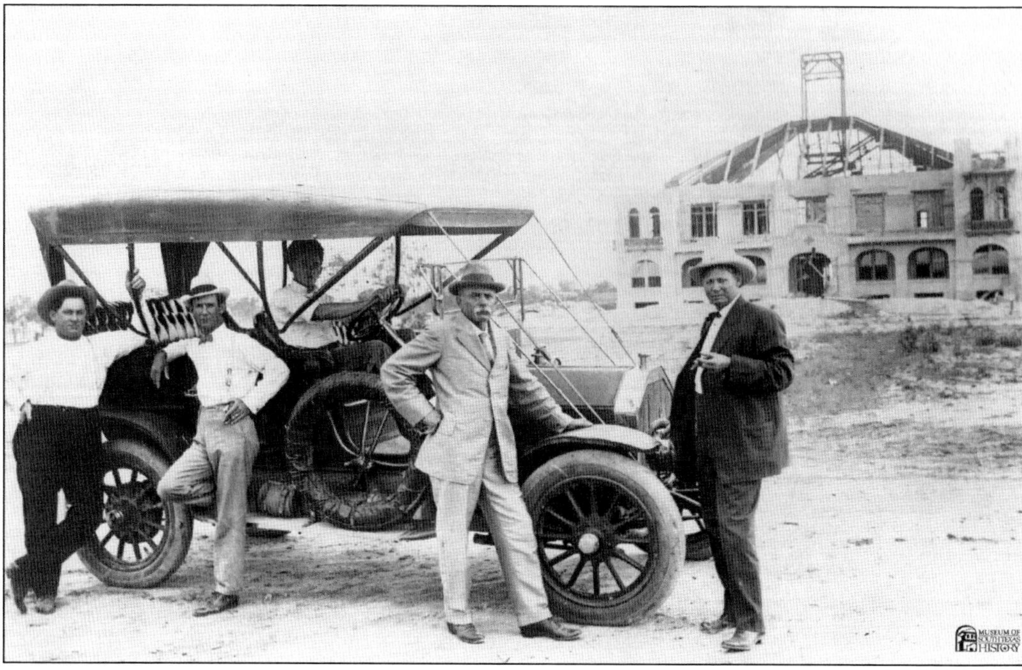

In 1912, John Closner traded positions with A.Y. Baker. Closner became the new county treasurer and Baker became the new county sheriff. The photograph above, taken in front of the courthouse, shows the "county VIPs" standing next to a car, from left to right: county treasurer A.Y. Baker, county judge Walter Moses Doughty Sr., sheriff John Closner, lawyer and Chapin secretary D.B. Chapin. Behind the wheel of the car is John James Closner (John Closner's son). In 1919, while Closner was serving as county treasurer, an audit of the county records revealed that many records were missing, and Closner was accused of mishandling county records. A year later, he was acquitted without the jury even leaving the box. (Above, courtesy of the Museum of South Texas History; below, courtesy of The University of Texas–Pan American Library.)

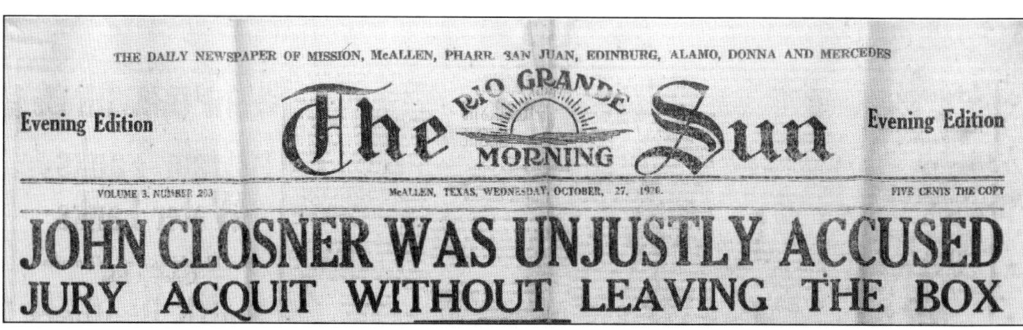
THE DAILY NEWSPAPER OF MISSION, McALLEN, PHARR, SAN JUAN, EDINBURG, ALAMO, DONNA AND MERCEDES

Evening Edition — The Rio Grande Morning Sun — Evening Edition

VOLUME 3, NUMBER 203 — McALLEN, TEXAS, WEDNESDAY, OCTOBER, 27, 1920. — FIVE CENTS THE COPY

JOHN CLOSNER WAS UNJUSTLY ACCUSED
JURY ACQUIT WITHOUT LEAVING THE BOX

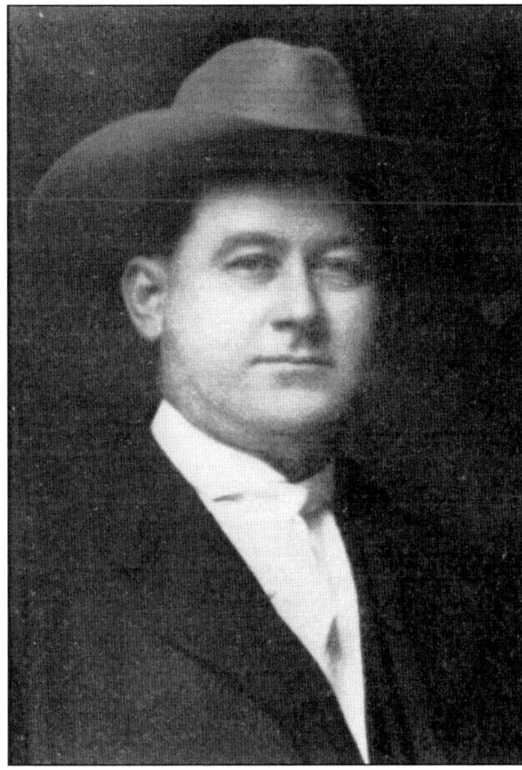

Anderson Yancey Baker (right), most commonly known as A.Y. Baker, first arrived in the Valley as a Texas Ranger. In 1907, he was appointed county treasurer, and in 1919, he became the first elected mayor when Edinburg became an incorporated town. He was loved by some and hated by others, but all could agree that Baker had a large influence in city and county events. As a ranger, Baker was accused of excessive violence. He acquired land inexpensively because of advance knowledge of seizures and foreclosures through his positions with the Customs Bureau and the county. The photograph below shows, from left to right, A.Y. Baker (1), George ? (2), ? Guerra (3), Ernest Horn (4), and Lee Welch (5). (Right, Museum of South Texas History; below, courtesy of The University of Texas–Pan American Library.)

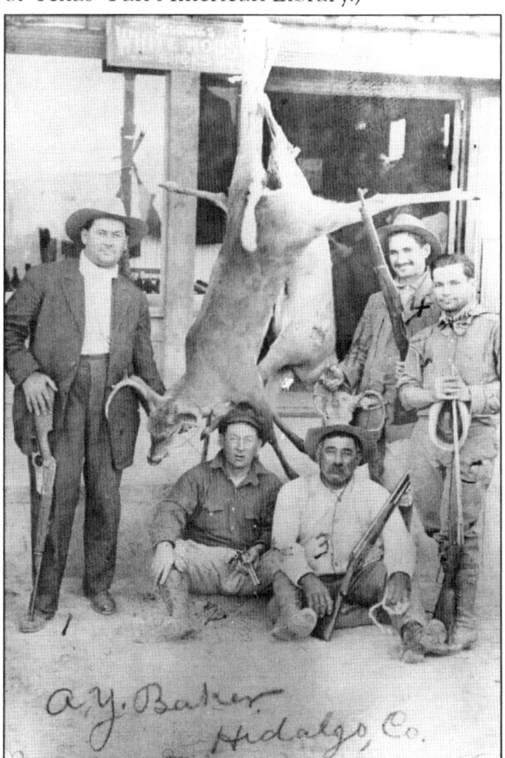

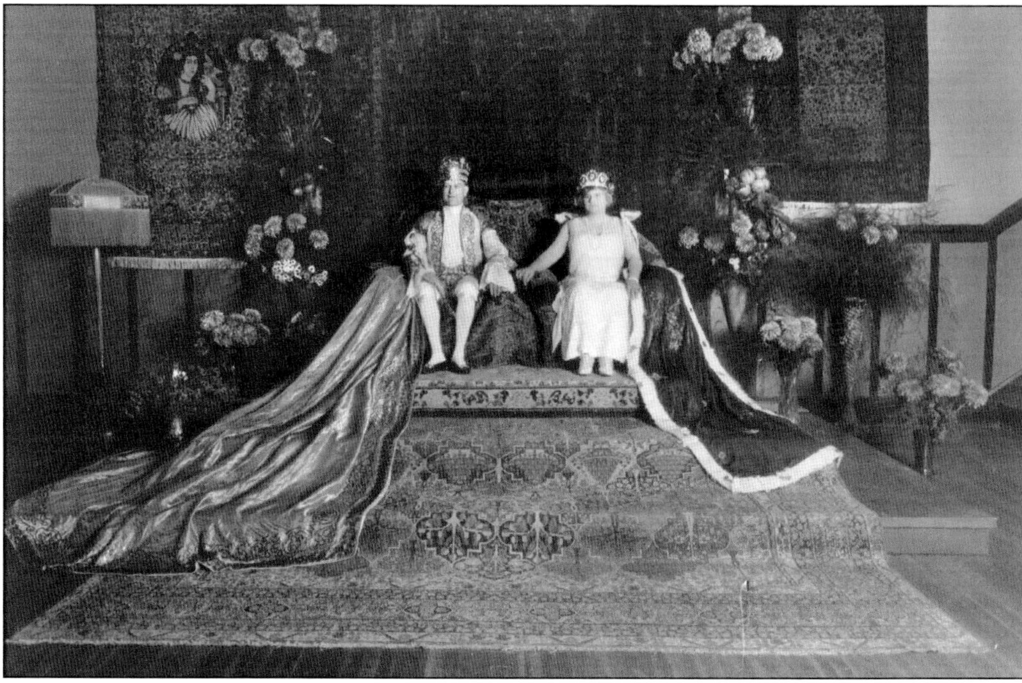

Most of all, A.Y. Baker is known as one of the most important political bosses of Hidalgo County. In 1928, the Hidalgo County Rebellion and Good Government League was formed largely in response to Baker's boss rule, political control, and questionable election practices. One of Baker's most famous actions was a bond election in 1927 for the so-called "Nickel Plated Highway to Hell," which supposedly cost taxpayers $100,000 a mile. The highway began in Edinburg and ended by the bridge in Hidalgo near a gambling and drinking establishment owned by Baker. Seen above are John Shary and Mrs. A.Y. Baker posing as Grapefruit King and Queen at the county fair. The photograph below shows the Baker house. (Above, courtesy of The University of Texas–Pan American Library; below, courtesy of the Museum of South Texas History.)

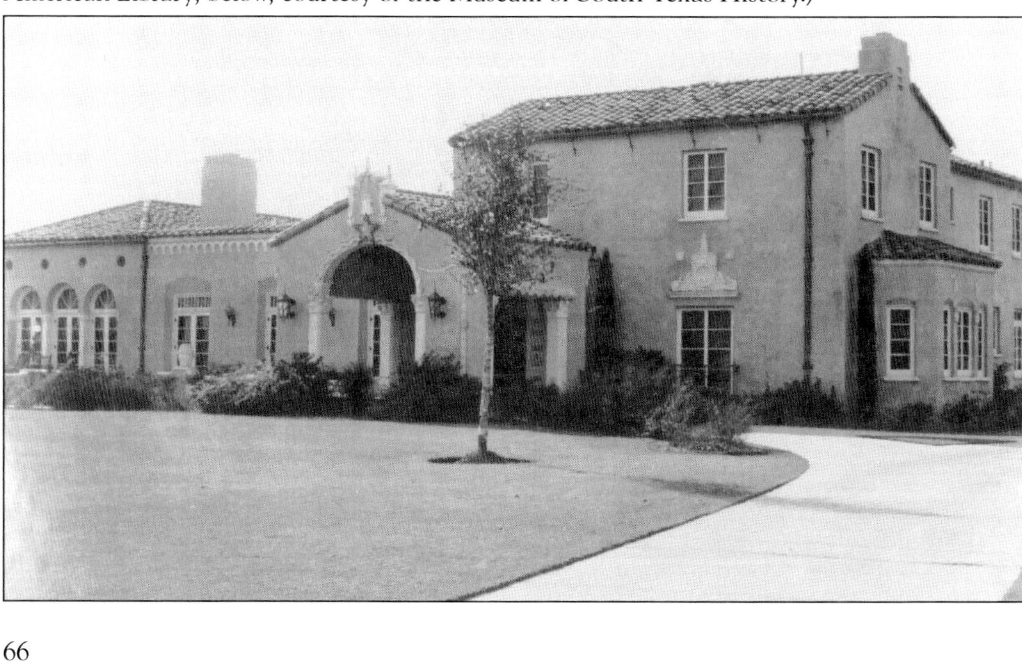

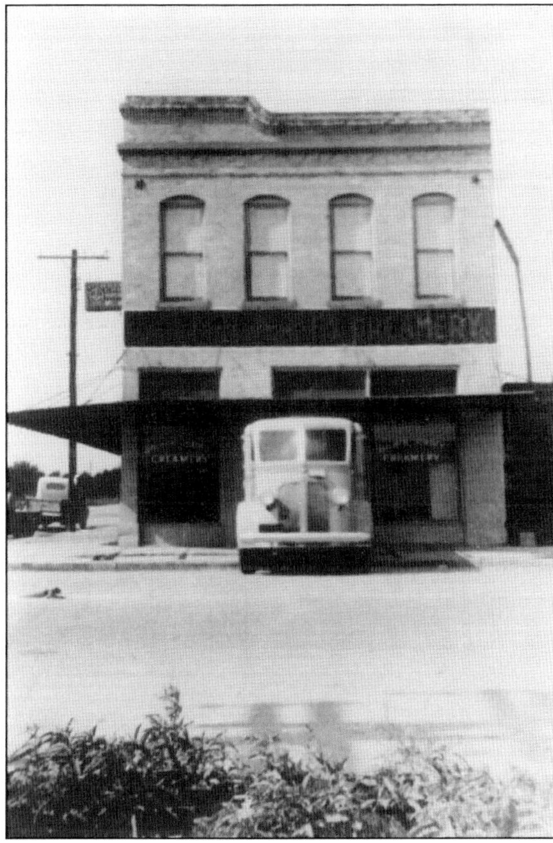

The building on the corner of McIntyre Street and Twelfth Avenue on the northeast corner of the courthouse square has alternately been known as the Miller-Everitt Building, the Hendrix-Cook Building, and the Golden-Jersey Creamery. John Closner built the structure in 1910. Rev. W.O. Miller rented it for the Rio Grande Hardware and Machine Company. A decade later, E.M. Everitt purchased it. He used it at first for a furniture store, then a grocery store. From 1930 to 1946, the Golden Jersey Creamery rented the building, as shown at right. After 1946, Golden Jersey Creamery moved to the opposite corner of the courthouse square to the corner of McIntyre Street and Tenth Avenue as shown. (Courtesy of The University of Texas–Pan American Library.)

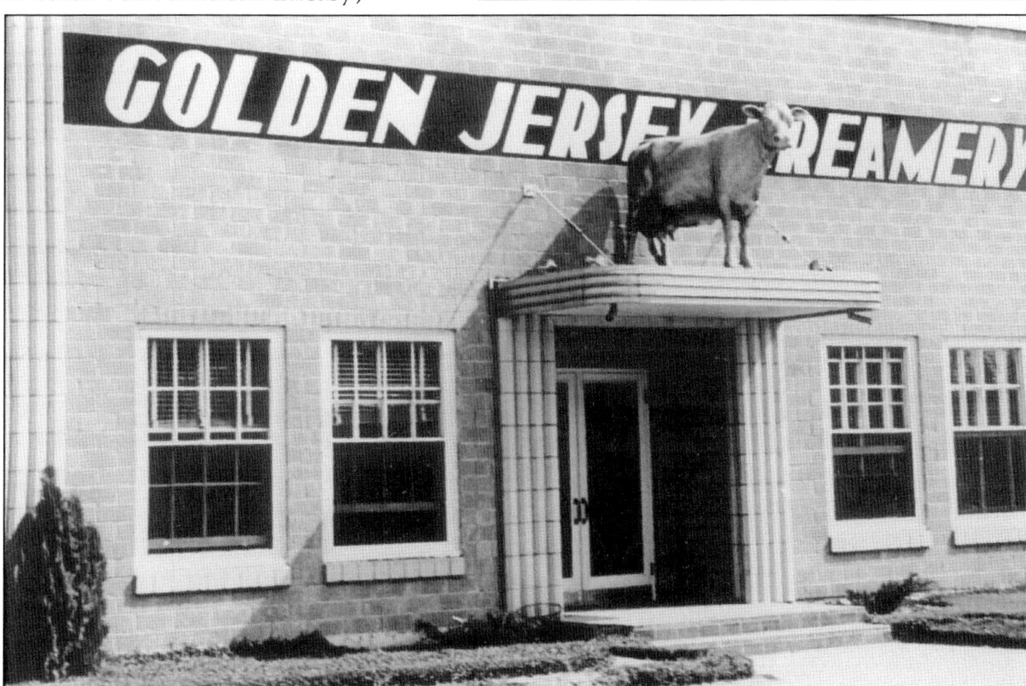

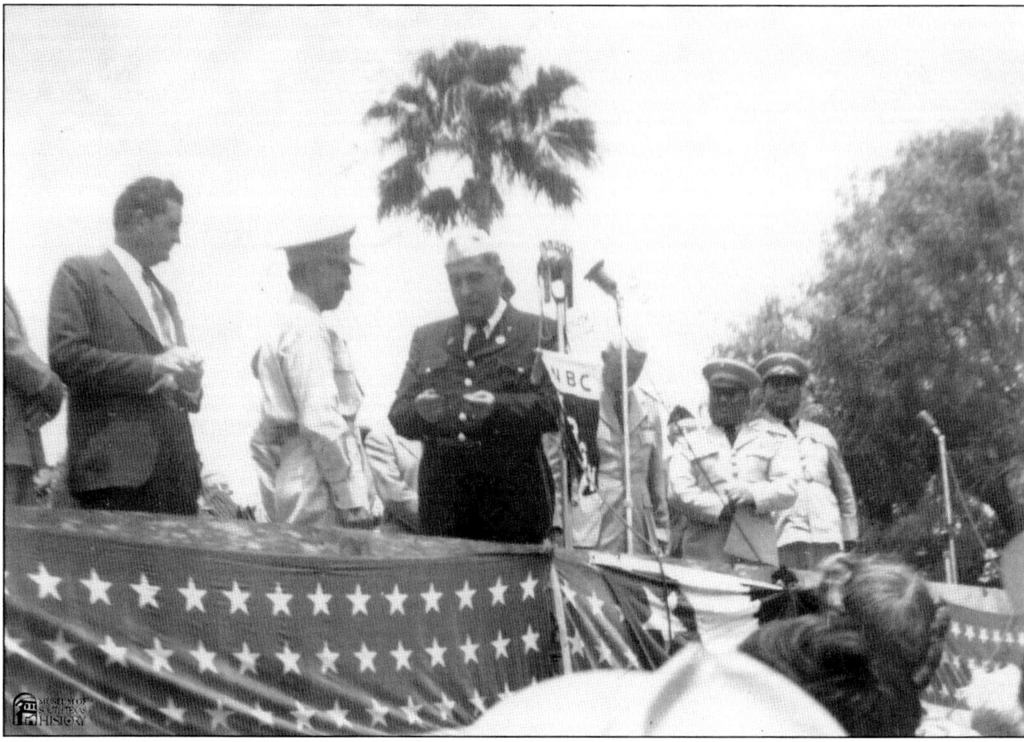

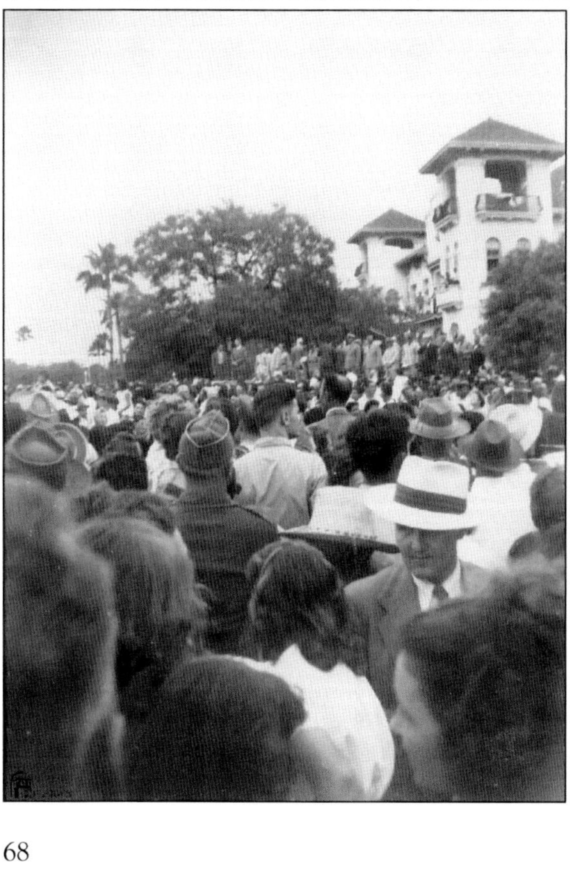

Over the years, the residents of Edinburg have wished to honor some of their citizens through street and school names. South of the courthouse was Kruttschnitt Street, named after J. Kruttschnitt, a chairman of the executive committee of the Southern Pacific. This street was renamed to Cano Street shortly after World War II to honor Pedro Cano, who received two Silver Star medals, a Purple Heart, and the Distinguished Service Cross, the country's second highest military honor, for his World War II service. The citizens of Edinburg honored Private Cano on April 26, 1946, for "Pedro Cano Day" during which businesses and schools closed to allow everyone to attend the ceremonies. In May 1946, Mexican-born Cano received his American citizenship. (Courtesy of the Museum of South Texas History.)

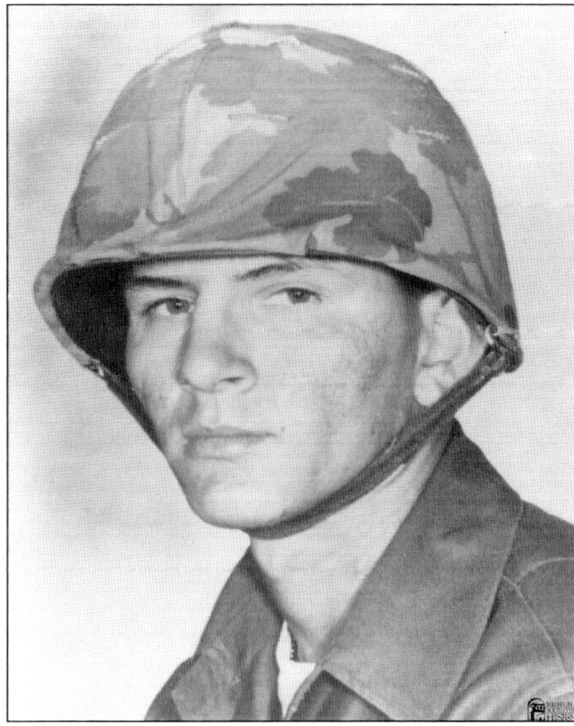

Another hometown hero, Freddy Gonzalez (Alfredo Cantu Gonzalez), received the Medal of Honor for his actions during the Vietnam War. Gonzalez displayed such bravery in action and rescuing a comrade despite his own injuries that he has been honored in Edinburg and elsewhere in America. In Edinburg, Freddy Gonzalez Street, an elementary school, and the Alfredo Cantu Gonzalez American Legion Post were named in his honor. Other cities have also honored Gonzalez including the Alfredo Gonzalez Dining Hall at the Naval Air Station in Corpus Christi, and Alfredo Gonzalez Boulevard at Camp Lejeune, North Carolina. The USS *Gonzalez* (below), a guided missile destroyer, is the first ship named for a Hispanic Texan hero. (Courtesy of the Museum of South Texas History.)

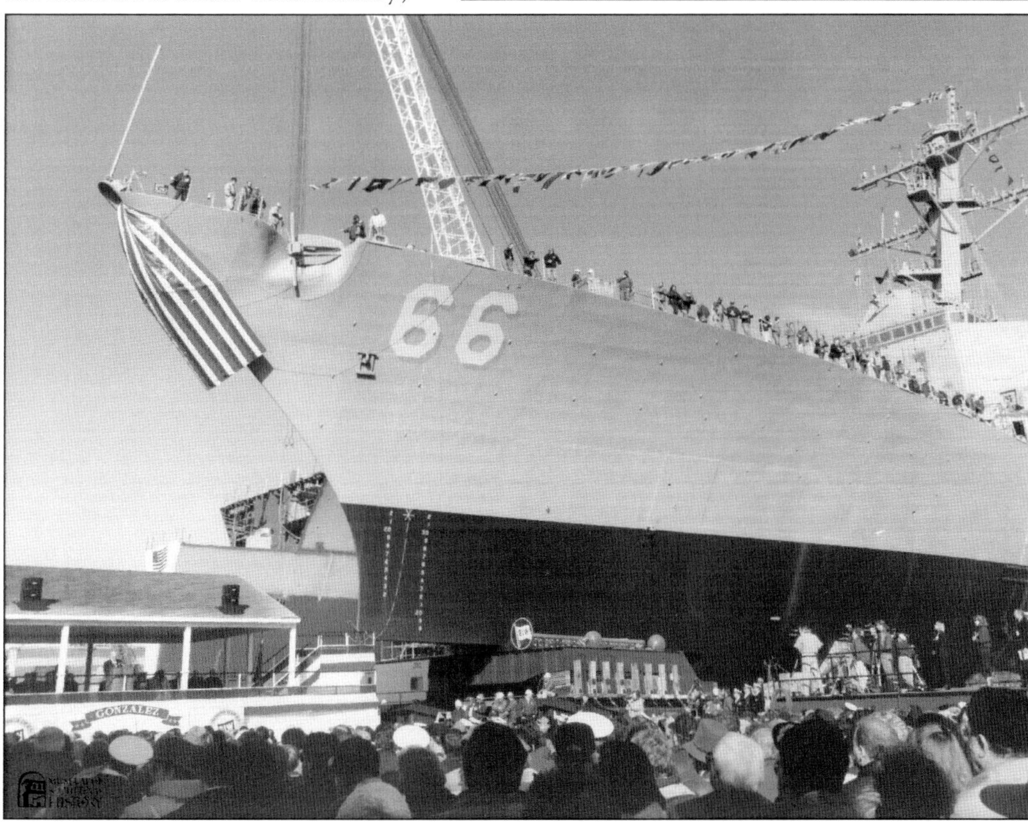

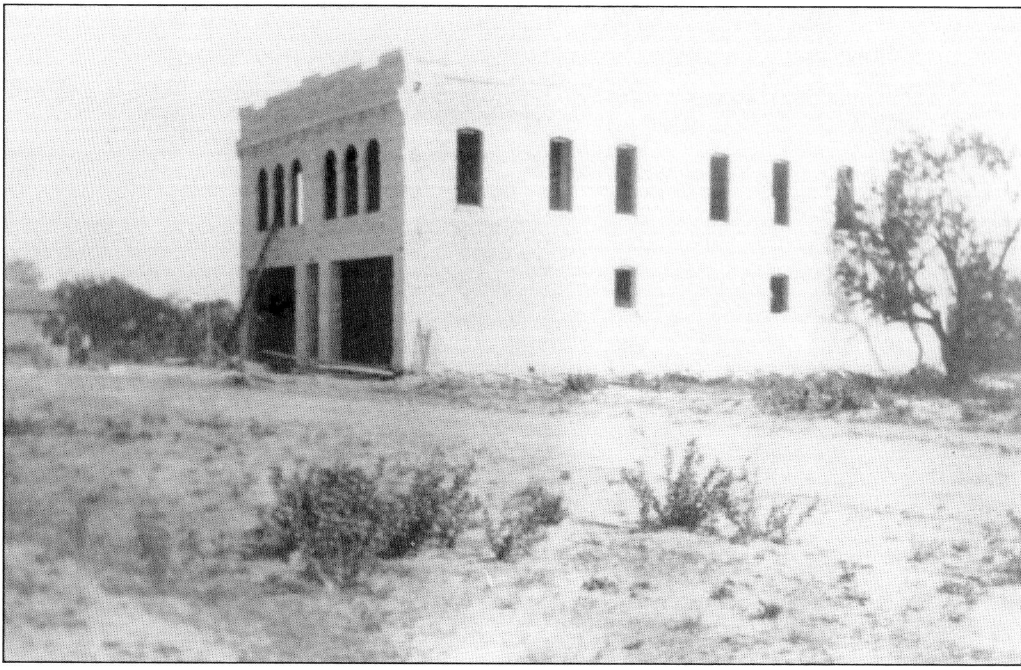

In 1908, the first drugstore was built by J.B.F. McMillan on the eastern side of the southeast corner of the courthouse square on Kruttschnitt (Cano) Street and Twelfth Avenue. McMillan was both a pharmacist and a medical doctor, and on that corner he originally built three small wooden buildings, which housed many doctors' offices through the years. The small wooden buildings were replaced with a larger brick building, which became known as the McMillan Building or the Corner Drug Store. The wooden drugstore is shown above. The brick corner drugstore building is seen below around 1932. Suites for doctors' offices were housed on the second floor. (Above, courtesy of The University of Texas–Pan American Library; below, courtesy of the Museum of South Texas History.)

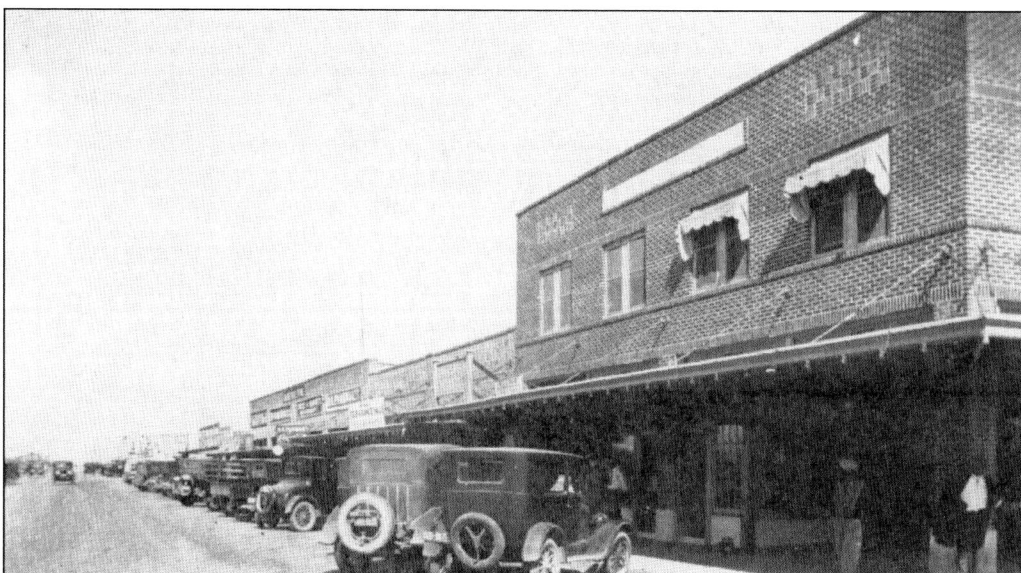

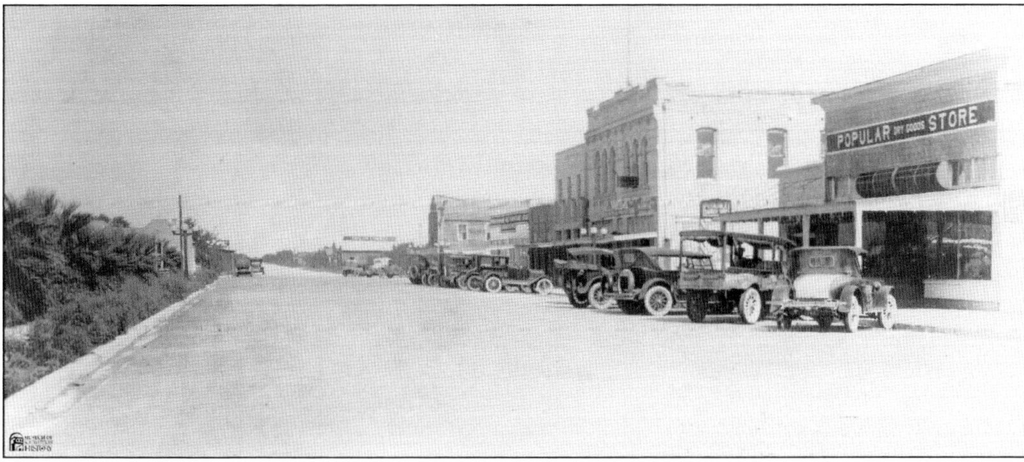

The first building to be built that is still standing on the southern side of the courthouse square is known as the Lipscomb Building as shown below. The building is in the middle of the block on Cano Street. The photograph above shows the building in 1910 after John Closner had just completed its construction. The photograph below was taken just 10 years later in 1920, after a sidewalk ordinance was passed requiring property owners to install sidewalks in front of their stores. It is apparent how quickly Edinburg grew in those intervening years. The Lipscomb building is easily identifiable with its distinctive facade (Courtesy of the Museum of South Texas History.)

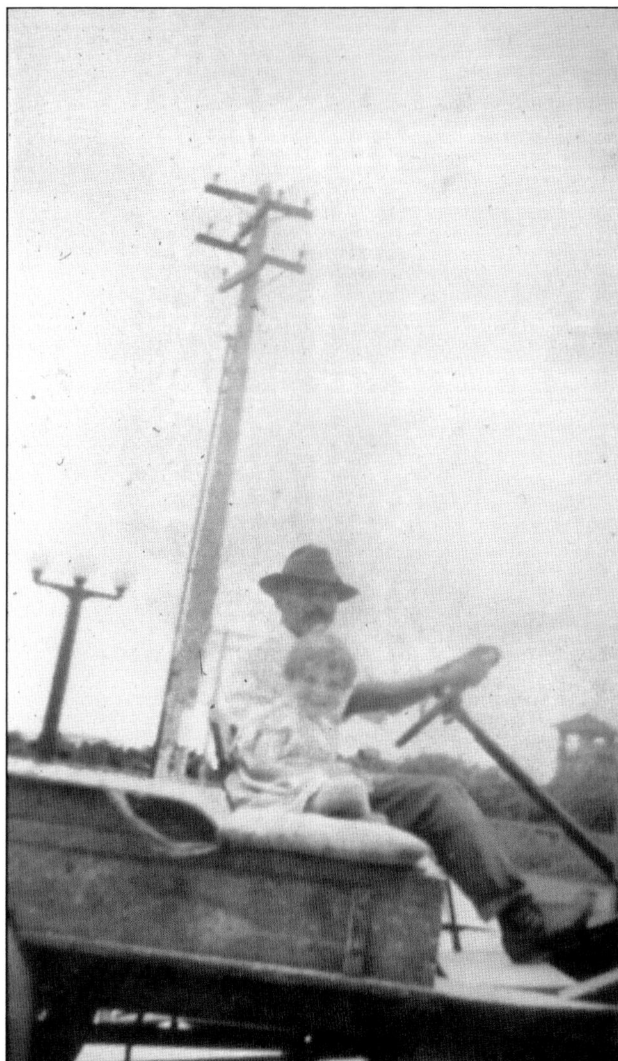

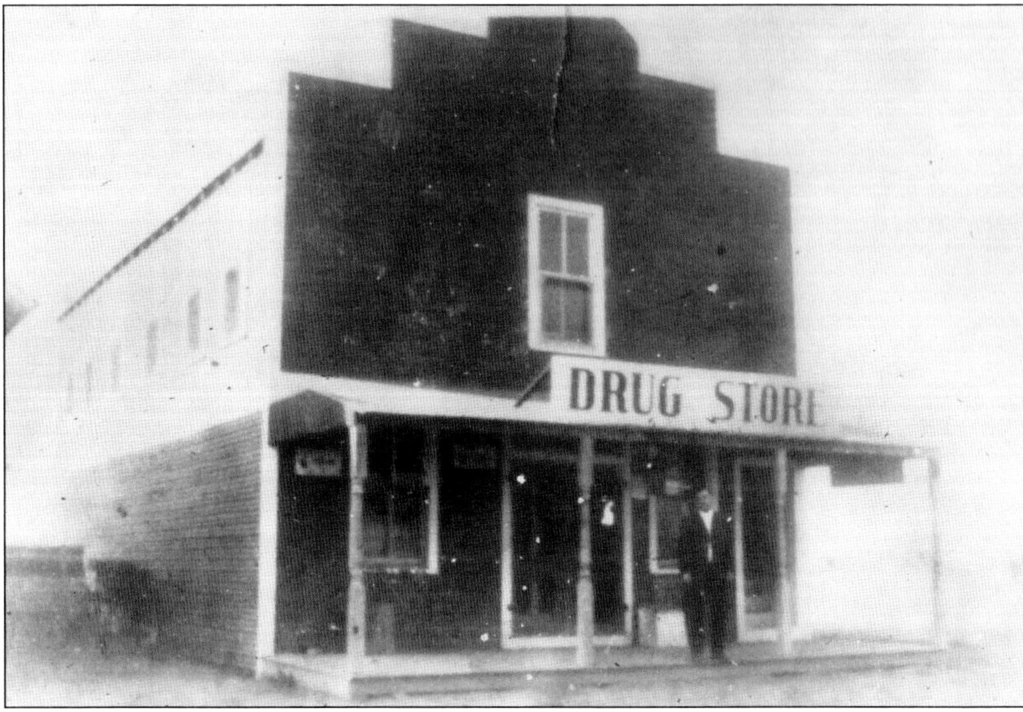

The Lipscomb building was to be used for the Chapin Improvement Company. W.L. Lipscomb and H.P. Griffin created the Lipscomb and Griffin General Merchandise store, with groceries on the east side, and general merchandise on the west side. Mr. Lipscomb eventually bought the property and stayed open for business for the next 34 years. Lipscomb is said to have called his customers daily to see what their grocery needs were, and then would deliver what was needed. The photograph below shows Henry Lopez and a child in the Lipscomb delivery truck. The building has since gone through a series of ownerships and businesses, including as Walgreens drugstore as shown in the photograph below. (Above, courtesy of The University of Texas–Pan American Library; below, courtesy of the Museum of South Texas History.)

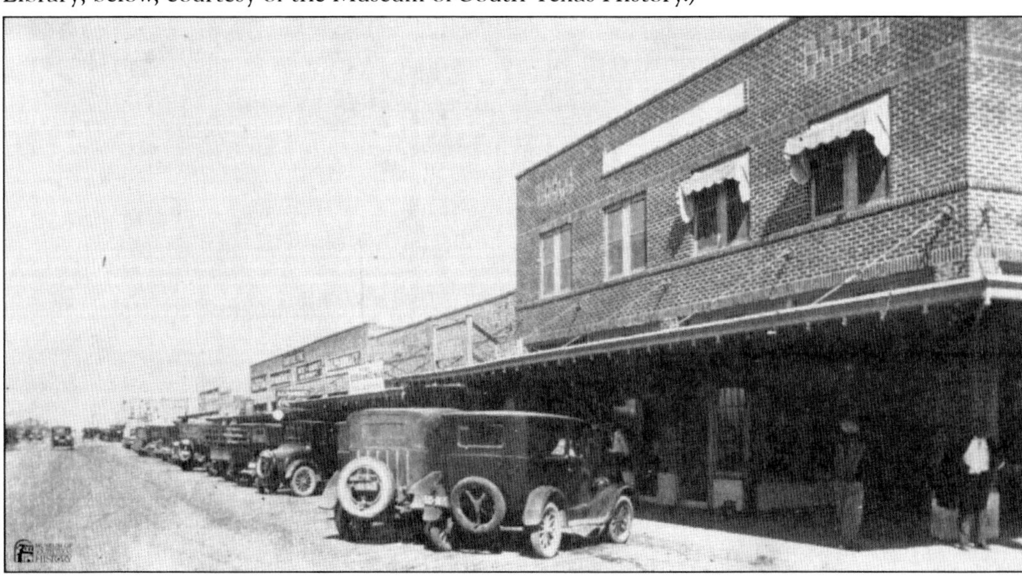

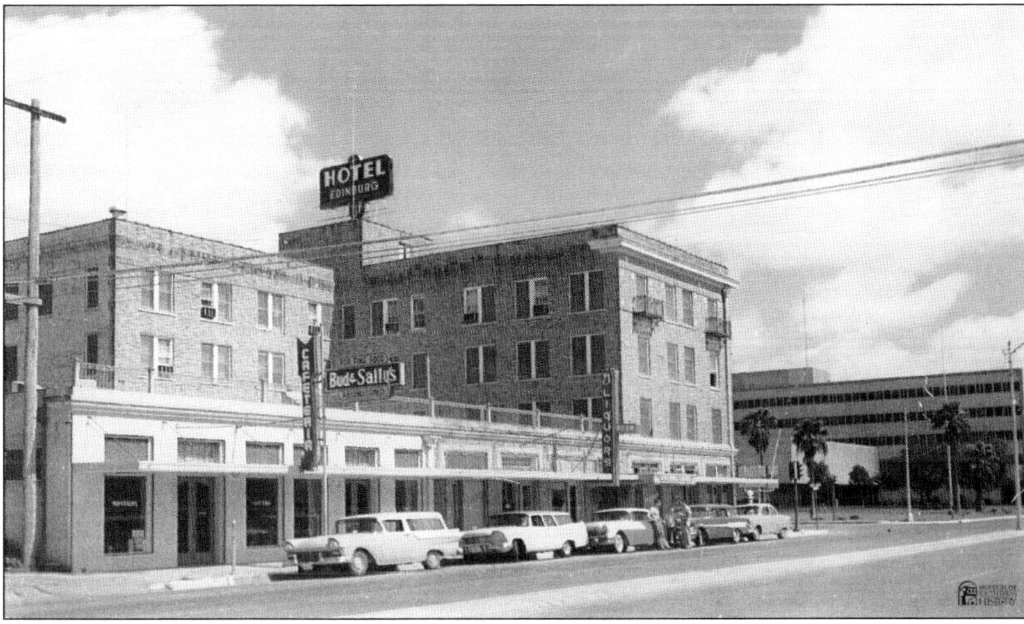

For decades the four-story Edinburg Hotel dominated the skyline. The hotel's sign, sticking up above the landscape, was captured in many photographs until the building was torn down. The two photographs on this page were both taken after the 1954 courthouse was constructed. Above, one can see the courthouse in the background. Even when the hotel was not the focus, it appears in many photographs, such as the scene below of a pumper race in front of the courthouse with George Paraskevas dragging and Gary Pierce catching as the crowd cheers, the hotel sign clearly visible in the background. (Above, courtesy of the Museum of South Texas History; below, courtesy of the Edinburg Volunteer Fire Department Museum.)

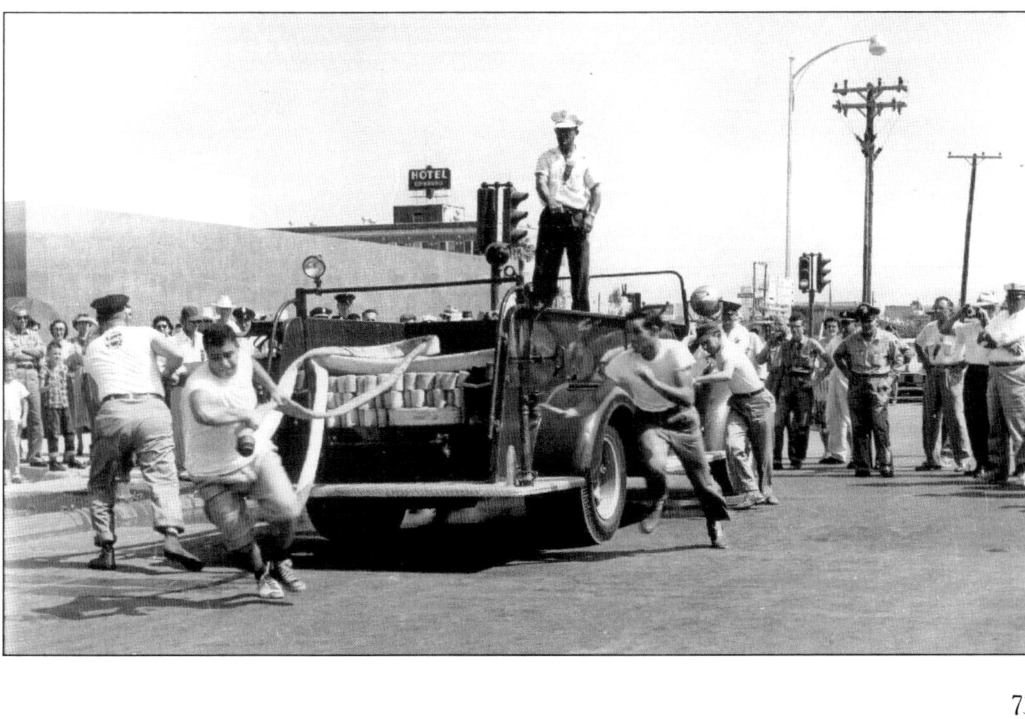

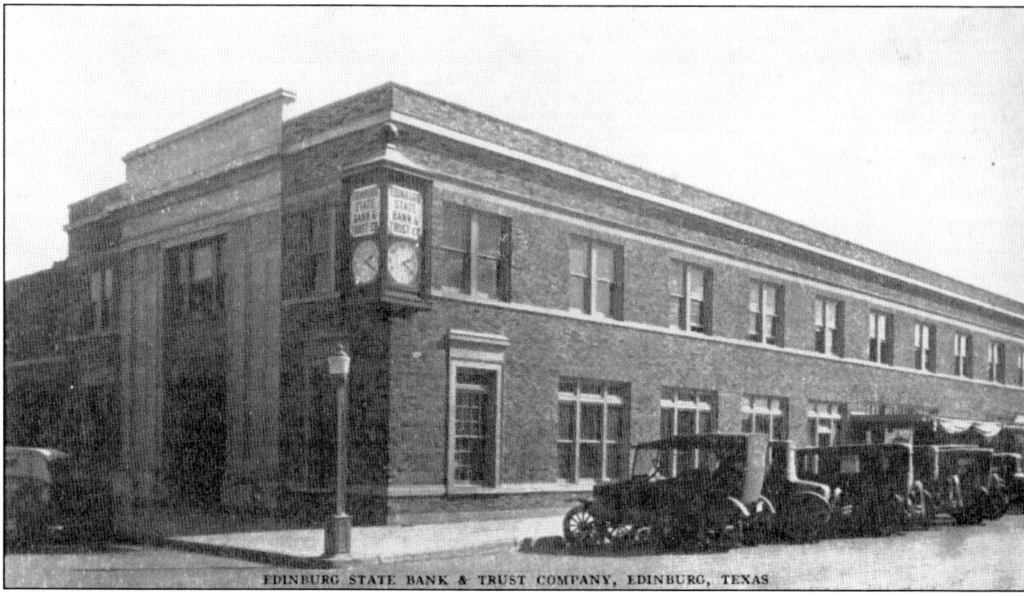

On the opposite corner of the Edinburg Hotel on the eastern side of Closner Avenue and Cano Street, the First State Bank and Trust Company was built in 1927. The photograph above was taken after the building opened. The photograph below shows both the bank building and the white Lipscomb building in the middle of the block in the 1950s. As the county continued to grow, the bank building was turned into an administrative annex housing additional offices. Today, in 2011, the courthouse is over 50 years old, county offices are spread out in various locations in the city, and there are once again discussions concerning renovating or building a new courthouse and how to revitalize downtown. (Courtesy of the Museum of South Texas History.)

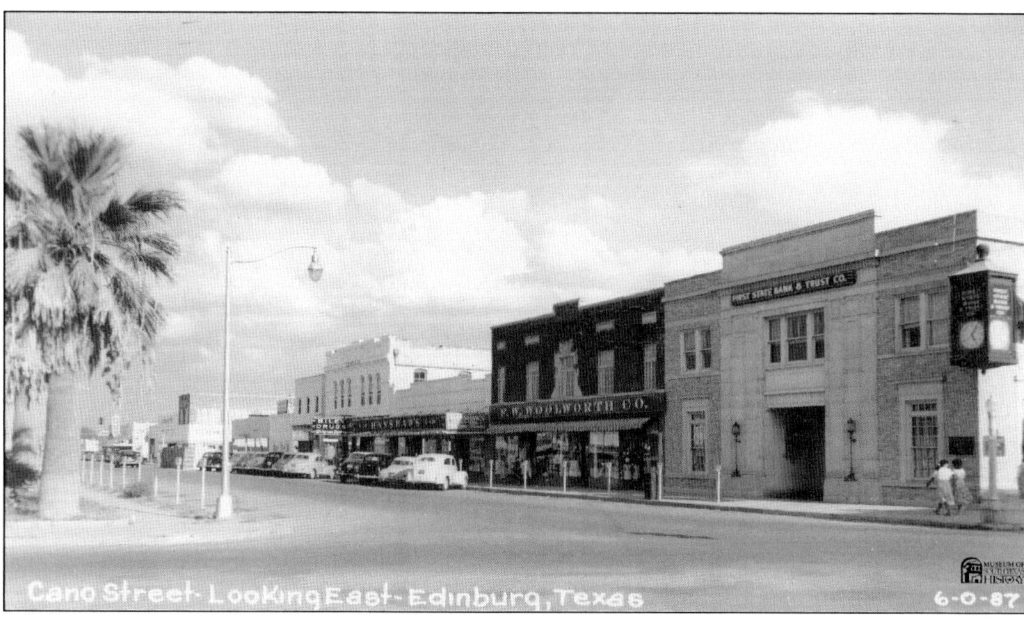

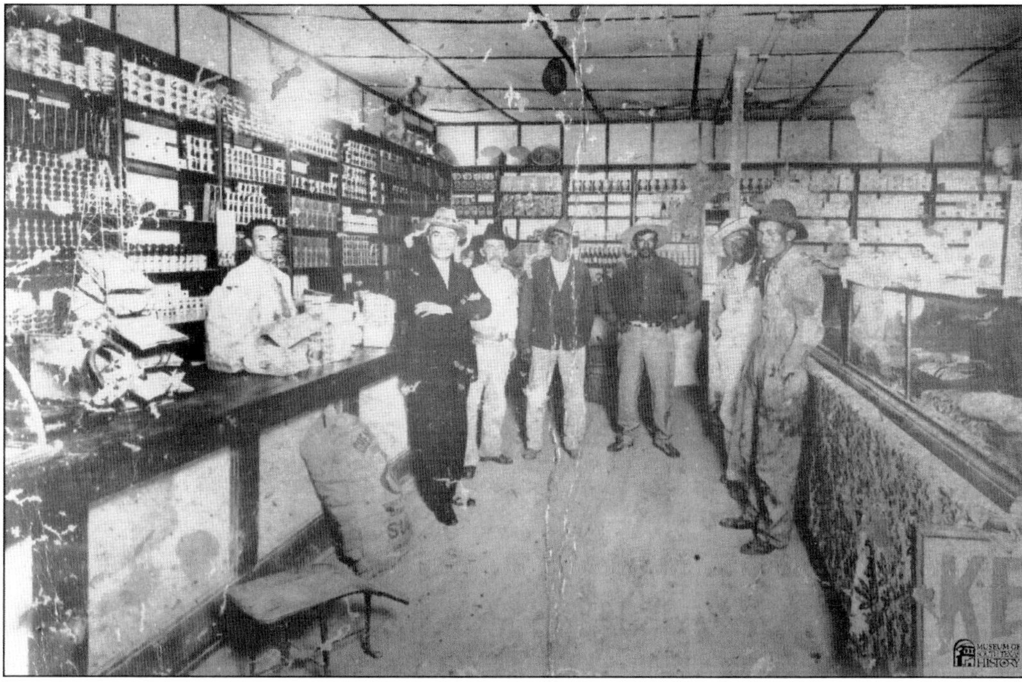

The photograph above was taken inside the Edinburg Drug Company store on East Cano Street in the 1920s. The photograph below was taken inside the Guerra Food Store on 323 E. University in 1933 and shows, from left to right, Mrs. José Guerra, her adopted daughter Maria Ponce, and José Guerra. The Guerra Food Store was eventually torn down and replaced with a shopping mall. The handled baskets in the photograph below are indicative of the change in shopping practice from taking customers' orders with pencil and pad to having the customers select their own merchandise and bringing it up to the counter. (Above, courtesy of The University of Texas–Pan American Library; below, courtesy of the Museum of South Texas History.)

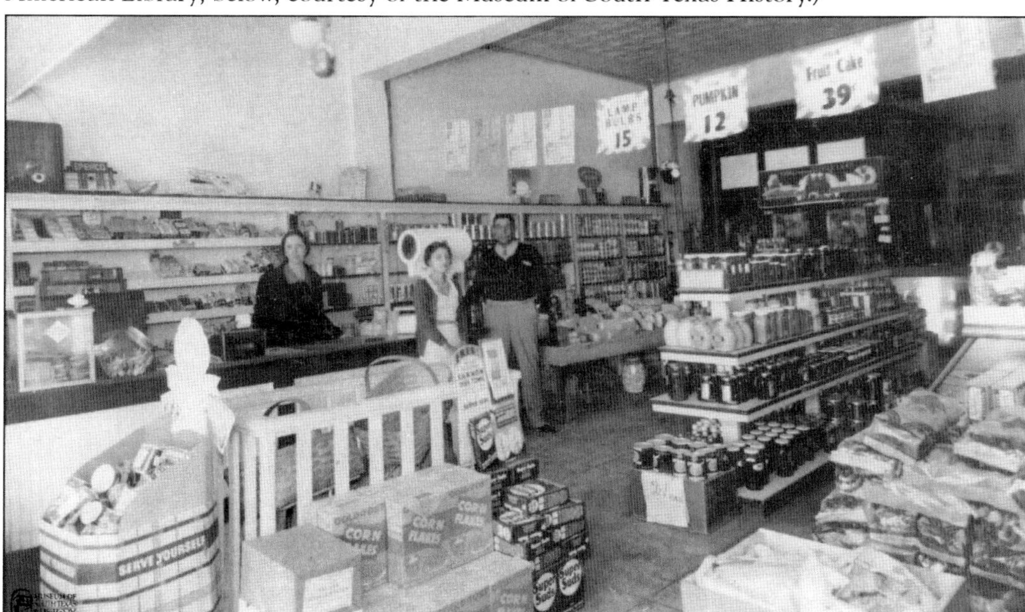

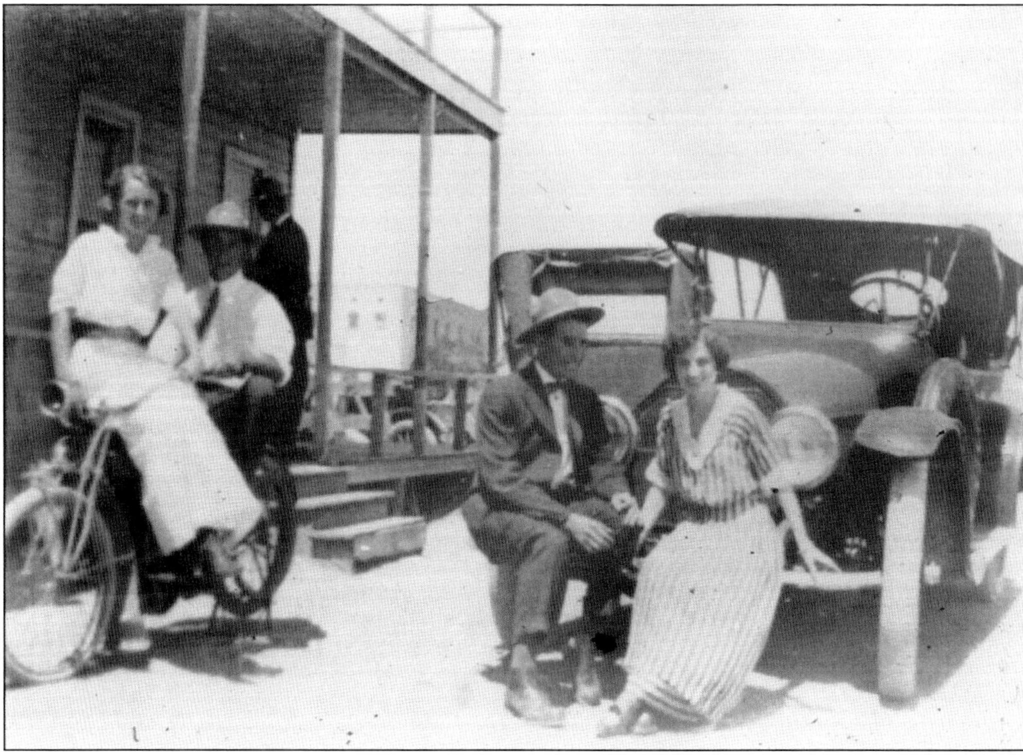

Mahl Street, one block south of the courthouse, was named for William Mahl, former comptroller for the Southern Pacific. At the corner of Mahl Street and Twelfth Avenue, Wilson "Daddy" Shaw operated the first hotel. It had a view of the Lipscomb Building and the courthouse. As well as hosting out-of-town guests, the Wilson Hotel also became a gathering place for the town's youth. The photographs on this page were taken in 1913; the people are unidentified. (Courtesy of The University of Texas–Pan American Library.)

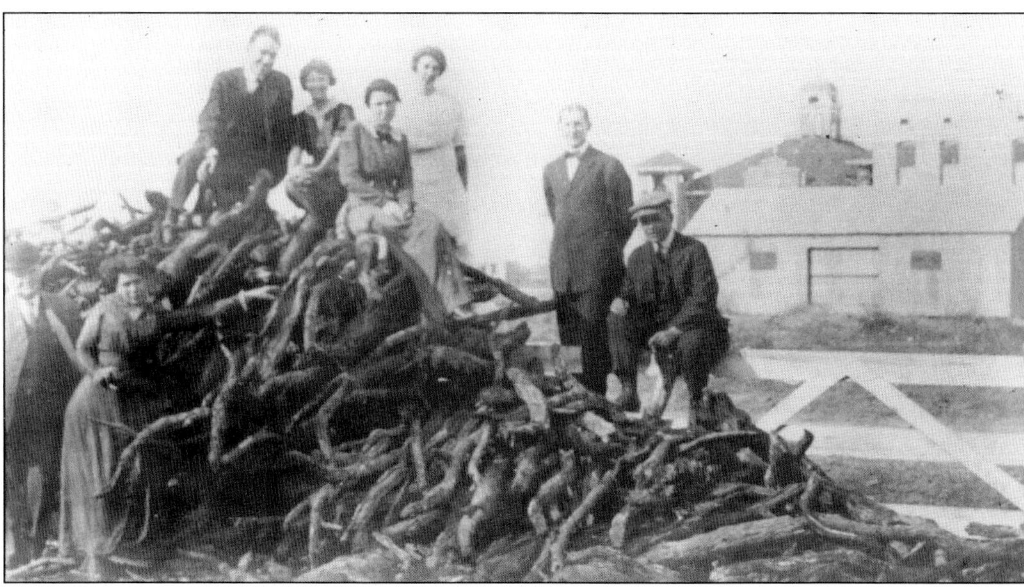

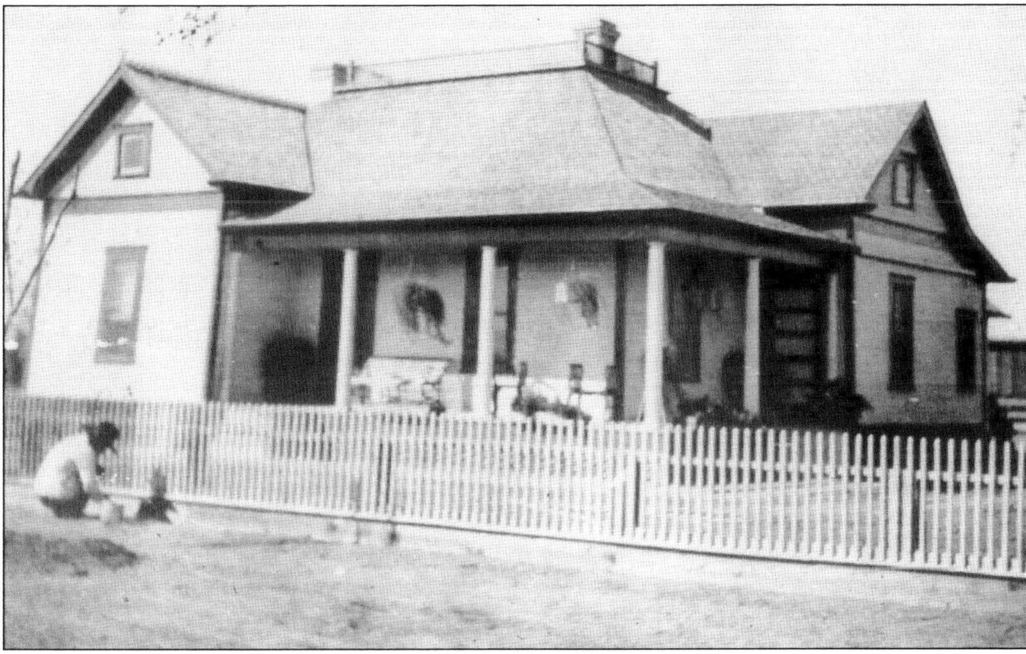

John Closner was one of the most important men in Edinburg. He was one of the town's founders, president of the Chapin Townsite Company, and served as a county sheriff and as a county treasurer, as well as owning several successful businesses including a very successful plantation in San Juan. As such, the town's citizens would have looked to him and he and his family would have entertained many visitors in his house. He built a showcase home on South Closner Boulevard in 1909. Later he built a bigger, second home. The Closner family also owned homes in Hidalgo, San Juan, and Brownsville. (Courtesy of The University of Texas–Pan American Library.)

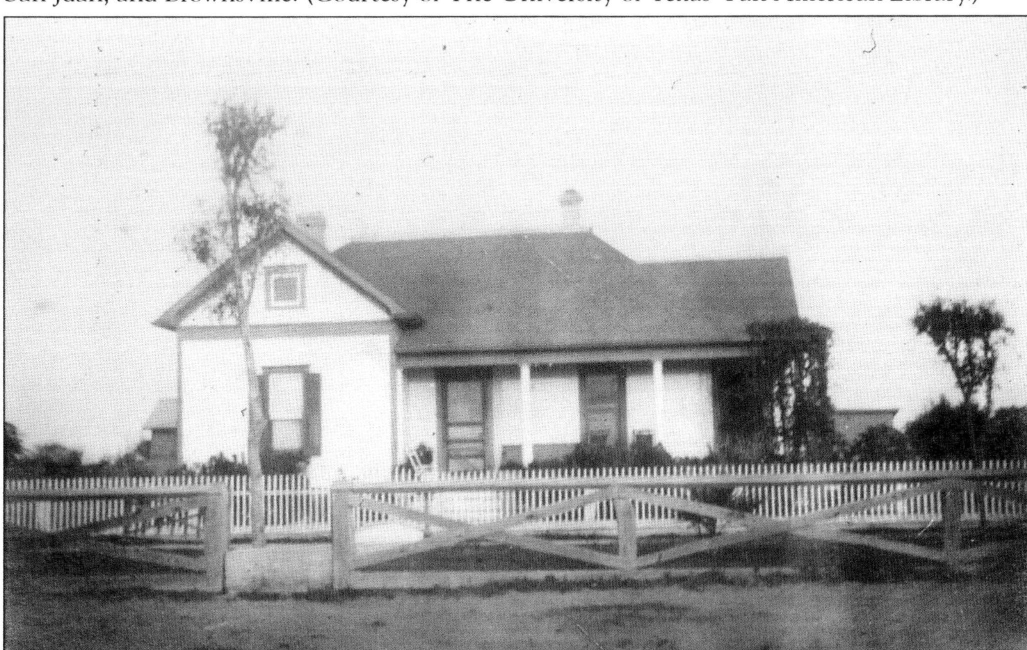

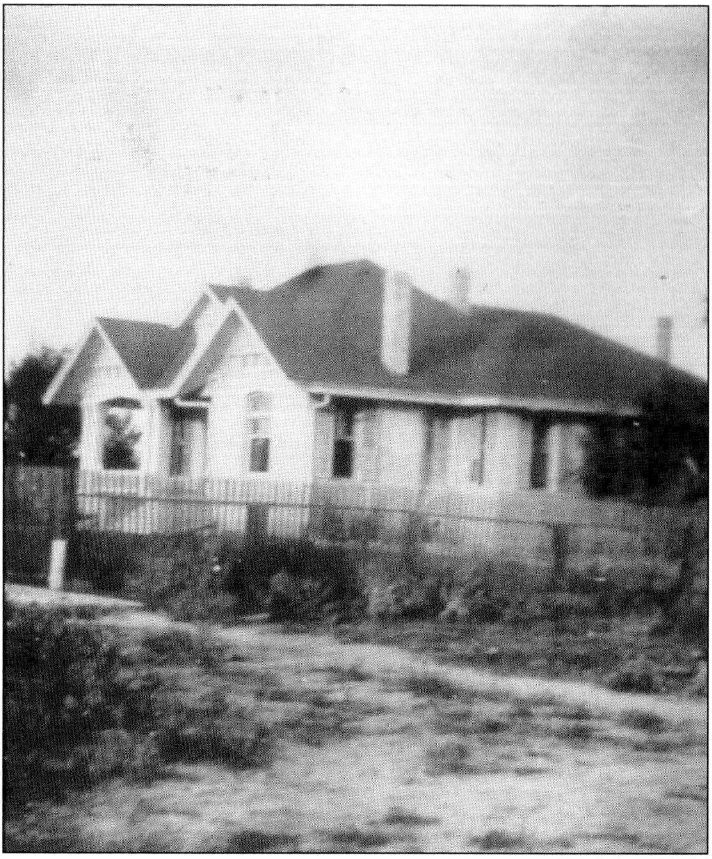

The two homes shown on this page are typical of the first homes in Edinburg. The first brick home (at left) was built for D.B. Chapin, although he never lived there. William Davis Day, the first postmaster and one of the first storeowners, owned the house below at 401 South Tenth Street. John Closner had also set aside a town site lot in the 600 block of East Stubbs for the first baby to be born in Edinburg. Closner Chapin Ramsey, born in May 1909 to Mr. and Mrs. J.G. Ramsey, had that honor, and was named after the two founders of the town, although his parents never did move to that lot. (Courtesy of The University of Texas–Pan American Library.)

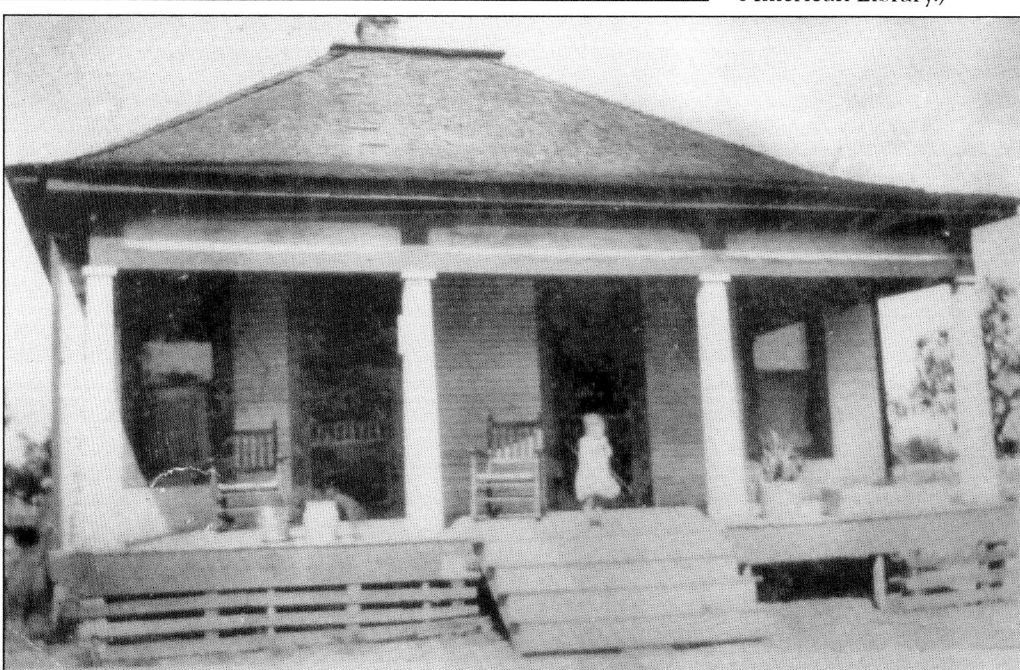

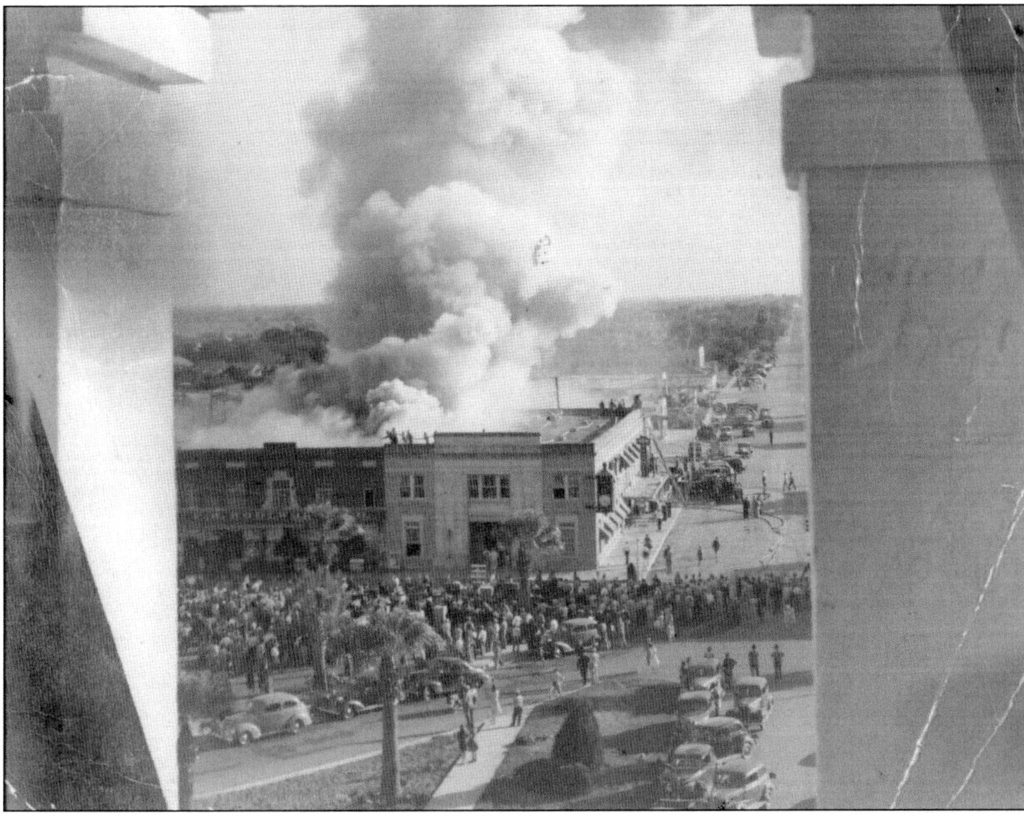

The two photographs on this page were probably taken 30 to 40 years after the photograph on page 38, one of the earliest photographs from Edinburg. From rough dirt roads and very few buildings, the town had grown with paved roads and brick buildings. Both of these photographs show the same street, but from opposite viewpoints. The photograph below was taken looking north towards the courthouse on Closner Boulevard. The photograph above was taken from the courthouse looking south on Closner Boulevard on the occasion of the Woolworth fire in 1939 (see page 74 for another photograph of the Woolworth building). Besides the fire, the smoke and the crowd, which are quite impressive, note also how there are no large buildings just two blocks south of the courthouse, only trees and houses. (Above, courtesy of The University of Texas–Pan American Library; below, courtesy of the Edinburg Volunteer Fire Department Museum.)

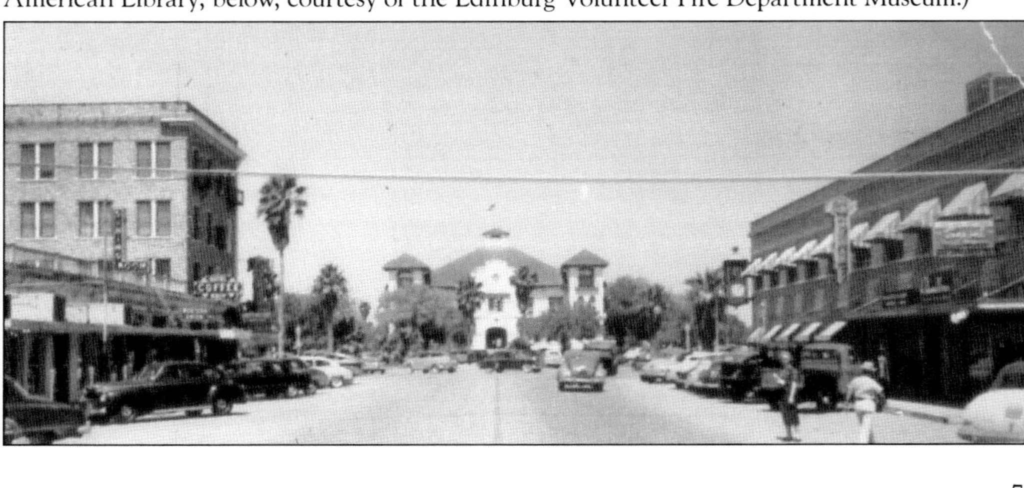

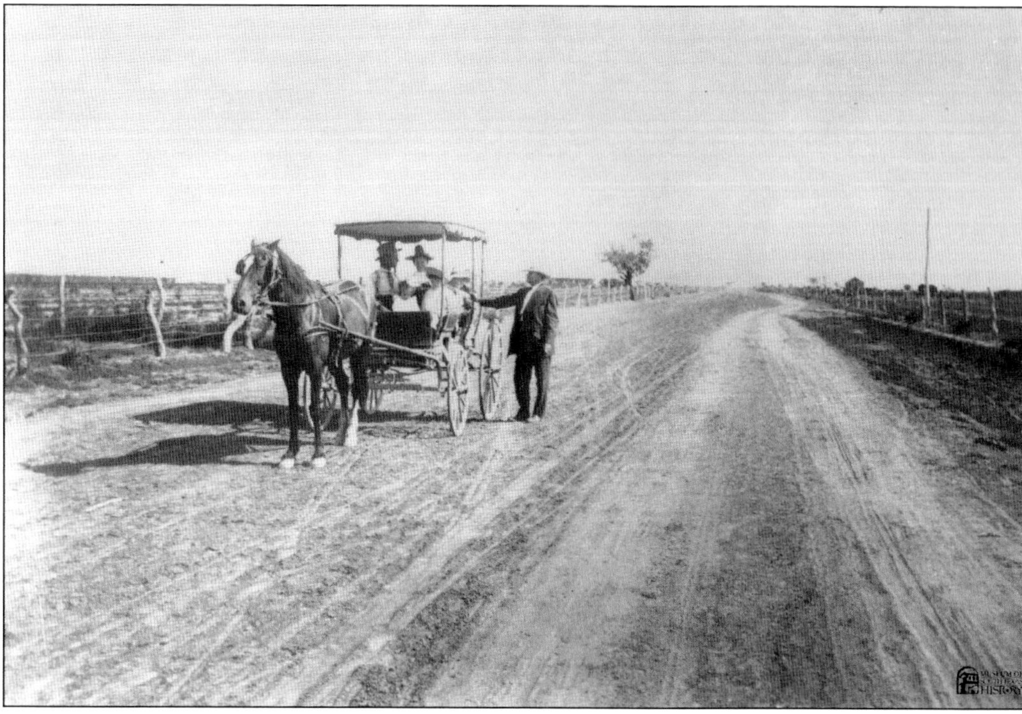

Good roads were essential to the growth and development of the city. Unpaved roads were particularly difficult for cars and other wheeled vehicles. The photograph above shows D.B. Chapin talking to a family in a surrey (horse carriage) on the road to the town of Chapin in 1910. Beginning in the 1920s, the town and the surrounding areas began fixing the roads. Lining the roads with a layer of caliche vastly improved the road surface for driving. It created a smooth surface that would not as easily form ruts or become as uneven as plain dirt roads. The photograph below shows a newly completed caliche road with a Model T Ford. (Above, courtesy of the Museum of South Texas History; below, courtesy of The University of Texas–Pan American Library.)

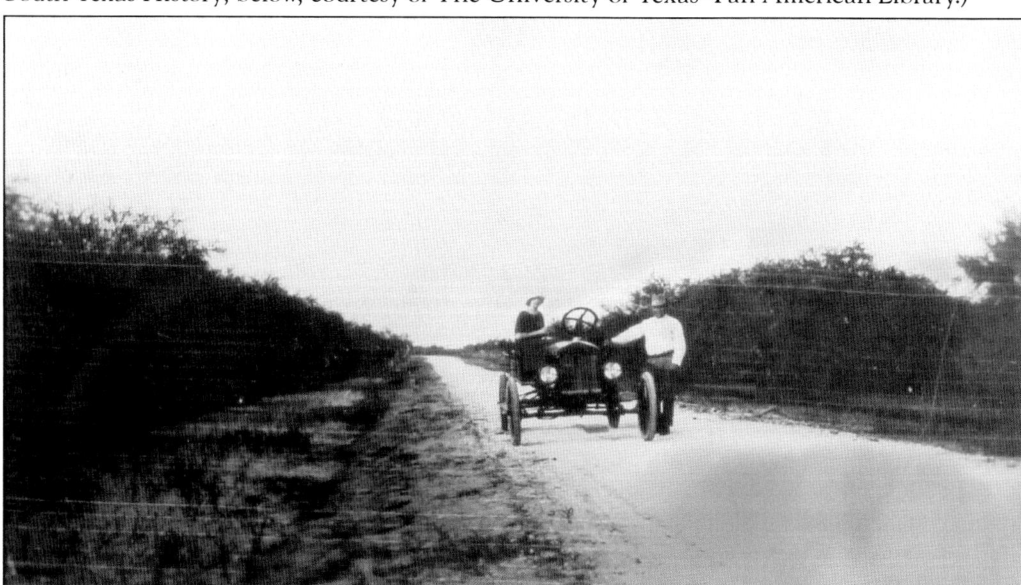

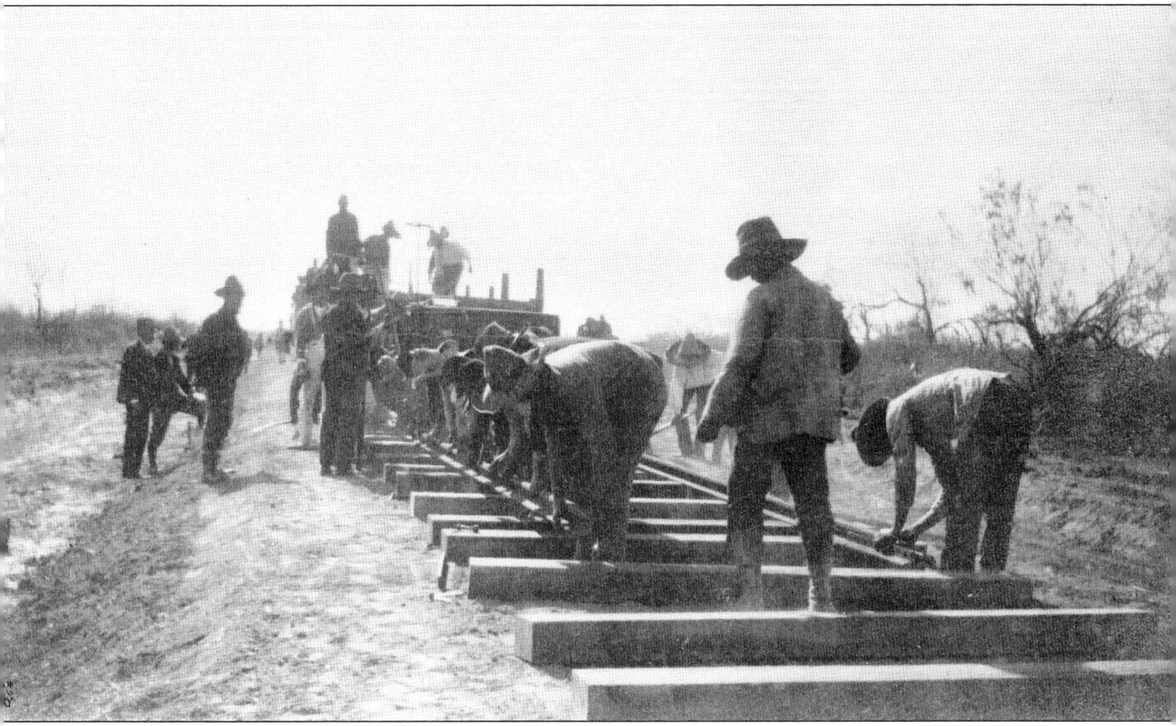

In 1908, John Closner worked with Sam Robertson, construction engineer of the St. Louis, Brownsville, and Mexico Railroad, along with E.M. Card and Henry Griffin to build a railroad spur that would connect Edinburg with the main railroad line from Brownsville to Mission. The deal ran into difficulties due to financing, but Closner and Sprague persevered in finding funds and arranged a deal with Dilly and Sons of Palestine, Texas, to purchase the necessary steel rails. The spur was eight miles long between San Juan and Edinburg and was called "the San Antonio–Rio Grande Valley Railroad." As is apparent from the name, the initial wish was to extend the railroad north to San Antonio via Falfurrias; however, the tracks never extended farther than four miles north of Edinburg. The line later became a branch of the St. Louis, Brownsville, and Mexico Railroad in 1912. The photograph shows Sam Robertson's crew laying the tracks between San Juan and Edinburg (Courtesy of the Museum of South Texas History.)

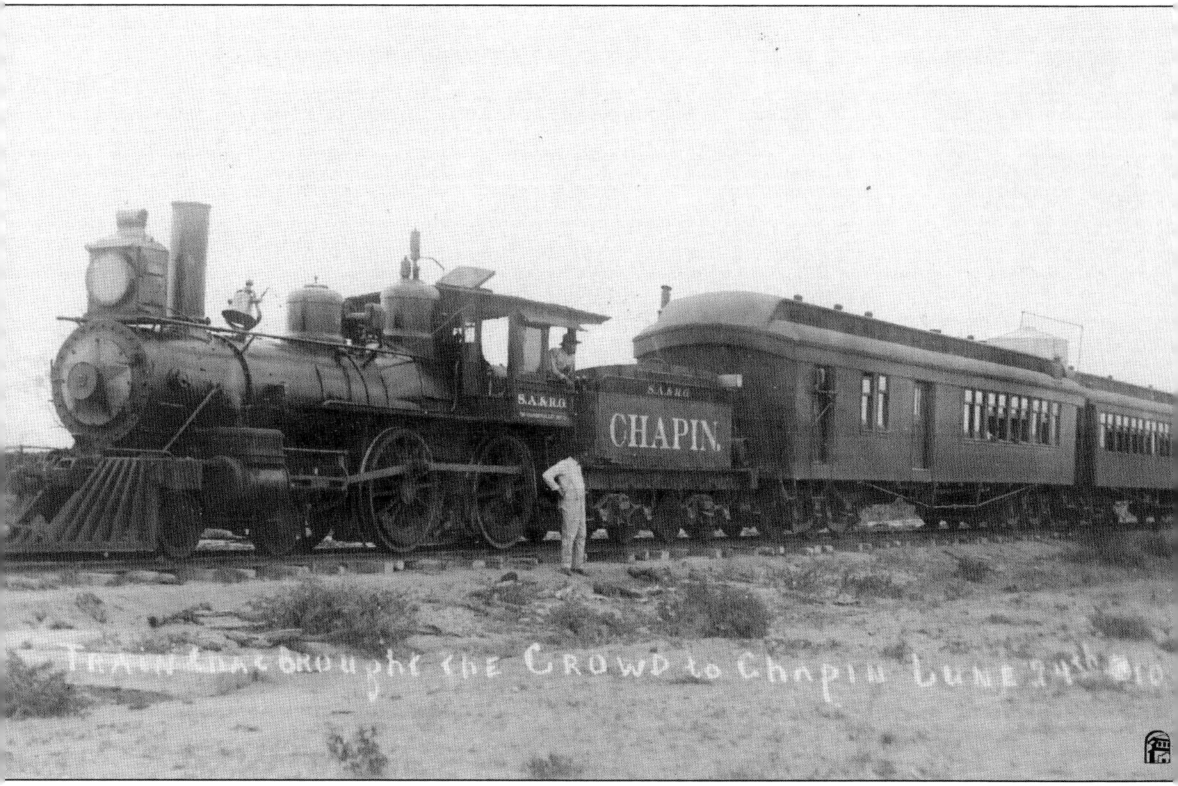

The train consisted of one engine and two boxcars and was affectionately known as Old Flossie. She was also called, perhaps more accurately, the Old Rattler or the Mesquite Special because she burned mesquite in her firebox. The first crew members were engineer Dick Houston and conductor Jim Crane. One of the two boxcars was dedicated for freight shipping; the second was a catchall for passenger, freight, express, baggage, mail, and livestock. As Closner Ramsey later related, there were "boards across one end for seats with freight and express rolling over your feet. The other end was loaded with cows, mules and hogs. If the passengers were offended, they rode on top of the car—needing enough athletic skill to hold on to the car as it swayed from side to side" (Above, courtesy of the Hidalgo County Historical Marker Applications Collection, The University of Texas–Pan American; below, courtesy of the Museum of South Texas History.)

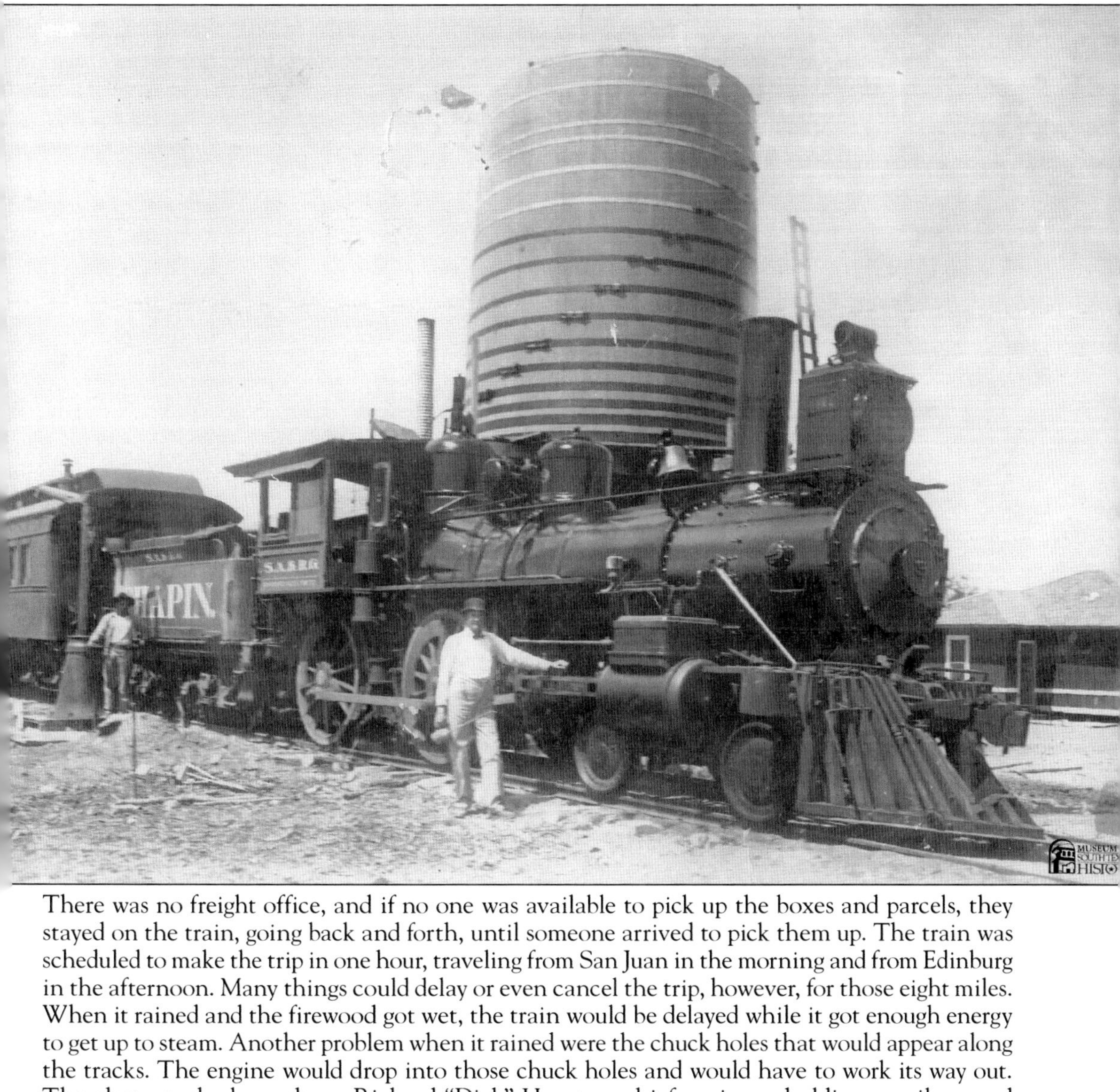

There was no freight office, and if no one was available to pick up the boxes and parcels, they stayed on the train, going back and forth, until someone arrived to pick them up. The train was scheduled to make the trip in one hour, traveling from San Juan in the morning and from Edinburg in the afternoon. Many things could delay or even cancel the trip, however, for those eight miles. When it rained and the firewood got wet, the train would be delayed while it got enough energy to get up to steam. Another problem when it rained were the chuck holes that would appear along the tracks. The engine would drop into those chuck holes and would have to work its way out. The photograph above shows Richard "Dick" Houston, chief engineer, holding an oilcan and checking the engine while it is being fired up and filled with water. The house behind the train belonged to the Houstons. (Courtesy of the Museum of South Texas History.)

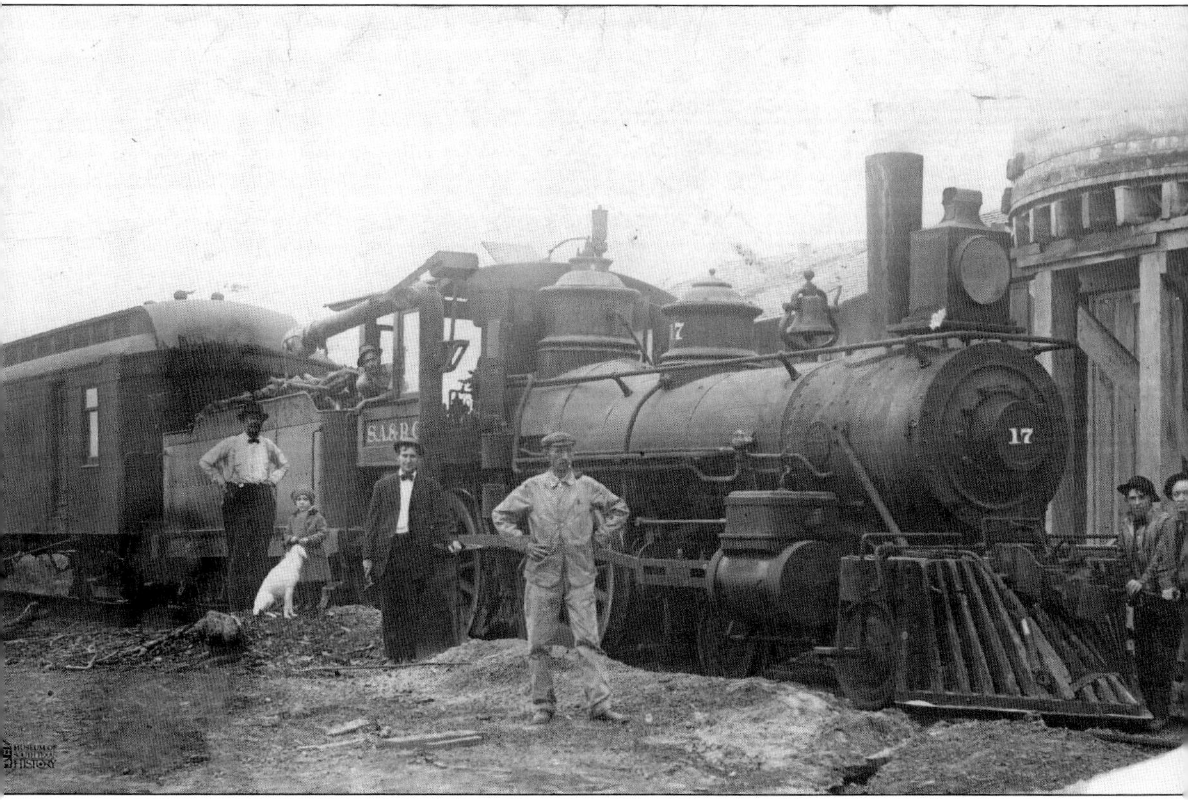

This photograph shows, from left to right, Richard (Dick) Houston; Annette Dottie Grover with her dog; Richard (Dick) Marsh, in the locomotive; an unidentified guest at the hotel; Charlie Heck, assistant engineer; and Johnny Geig, conductor; with Gene Diaz standing behind him. A turntable to allow the train to turn around was never built in Edinburg, thus Flossie would run forward from San Juan to Edinburg, and then backwards all the way on the return trip. The train ran twice daily except on Sunday, leaving at 11:30 a.m. and 3:15 p.m. from San Juan and returning from Edinburg at 12:00 p.m. and 3:30 p.m. Old Flossie was eventually replaced with the Southern Pacific Railroad, which, in turn, was replaced by the highway as the primary transportation mode in Edinburg. In 1968, after a car ran into a train, killing two people, the city decided to remove the train tracks. (Courtesy of the Museum of South Texas History.)

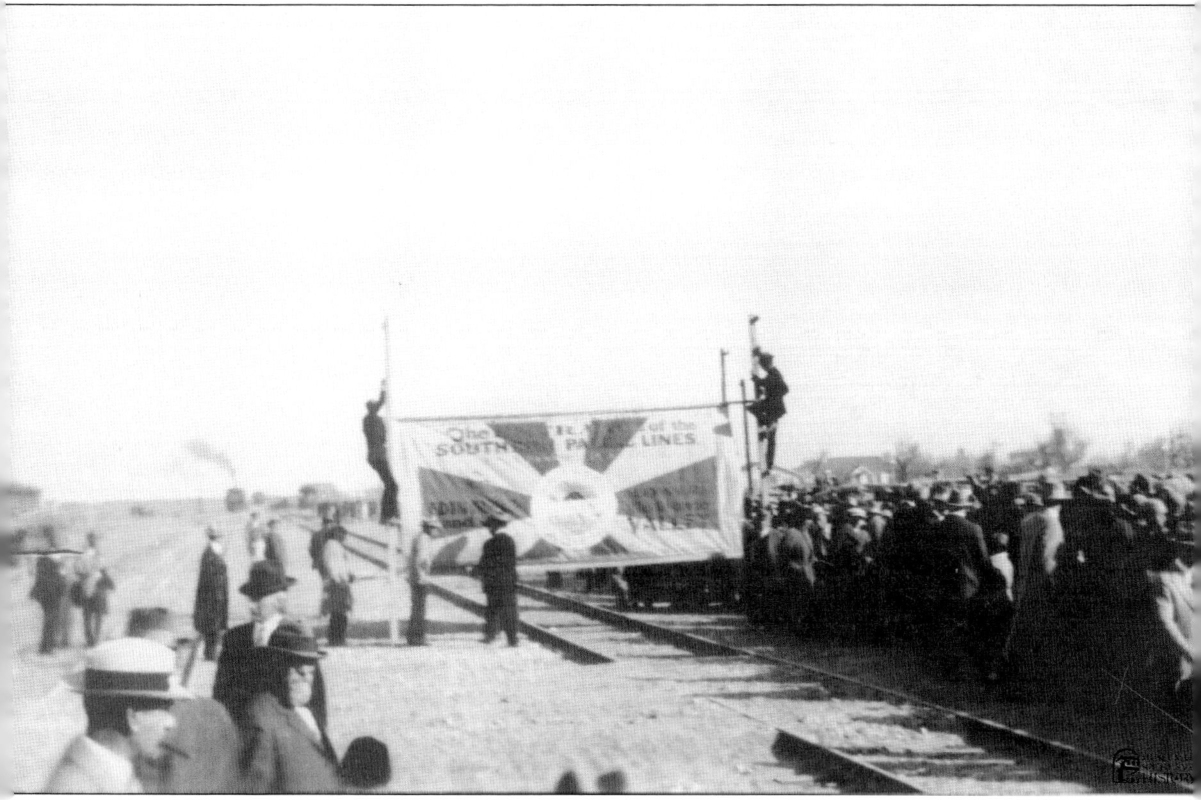

In 1927, the much-anticipated Southern Pacific Railroad arrived. The Edinburg Depot was built, and the whole town of Edinburg celebrated the arrival of the new train. The Southern Pacific railroad made its first run into Edinburg, and H.M. Lull, then vice president of Southern Pacific Railways, drove the "Golden Spike." Dignitaries from the Valley and Southern Pacific rode on the train as it burst through a banner stretched across the tracks that read "The entry of Southern Pacific means the dawn of a new era for Edinburg and the Lower Rio Grande Valley." In honor of the occasion, all schools were closed and thousands gathered for the grand ceremony, with food and a band playing on the town square. (Courtesy of the Museum of South Texas History.)

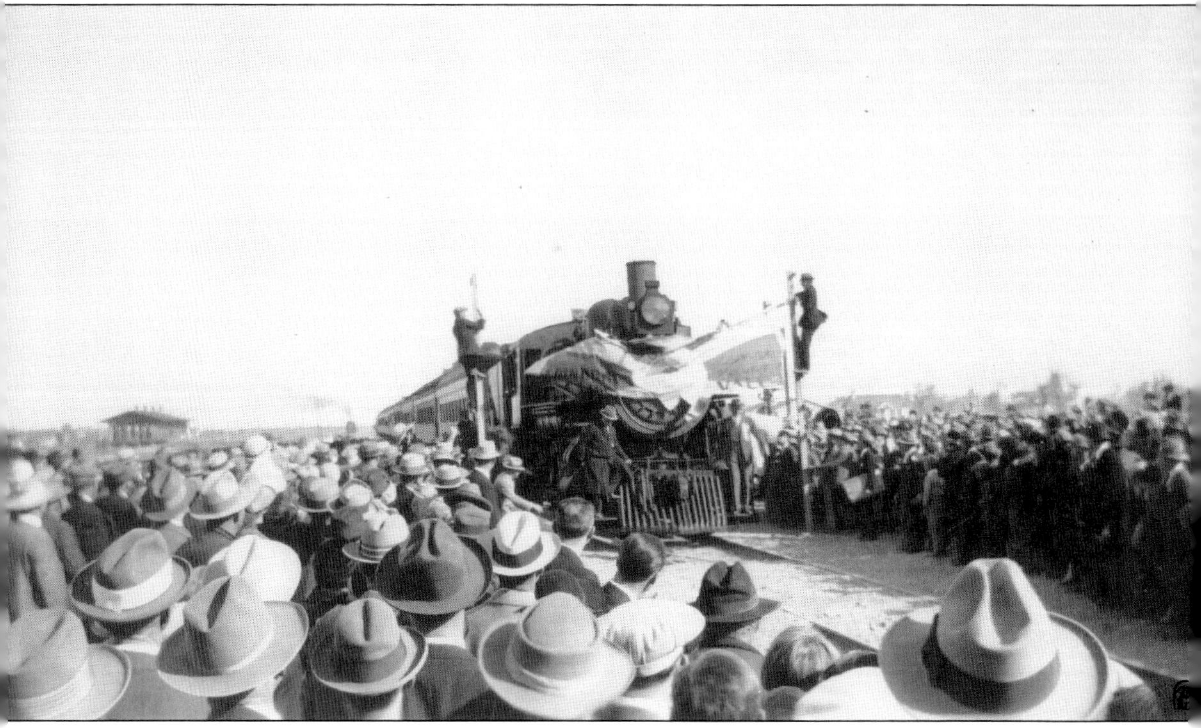

This image shows the train bursting through the paper banner welcoming Southern Pacific. (Courtesy of the Museum of South Texas History.)

Four

EDINBURG
THE GATEWAY TO EDUCATION

Edinburg, as the county seat, serves not only as the center of government for Hidalgo County, but also as the center of education. It is home to the Edinburg Consolidated Independent School District, one of the largest school districts in the United States, covering an area of 945 square miles, over half the size of Hidalgo County. Edinburg is also home to the University of Texas–Pan American, the oldest institute of higher education in Hidalgo County, and just one year younger than Texas Southmost College, the oldest educational institution in the Lower Rio Grande Valley. It is the home and birthplace of Region One Educational Service Center, which serves public schools in seven counties in South Texas. It is where the Rio Grande Bible Institute was established, which trains missionaries in Spanish language and Bible studies. The missionaries who graduate from the Rio Grande Bible Institute travel throughout all of South and Central America. Edinburg is also the birthplace of South Texas Independent School District, which currently operates magnet schools throughout the Lower Rio Grande Valley in specialized educational settings.

This center for educational prominence, however, had humble beginnings. Richard Alvis Marsh, one of the first and best-known educators in Hidalgo County, is quoted as saying, "the early settlers thought more of protecting their homes from the raids of the Indians and bandits than they did of educating future generations, but since the year 1875, interest in education has gradually been awakening, and today the lower Rio Grande counties can be said to be in line with other sections of the state educationally." Marsh was initially a traveling teacher, going from one ranch to the next to teach children. He eventually became superintendent of schools from 1902 to 1914, and continued to teach until his death in 1917. Through his influence and his teachings he can be credited, either directly or indirectly, with educating and training many of the future teachers of Hidalgo County.

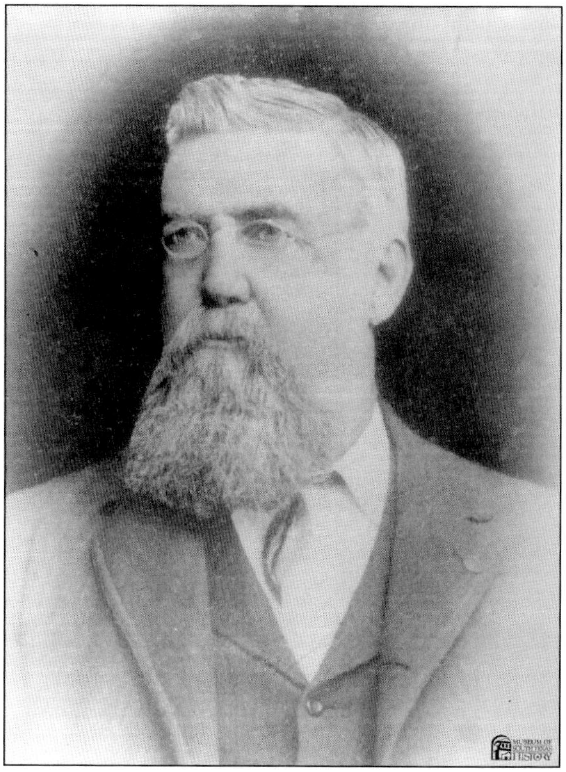

Richard A. Marsh (left) arrived in the Lower Rio Grande Valley in 1880 as an ex-Confederate soldier. He taught school at Fort Ringgold in Rio Grande City but soon discovered the great need for education on the ranches. He began traveling from ranch to ranch, teaching classes. He was so well beloved by his students and their parents that the children would often follow him from one ranch to the next. The photograph below is from the Laguna Seca Ranch, where he also served as postmaster. Shown in the photograph are Bessie Marsh, his daughter, and other children from the ranch. The caption on the photograph reads, "*Un recuerdo para me madrina Carlota, Bessie Marsh.*" ("A remembrance for my godmother Carlota, Bessie Marsh.") (Left, courtesy of the Museum of South Texas History; below, courtesy of Carola Chapa.)

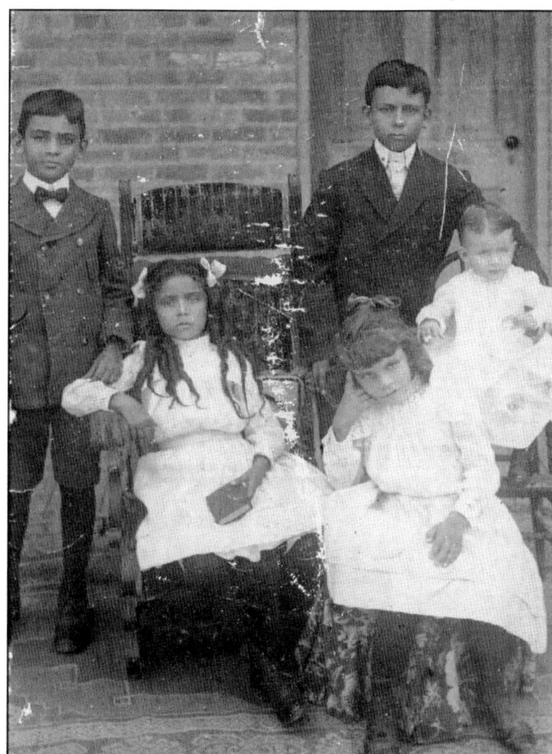

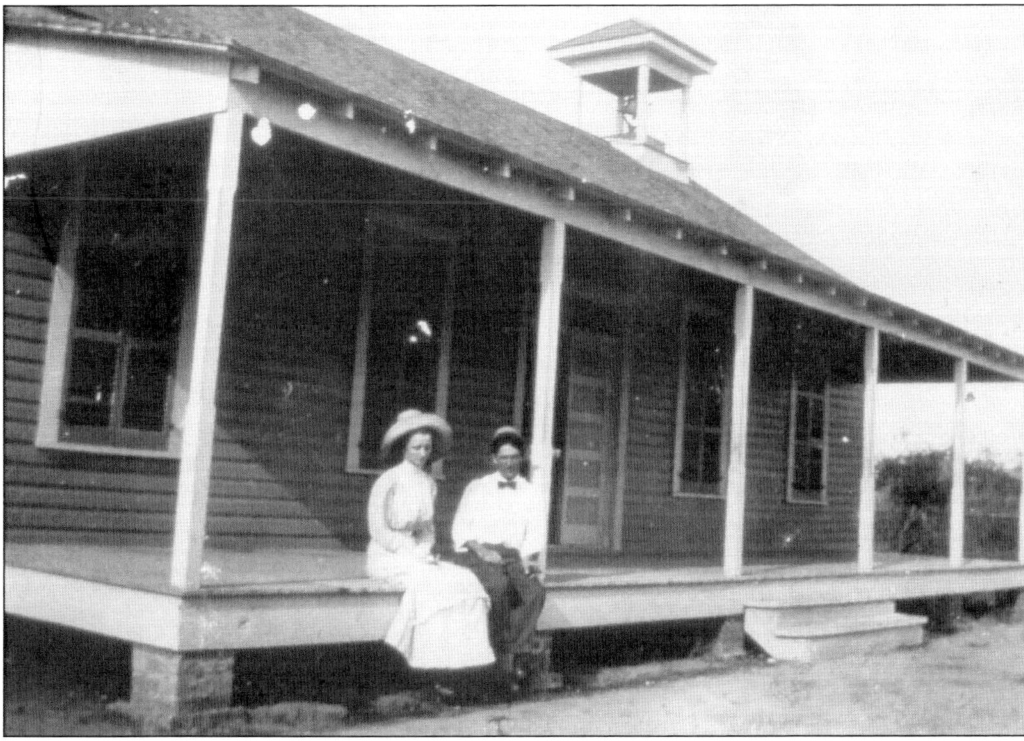

The first school building in Chapin was a two-room frame schoolhouse, shown above. By 1912, a larger school building was needed, and a four room brick building was erected near North Eighth Avenue and Peter Street with two rooms upstairs and two downstairs. Miss Mabelle Umland taught the upper grades and served as principal. Miss Venette Klossner taught the lower grades. The students were assigned to the four classes according to their ability to learn. The brick building was torn down in 1927 and was replaced with a larger school building. In 1926, the Edinburg School District joined with two common school districts in the northern part of the county, consolidating into one of the largest school districts in the United States in land area. In 1930, just 18 years after the first two room schoolhouse, Edinburg hosted a multi-building combined high school and college (below). (Above, courtesy of the Museum of South Texas History; below, courtesy of The University of Texas-Pan American.)

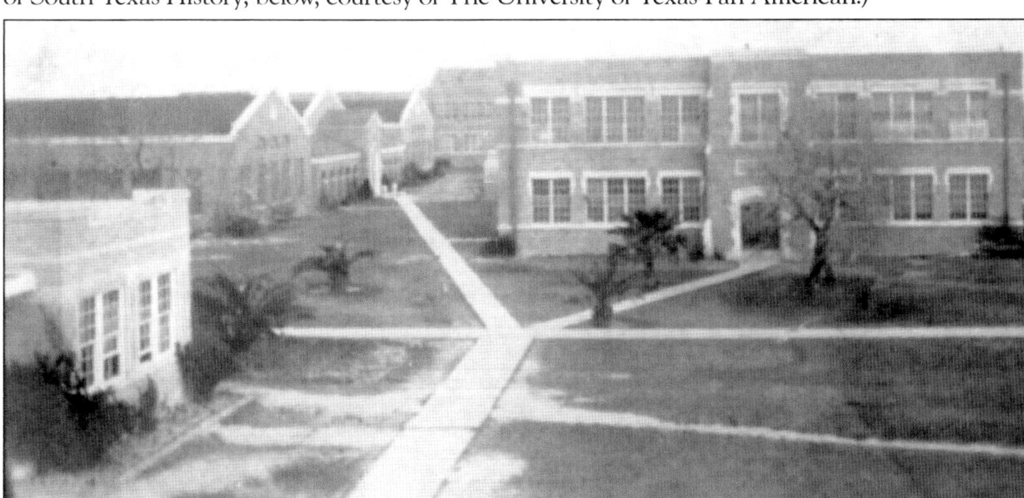

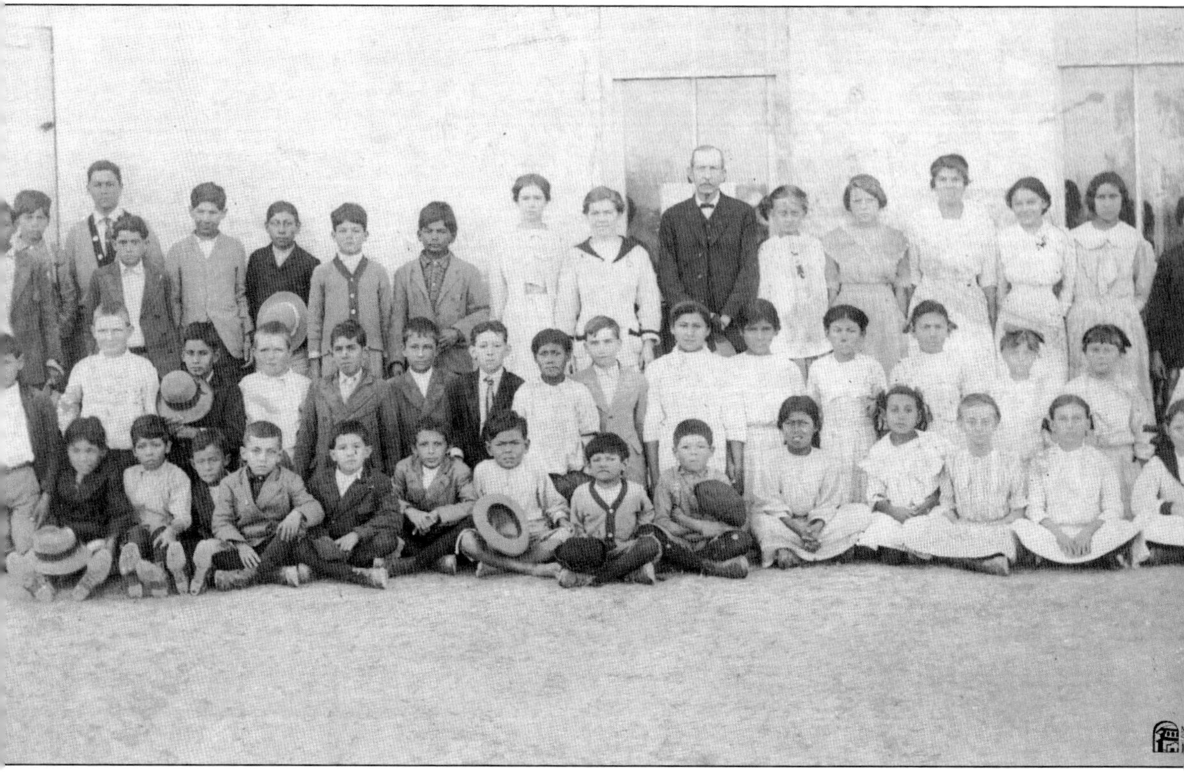

This photograph shows the students and faculty of Edinburg in the 1912–1913 school year. Many of the family names in this school picture appear often in Edinburg's history. The children identified in the photograph are, from left to right, (first row) two unidentified, Andres Chavez, Plutarco de la Vina, unidentified, Pete Alamia, Benacio Lopez, Taurino Reyes, Ladd Simmons, Theresa Alegria, Dora Marsh, Roxanna Klossner, unidentified, and Velma Curry; (second row) unidentified, Charles Ramsey, Richard Marsh, Leon Ramsey, Martin Guerra, James Edwards, Frank Estimbo, unidentified, George Wright, four unidentified, Laura Ramsey, Leola Schoenfeld, and Fonda Doty; (third row), unidentified, Primitivo Nino, Tom Simmons, Benito Estimbo, Juan Olivarez, William Simmons, Pedro Lopez, teacher Beulah Moye, teacher Rhoda Hatch, Professor Kirkpatrick, Susie Edwards, Mary Foster, Jennie Marsh, Maria Lejia Chavez, Emma Estimbo, and Maria Longoria. (Courtesy of the Museum of South Texas History.)

Every school day, a rope was pulled, ringing the bell to call the children to school. Stories were told that children had to watch for rattlesnakes on the way to school. The first class had 25 pupils, two teachers, and a principal. The school grew quickly, so by 1912, there were 125 students and four teachers. In 1917, the high school was organized, and two years later, the first two graduates, Emilia Schunior (educator and mother of Al Ramirez, Edinburg's first Hispanic mayor) and Anne Lipscomb (later Anne Magee, an educator), graduated from the 11th grade. Their graduation picture is shown at right. Less than 20 years later, the number of graduates had jumped to 71, as shown in the 1936 senior collage below. (Courtesy of The University of Texas–Pan American Library.)

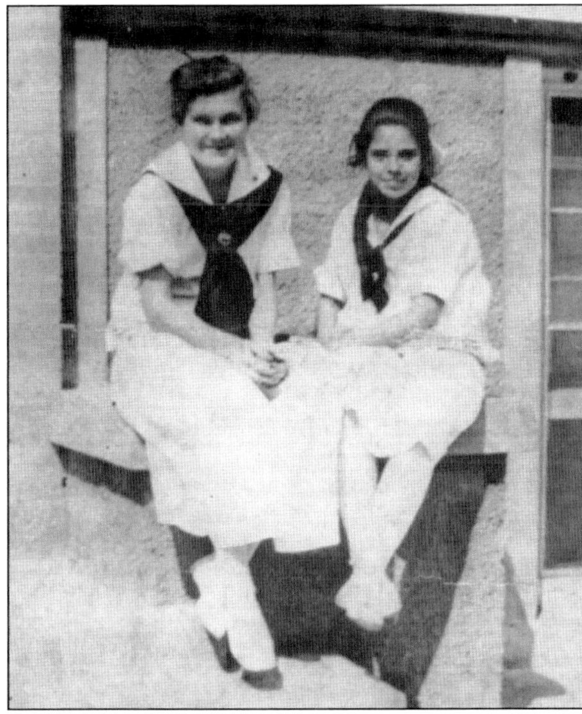

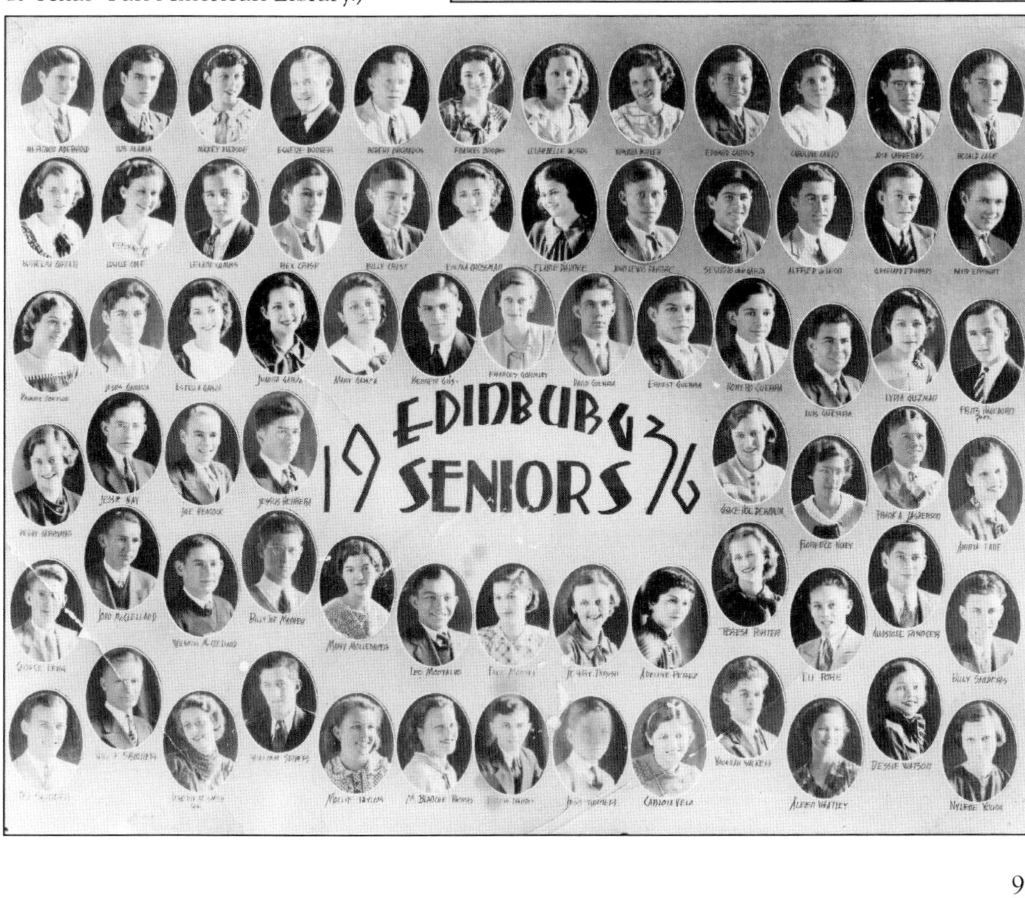

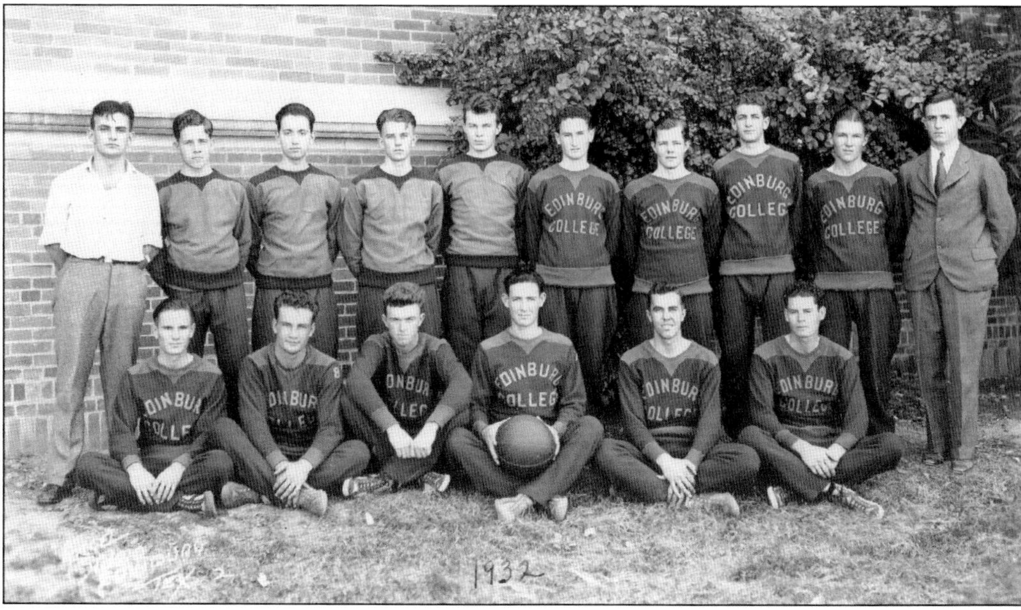

"Hit 'em high, hit 'em low; Come on Edinburg, Let's go! Come on Edinburg, Let's go!" Friday nights and high school football have become iconic in Texas. Football players start young these days, playing in clubs and schools long before they reach high school. That has not always been the case, however. Edinburg High School's first team (above) was formed in 1921, and only two of those players had experience playing football. Football helmets in the 1920s were made of soft leather. Hard plastic helmets weren't introduced until the 1950s. Crowds would have also cheered for the girls' teams, such as the 1921 basketball team shown below in their dress-style uniforms. (Courtesy of the Edinburg Consolidated Independent School District.)

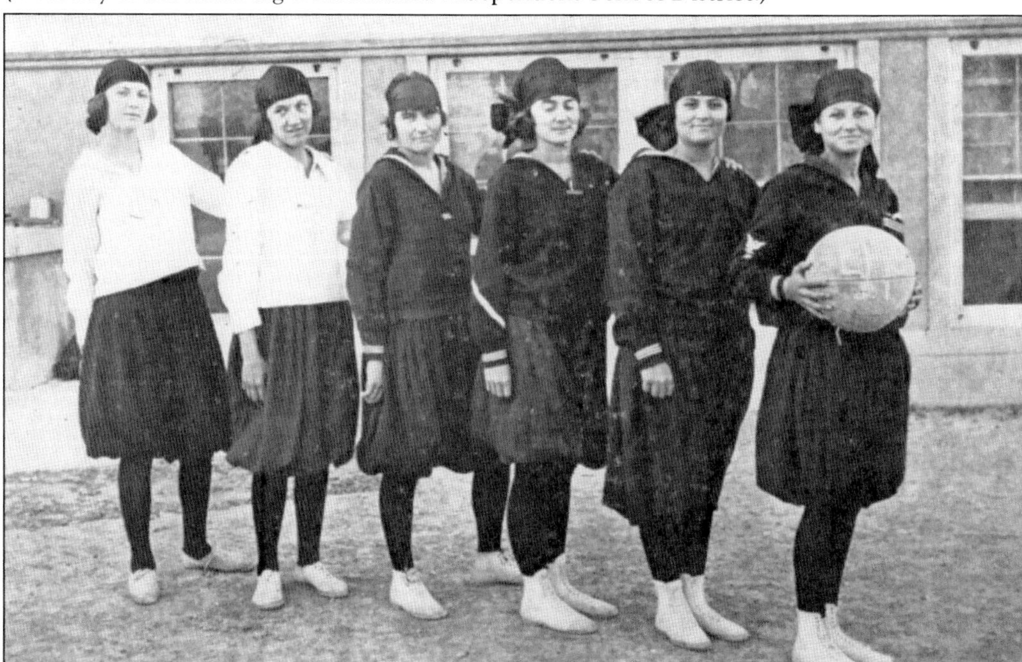

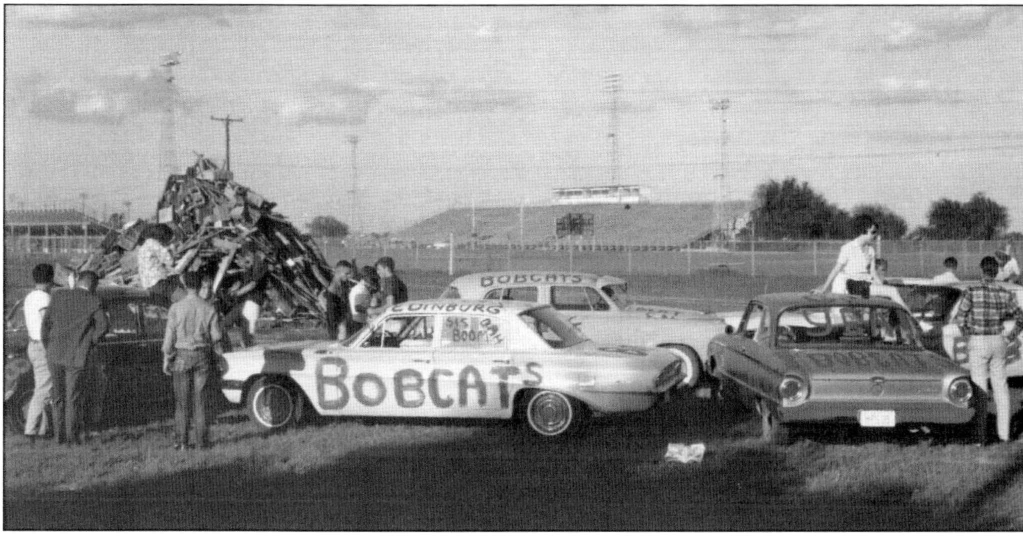

Bonfires, football games, homecoming dances, and other traditions were all popular ways for the Edinburg Bobcats to show their school spirit. The Edinburg High School students would gather wood from all over town to pile into larger and larger heaps. The Bobcat fans would gather near the football field, some students painting their cars with their team name, as shown in the 1966 photograph above. On occasion, Edinburg High students would find things other than wood to burn, such as the white "McAllen city limits" sign on top of the 1967 bonfire shown below. (Courtesy of the Edinburg Consolidated Independent School District.)

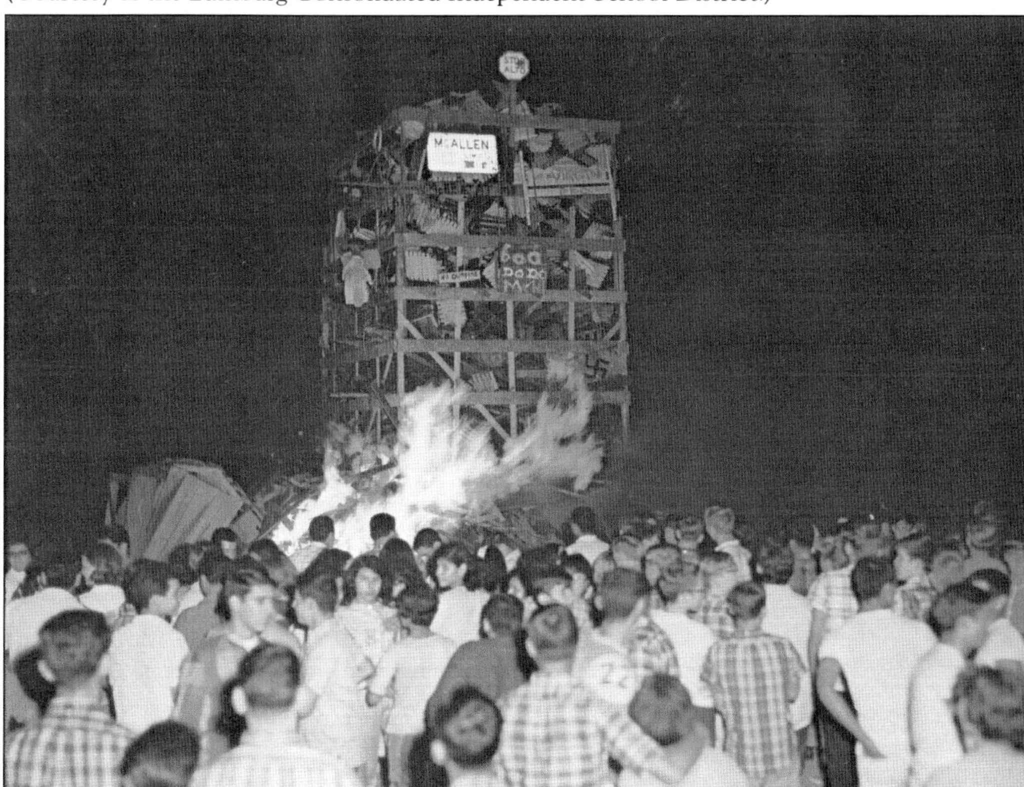

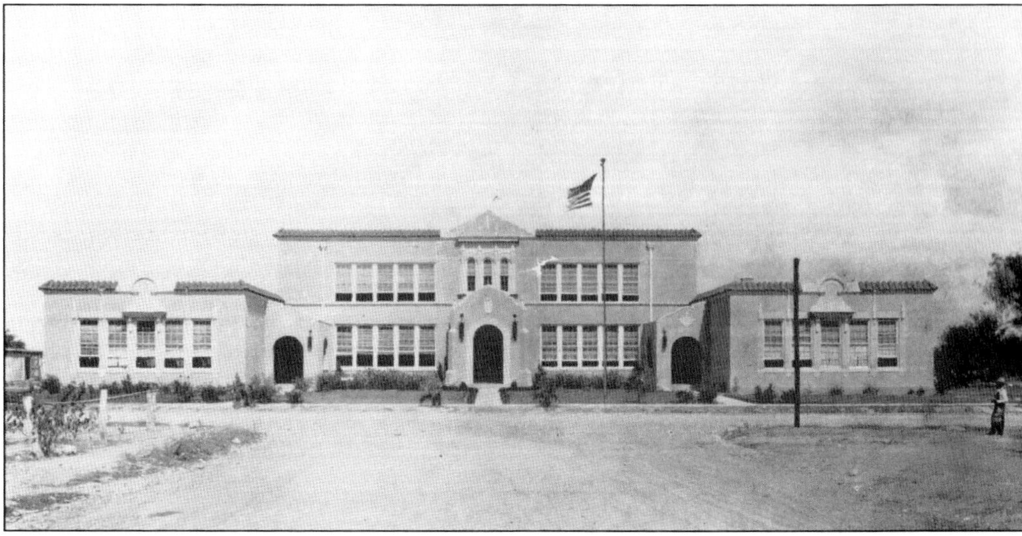

In 1927, after 15 years of rapid growth, the Edinburg School District hired the architectural firm of Giesecke and Harris to assist with planning and constructing school buildings. The architects described their plan in "A Texas Community School Plant—The Edinburg, Texas, Consolidated Schools" printed in the December 1927 *American School Board Journal*. They described the Stephen Austin School for Mexican children as located in the center of the Mexican population. Their first step was to enlarge the Mexican school from the previous four-room building and add an auditorium large enough to serve as the civic center for the Mexican population. The photograph above shows the front of Stephen Austin School; below is the auditorium. (Courtesy of The University of Texas–Pan American Library.)

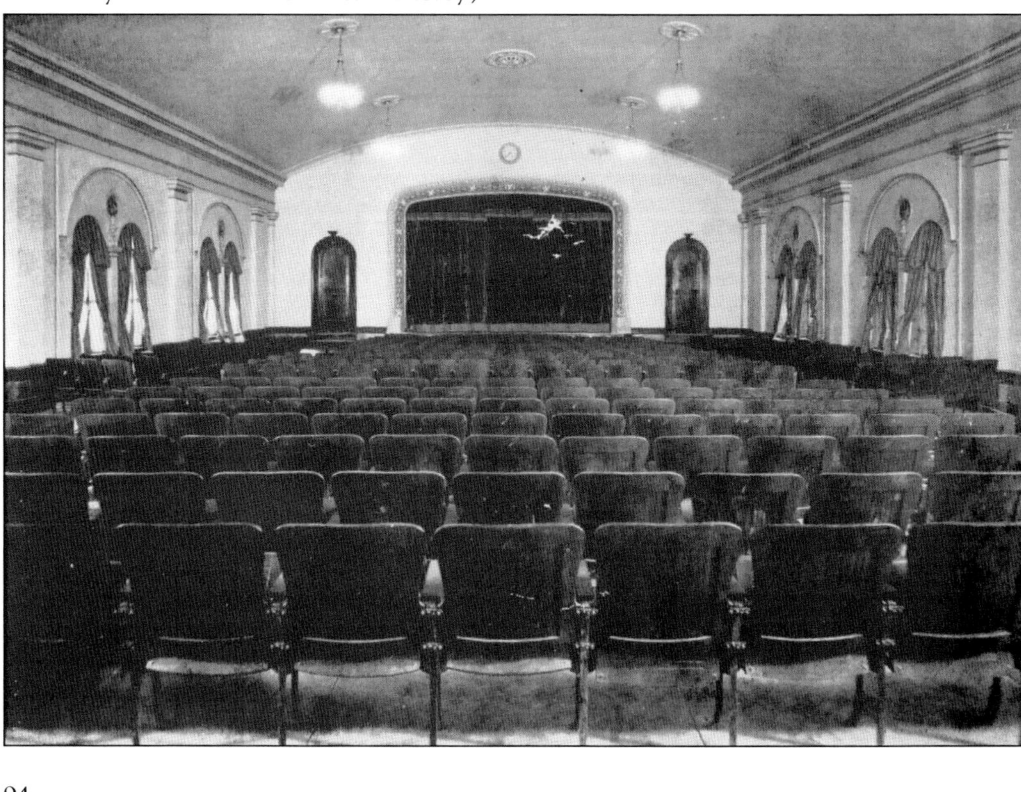

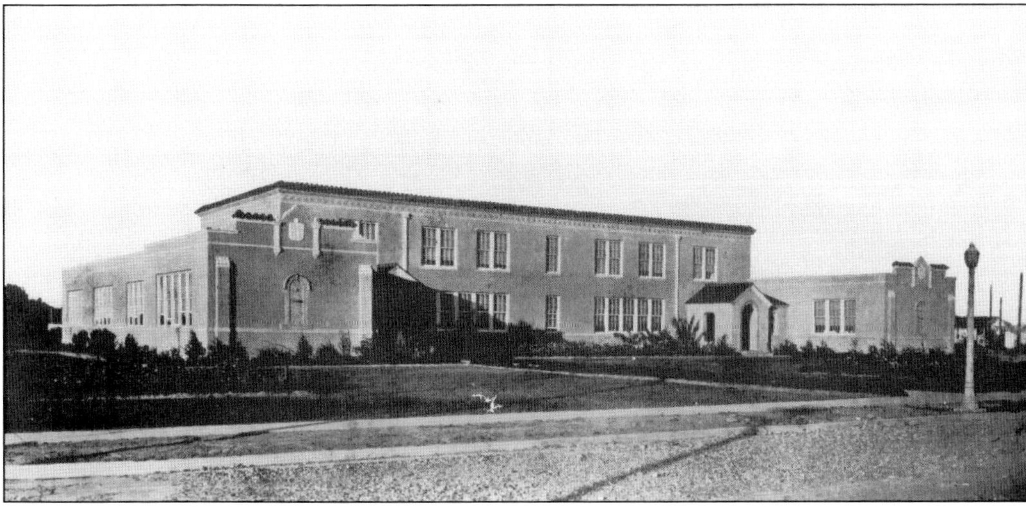

Sam Houston Elementary (above), the school for white children, was planned and equipped much along the lines of the Austin School for Mexican children. The high school was remodeled at the same time, then an auditorium was built large enough to seat 1,200 for dramas and operas. A science building was erected with laboratories, home economics classrooms, and a commercial department, and an industrial arts building was erected with classroom space for vocational and prevocational space for boys. A.Y. Baker Junior High School was the final step in construction in Edinburg. The architects also designed rural school buildings for the smaller towns within the school district. The teacherage, as shown in the photograph below, rivaled teacher dormitories at many colleges. (Courtesy of The University of Texas–Pan American Library.)

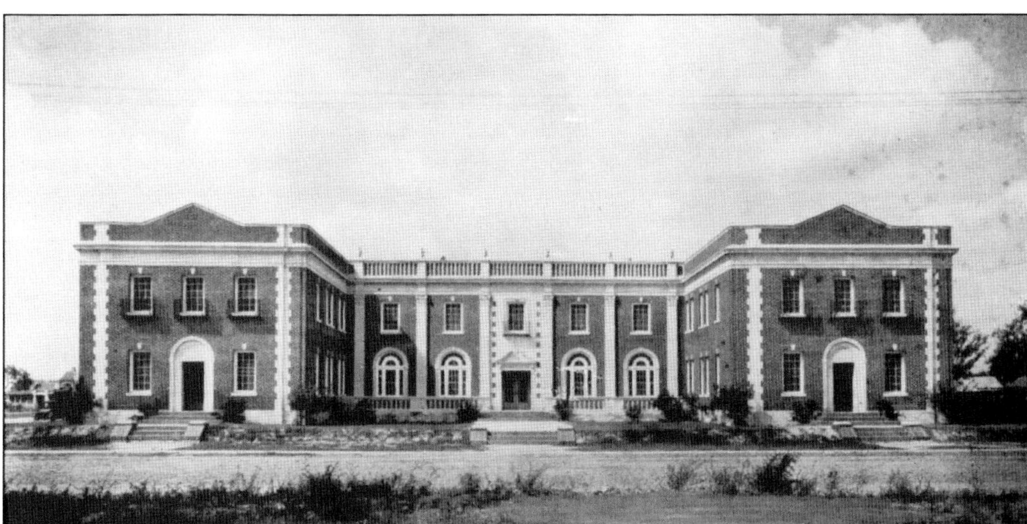

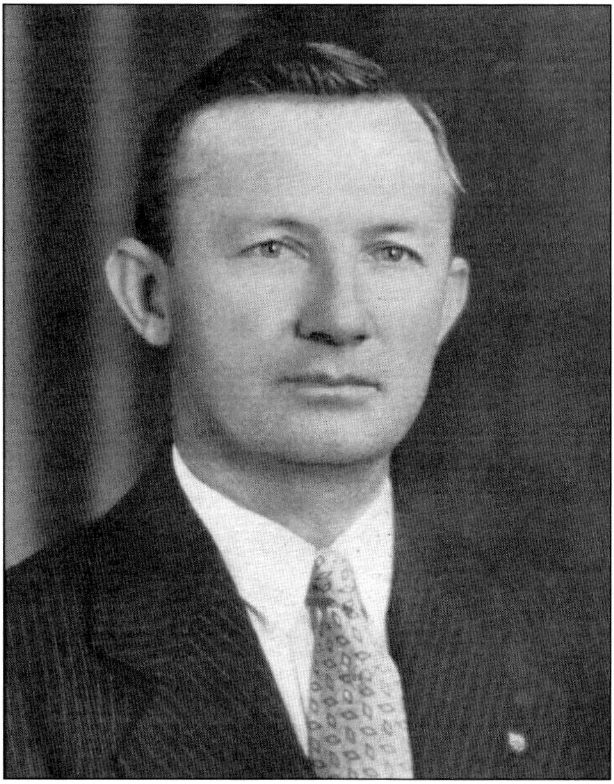

In 1925, Edinburg School District superintendent H.C. Baker, shown at left, asked faculty if they were interested in expanding to allow the students to be able to continue their education without having to travel to colleges in distant cities. Two years later, Edinburg College became a reality, opening the doors to its first classes in September 1927. That first year, 12 faculty members taught 180 students. Among the 12 faculty members, eight held master's degrees and four held doctoral degrees. H.C. Baker was named the college superintendent. H.U. Miles, shown below, followed Baker in presidency. He served as president for one year, from 1930 to 1931. (Courtesy of the Edinburg Consolidated Independent School District.)

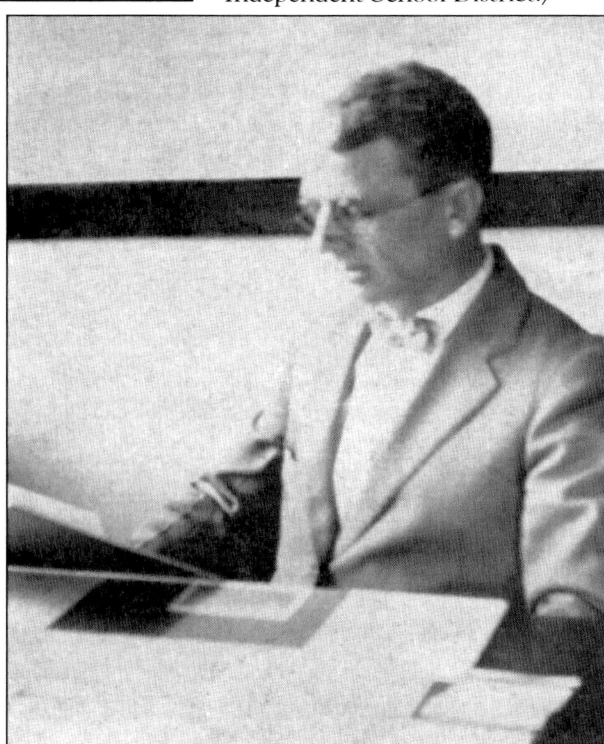

R.P. Ward, shown at right, became the president of the college in 1931, a post he held with honor and distinction until he resigned in 1959. Valley citizens have always been ready and willing to answer the call for service, and World War II was no exception. During 1944 and 1945, there were no male graduates and the total number of college students greatly decreased. Even President Ward took leave to serve in the military. H.A. Hodges, shown below, served as interim president during that time and after Ward resigned in 1959. (Right, courtesy of The University of Texas–Pan American Library; below, courtesy of the Edinburg Consolidated Independent School District.)

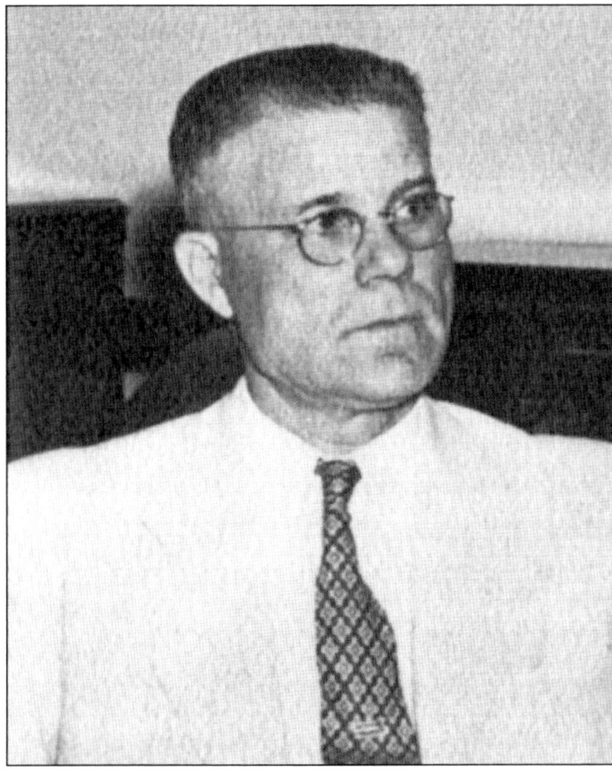

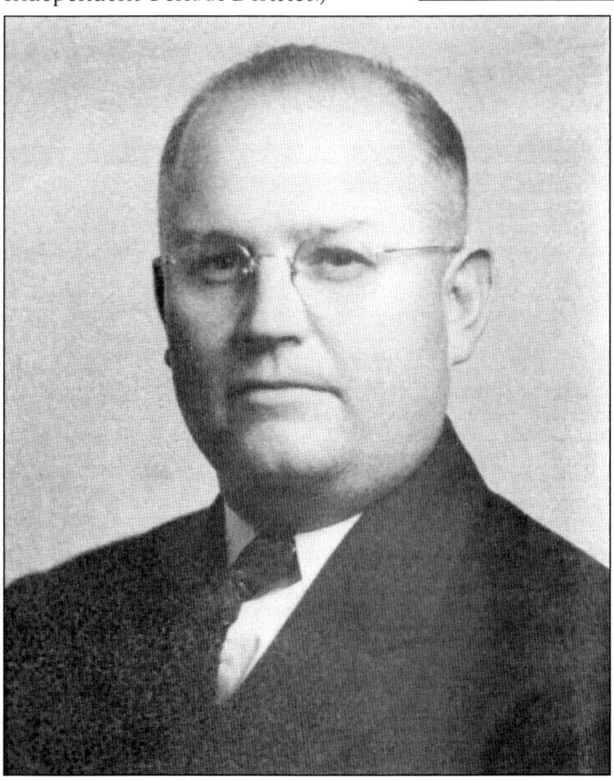

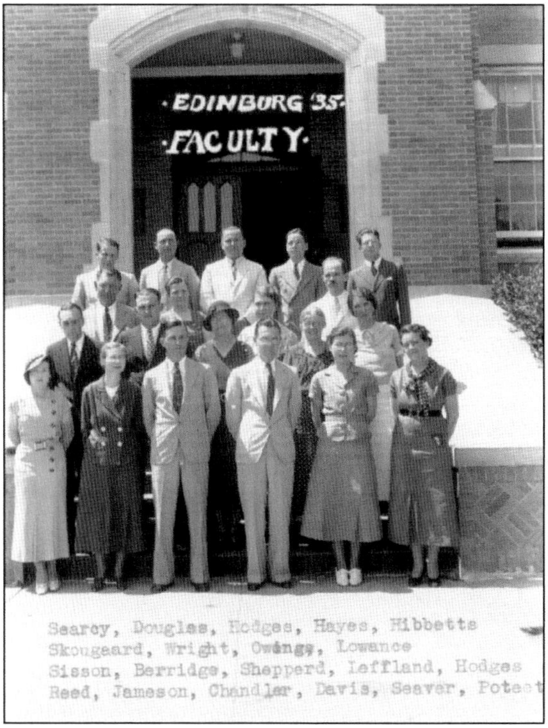

For several years, the high school and the college shared buildings and some faculty. The photograph at left shows faculty and staff from 1935, including H.C. Searcy, ? Douglas, H.A. Hodges, E.S. Hayes, Robert J. Hibbetts, Ivar Skougaard, Carrie E. Wright, Ruth M. Owings, F.E. Lowance, C.A, Sisson, H.L. Berridge, Enola Shepperd, Rigmor Leffland, ? Hodges, ? Reed, Grace Jameson, L.E. Chandler, C.A. Davis, Frances Seaver, and E. Poteet. The photograph below shows a group of students posing on campus. The continually increasing student enrollment and the ever-increasing distinction between high school and college led to a need for more campus space. This was accomplished in 1950 with the purchase of the "West Campus," the site of the current university campus. (Left, courtesy of The University of Texas–Pan American Library; below, courtesy of the Edinburg Consolidated Independent School District.)

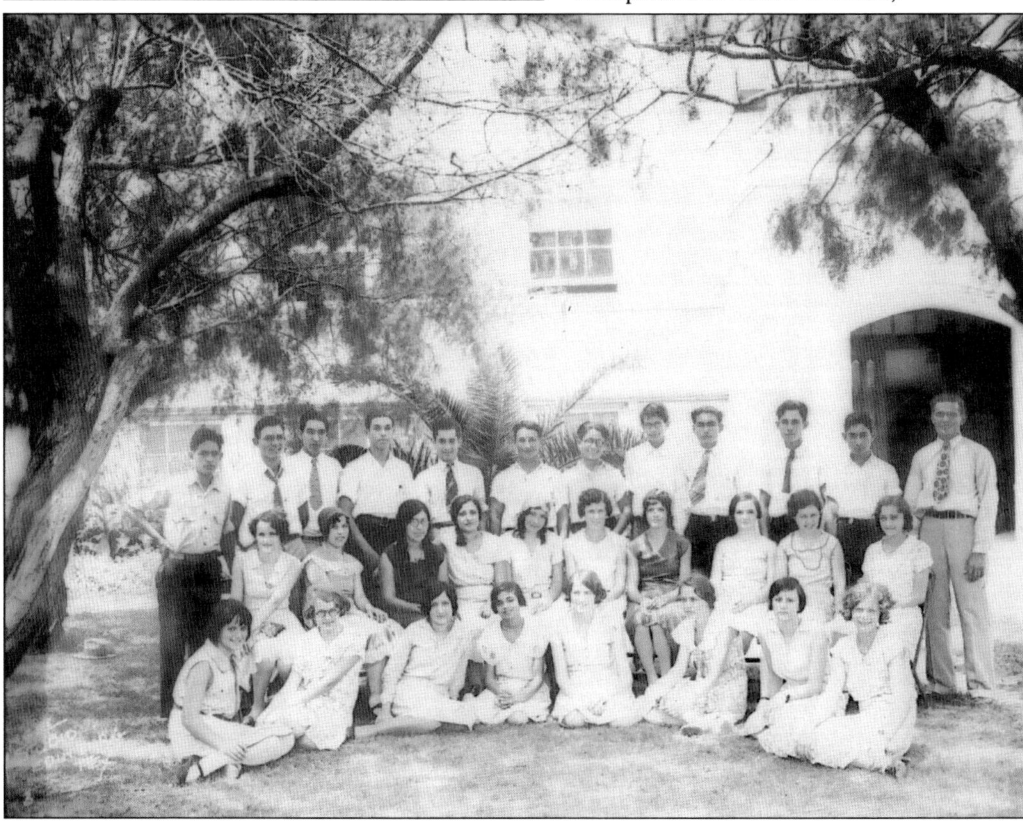

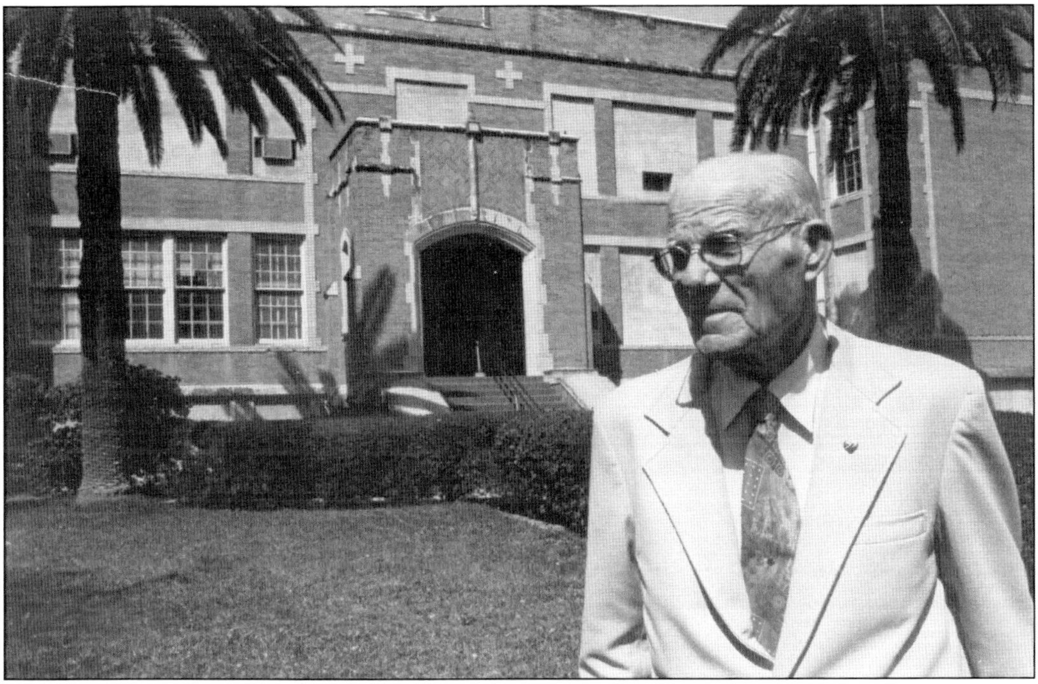

R.P. Ward oversaw significant changes during his tenure as president, including three name changes, the opening of the West Campus, and the change from a two-year to a four-year institution. The photograph above shows Ward in 1983. In 1933, Edinburg College changed its name to Edinburg Junior College to better describe its scope. The photograph at right shows Evelyn Milligan and Vida Burch with the Edinburg Junior College sign. In 1948, the college became a separate entity from the Edinburg School District, was granted partial state support, and was renamed Edinburg Regional College. In 1952, it became a four-year college. The name Pan American College was chosen to emphasize the regional aspect of the college both in the Valley and at the North America–Central America border. (Courtesy of The University of Texas–Pan American Library.)

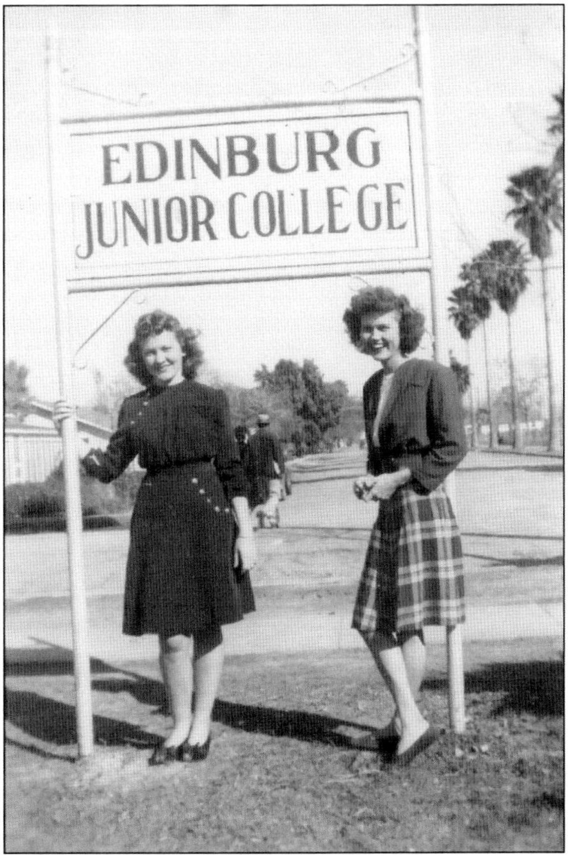

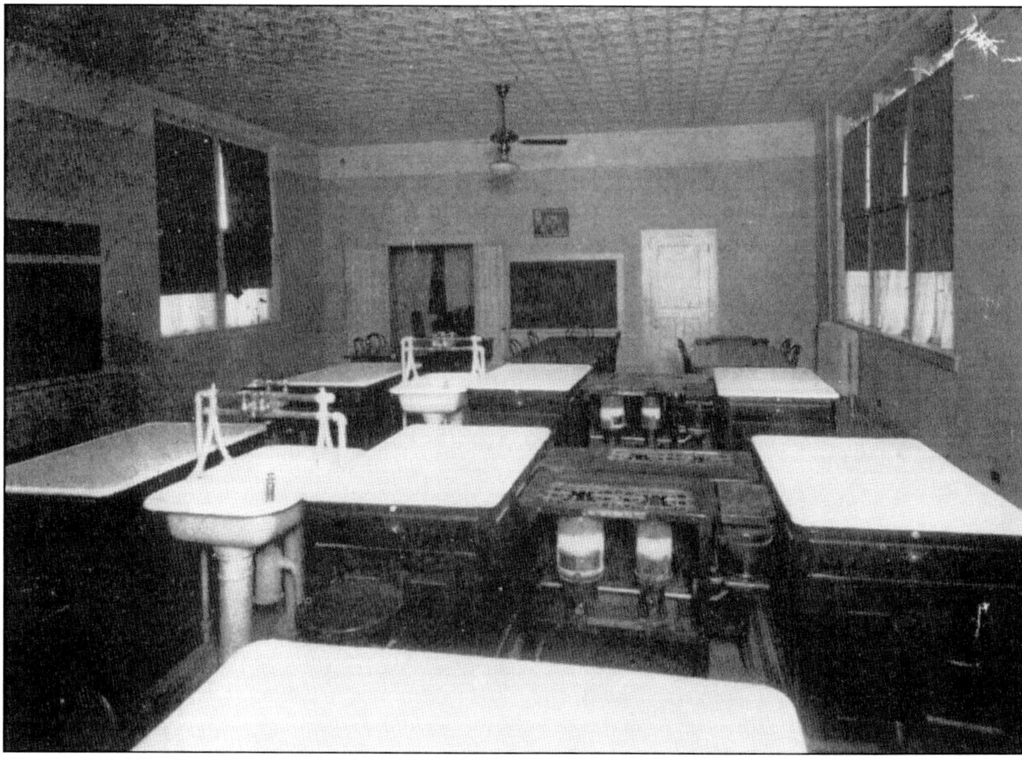

Courses at Edinburg College were arranged in three principal fields of instruction: General and Cultural; Professional and Vocation; and Fine Arts. Students of today may not recognize the classes that were once taught in high school and college. Besides the typical English and math subjects, classes also included home economics and mechanical classes. Home economics classes were taught in labs such as the one shown above. Future homemakers learned the proper way to prepare meals, dress and sew, and care for children. Mechanical courses also included hands-on experience, such as automotive mechanics in the "bus barn" shown below. (Courtesy of The University of Texas–Pan American Library.)

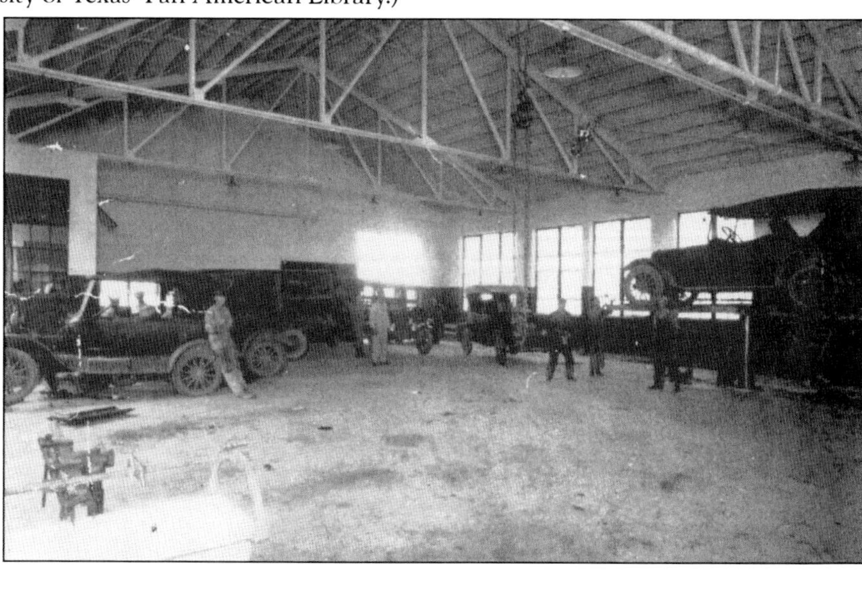

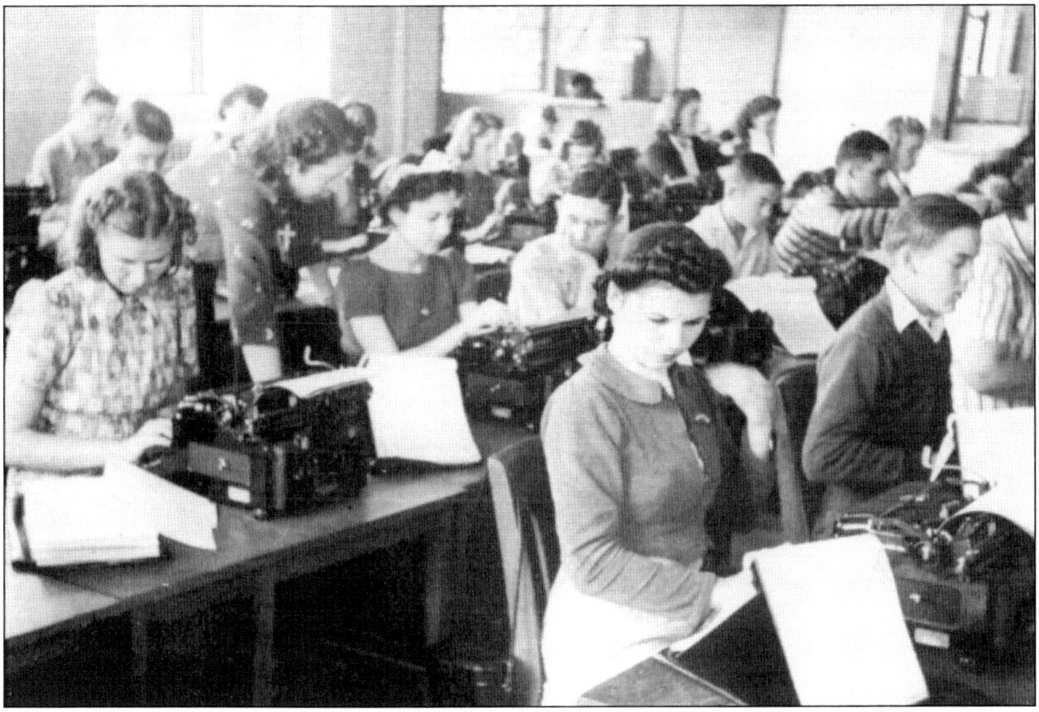

For many years typewriting was a regular course in the college catalog. A student taking business courses could also learn shorthand, stenography, and transcribing. As technology changed, so did the courses, as seen below in the photograph of a woman typing on the Digital Decscope computer. The Decscope was manufactured in the late 1970s when desktop computers were so new, the manuals explained what computers were and how to turn them on. (Above, courtesy of the Edinburg Consolidated Independent School District; below, courtesy of The University of Texas–Pan American Library.)

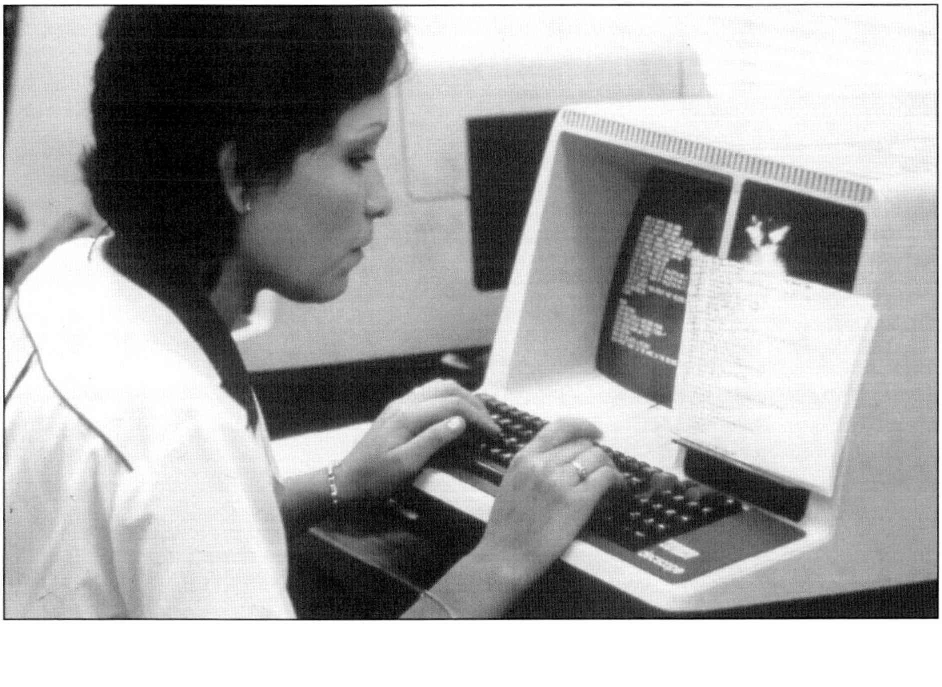

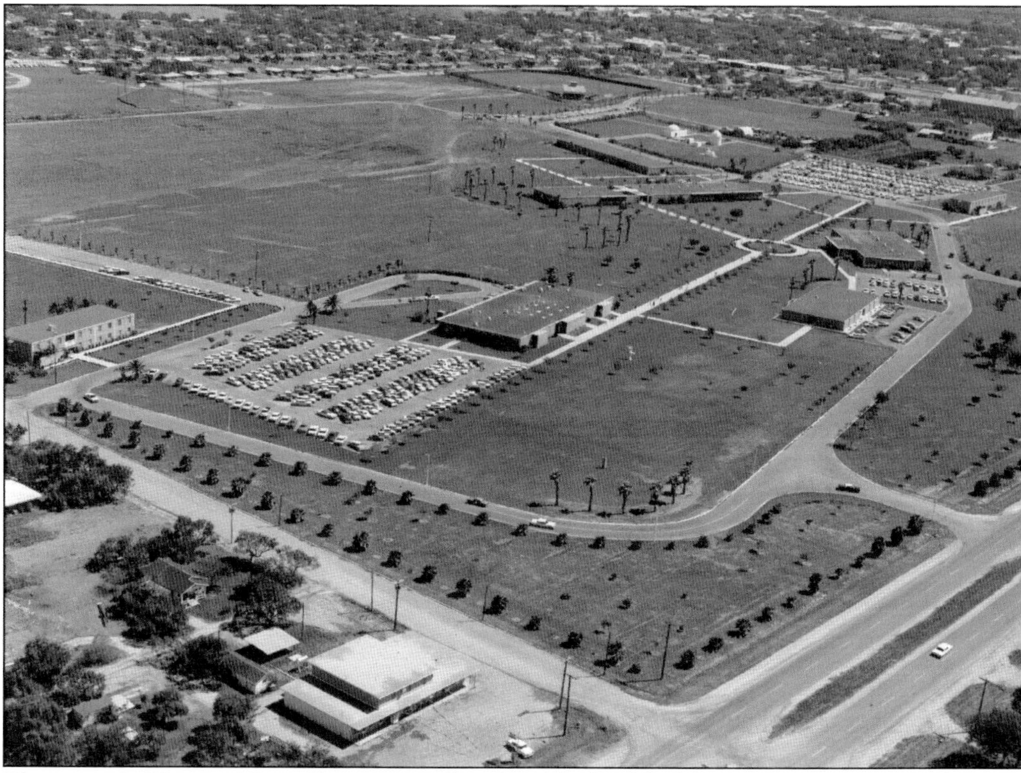

The expanded focus of the college meant that the old school buildings were no longer sufficient to meet the needs of the students and faculty. A move to McAllen was considered, but the Edinburg Chamber of Commerce and the citizens of Edinburg knew they wanted to keep the college in their town so they worked together, contributed money, and helped organize part of the purchase of what was known as the West Campus (now the main campus) across the railroad tracks. The first new building on the West Campus was a gymnasium. The photograph above shows the West Campus before the covered sidewalk was built around the campus. The photograph below of the West Campus is described on the back as "Pan American College in a cotton field" (Courtesy of The University of Texas–Pan American Library.)

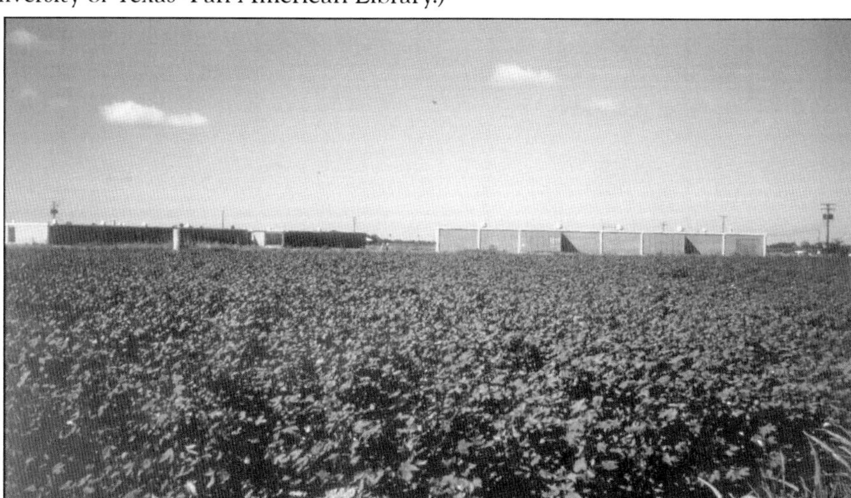

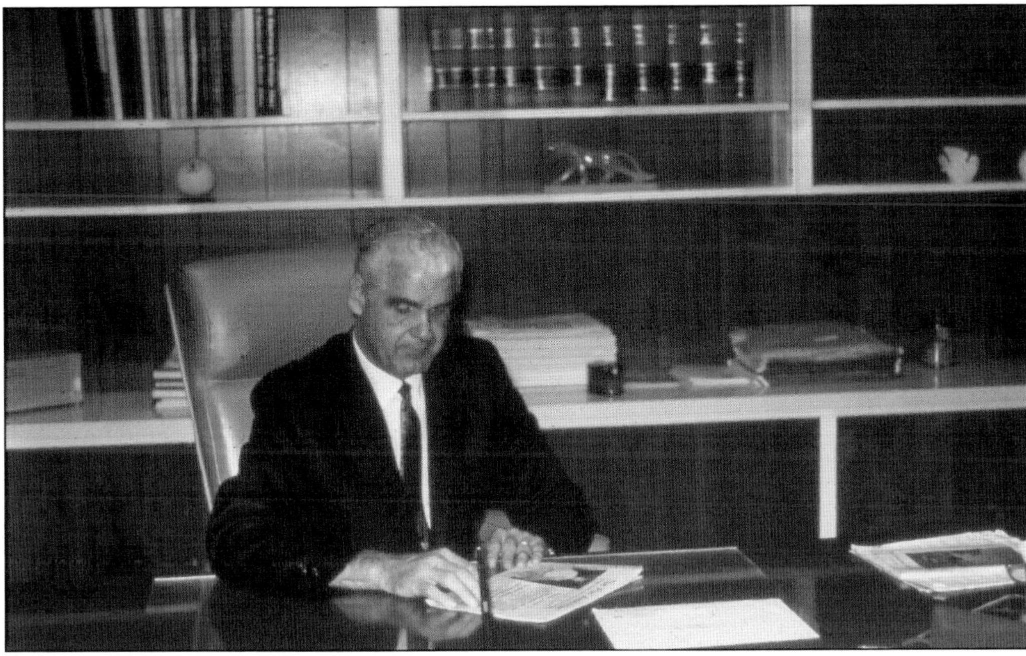

In 1960, Dr. Ralph Schilling (above) became the new president of the college. He served for the next 21 years, and like R.P. Ward, saw the college through tremendous change and growth. During Schilling's tenure, the college officially became accepted as Texas's 22nd state-supported senior college in 1965. After the college received permission to grant masters degrees in 1971, the name was changed to Pan American University, as can be seen on the tower in the photograph below. Upon Schilling's retirement in 1981, Dr. Miguel Nevárez, a Valley native, became the first Hispanic president of a major university in Texas. Dr. Nevárez led the university through a successful merger with the University of Texas system, and in 1989, the University of Texas–Pan American was created. (Courtesy of The University of Texas–Pan American Library.)

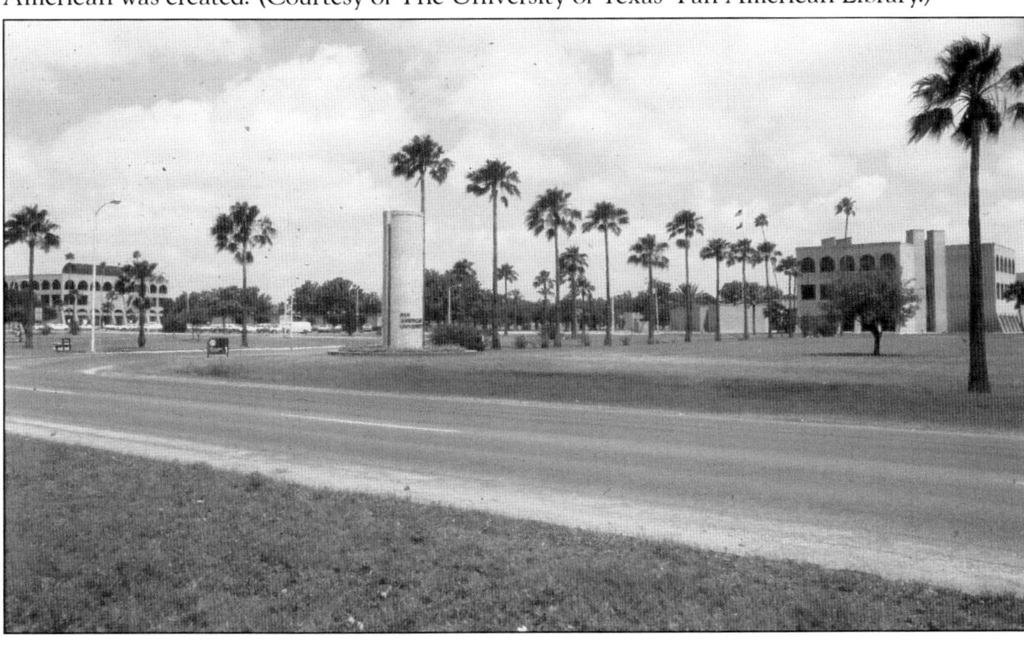

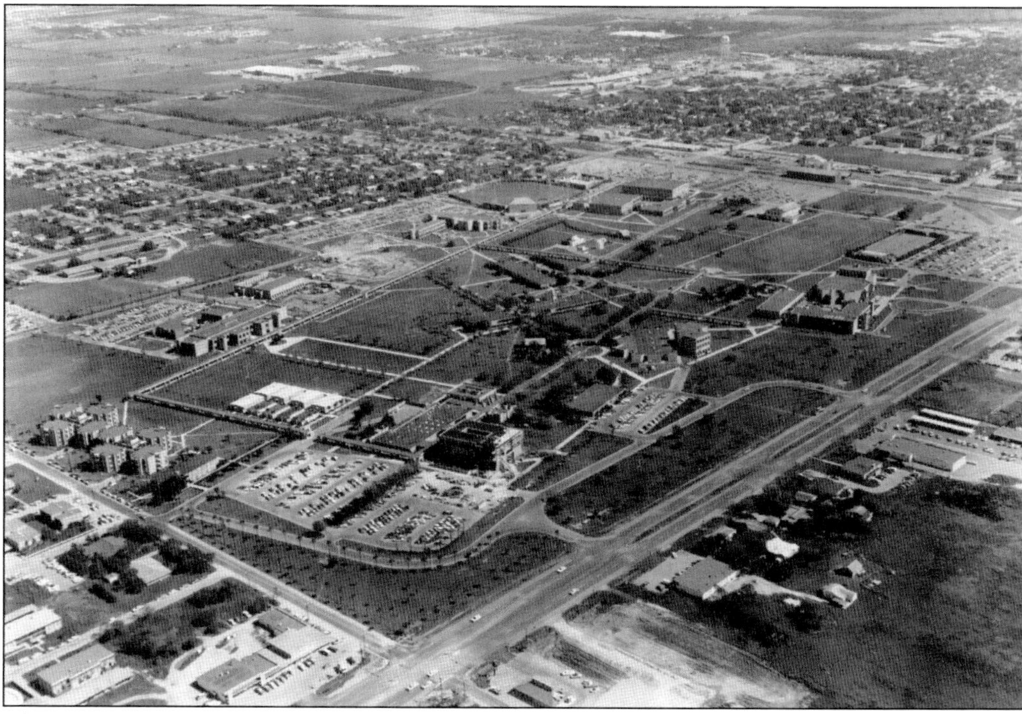

The West Campus, now the main campus for the university, just had a few buildings when Dr. Schilling became president in 1960. The campus grew quickly as enrollment continued to increase, and more buildings were constructed. A unique system of covered walkways was developed, which served a dual purpose of carrying cold water pipes and providing a sheltered and shady place for students to walk to class, as can be seen in the aerial photograph above. Two dormitories were also built on the West Campus—Emilia Hall for women and Southwick Hall for men. Emilia Hall was named after Emilia Schunior Ramirez, shown on page 91 as one of the first graduates of Edinburg High School. Three students are shown below studying in Emilia Hall. (Courtesy of The University of Texas–Pan American Library.)

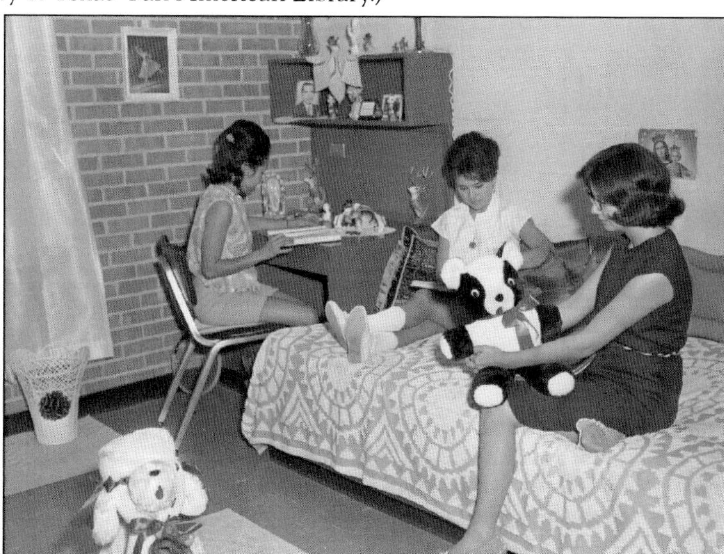

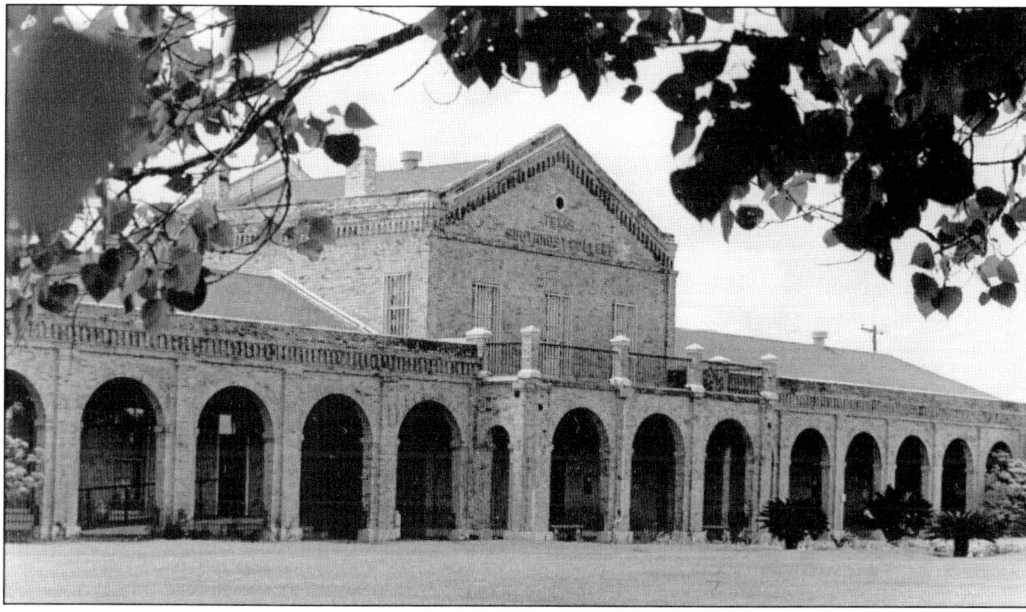

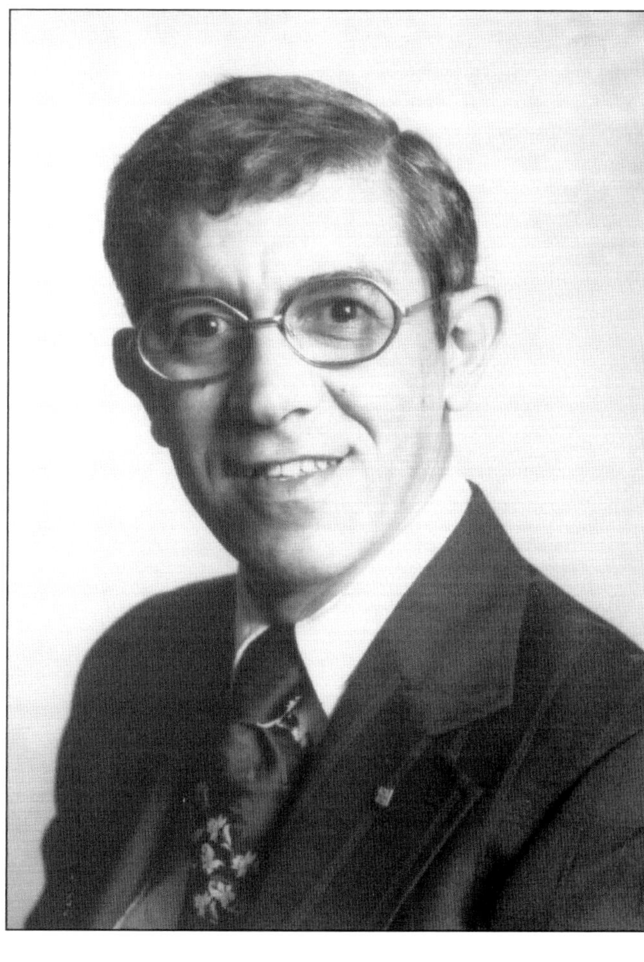

In 1973, Pan American University began working with Texas Southmost College to offer upper-level and graduate courses in Brownsville. In 1977, the Texas legislature authorized the creation of Pan American University at Brownsville (PAU-B). Dr. Arnulfo Oliveira (right), was selected as the first president of PAU-B. He was the president of Texas Southmost College, and a former professor of history on the Edinburg campus. Oliveira served until his death in 1981. In 1989, the University of Texas–Pan American at Brownsville was created as part of the University of Texas merger. In 1991, the University of Texas at Brownsville (UT-B) was created as a freestanding upper-level component of the University of Texas system. UT-B maintained a unique partnership agreement with Texas Southmost College that merged their administrative functions and allowed for a seamless affiliation of the junior and senior institutions.

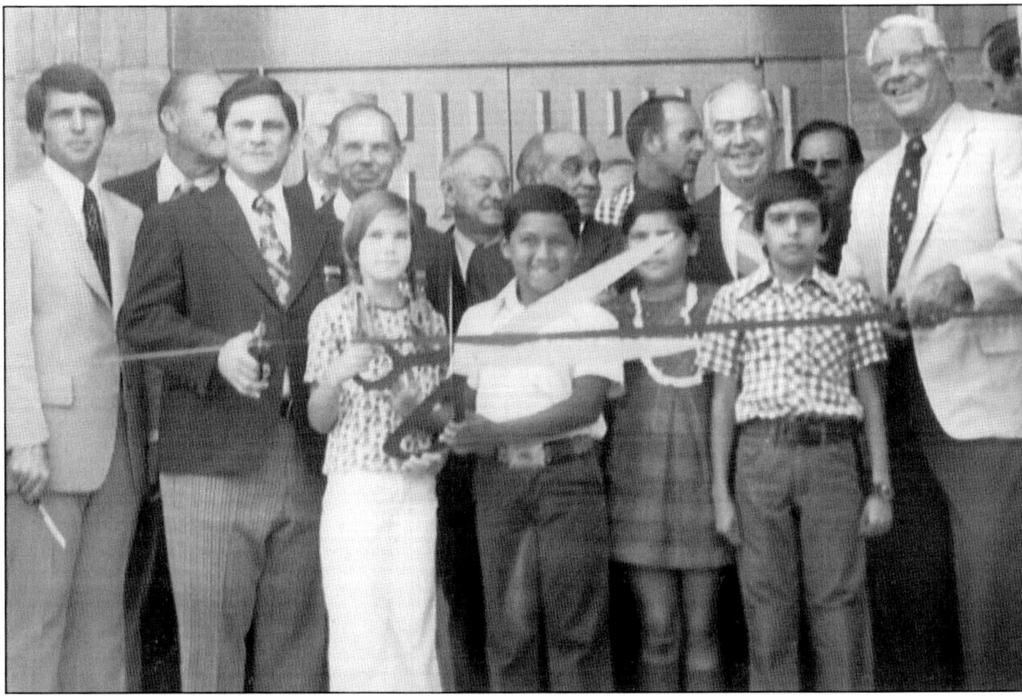

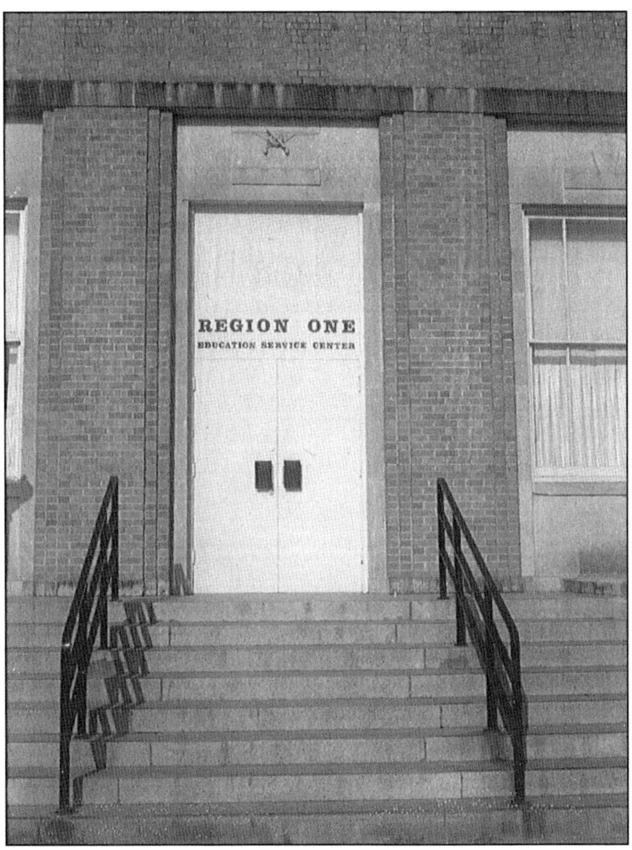

In 1968, the Region One Education Service Center was established in Edinburg. The center began when Harold Dooley, an Edinburg school administrator and director for the Elementary and Secondary Education Act Title III Project, foresaw the need to acquire and distribute resources for teaching English as a second language. As Region One grew it rented various locations throughout Edinburg to house its materials and staff. By 1974, the need for a larger permanent building was apparent. The City of Edinburg, the Edinburg Industrial Foundation, and the First State Bank and Trust of Edinburg worked together to provide funding for a new building. Roughly 300 employees all pitched in to help move into the new center. In 1974, the grand opening ceremonies were held to celebrate the new location on West Schunior. (Courtesy of the Region One Education Service Center.)

Today, Region One serves local school districts in the seven counties of Cameron, Willacy, Hidalgo, Starr, Zapata, Jim Hogg, and Webb by providing a variety of equipment and educational materials including books, pamphlets, film, slides, visual aid materials, and teaching aids to support a wide range of subjects. Region One also assists with a variety of issues including providing quality ideas and service information to aid with curriculum development, data processing, driver education, migrant education, teacher training, media services, special education, bilingual education, occupational education, guidance, and counseling. The photograph at right shows one of the driver's education simulators. The photograph below shows reel-to-reel equipment. (Courtesy of the Region One Education Service Center.)

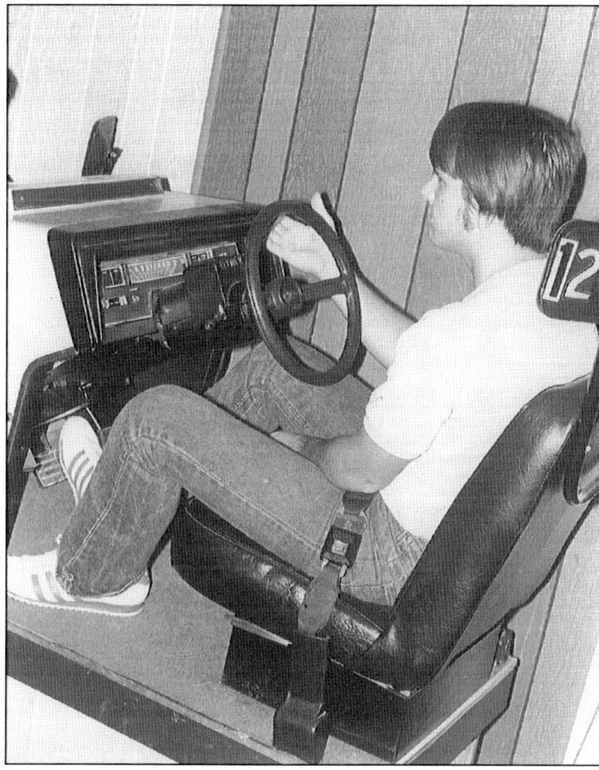

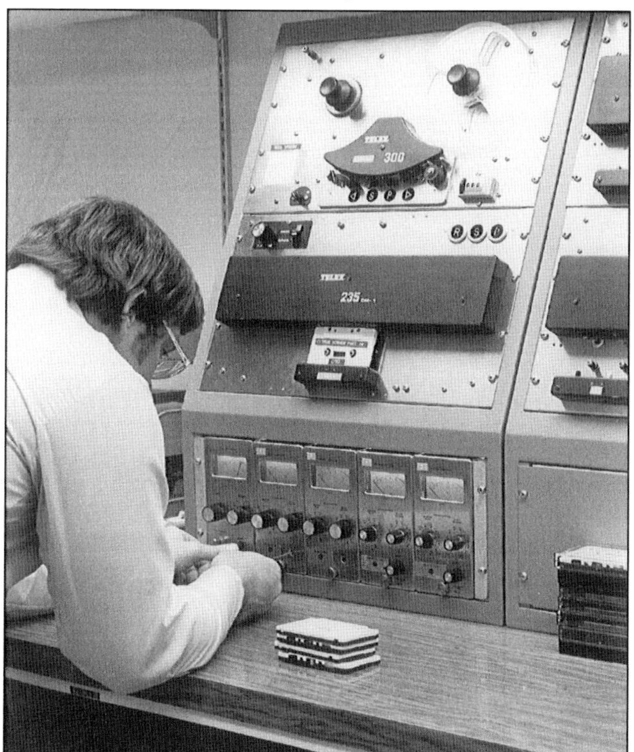

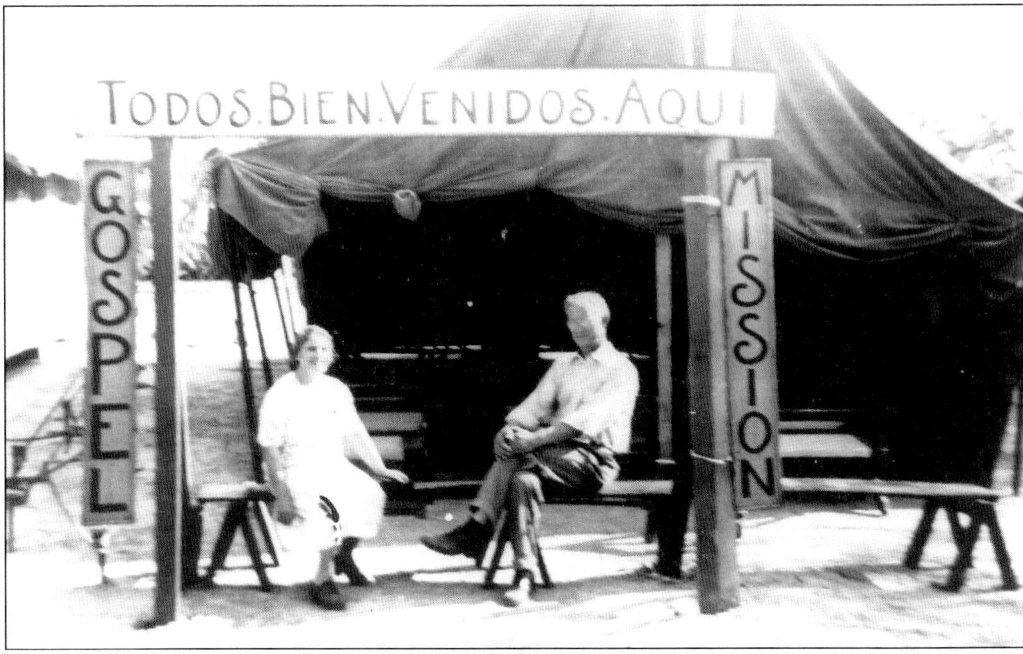

In 1946, Rev. Mack Carl Ehlert, a Baptist pastor and evangelist, founded the Rio Grande Bible Institute. Ehlert and his wife, Elizabeth, arrived in the Valley in 1937 to teach the gospel by trailer and tent as shown above. Ehlert saw a need to train Spanish speakers to spread the word in the Rio Grande Valley and Latin America. In 1946, he and two other teachers opened the Rio Grande Bible Institute as a three-year bilingual school. In 1955, English courses were discontinued and the one-year Spanish Language School was added to the Spanish Bible Institute. The Language School employed the latest language teaching techniques, including the assistance of native speakers such as Teófilo de la Torre, seen below. (Courtesy of the Rio Grande Bible Institute.)

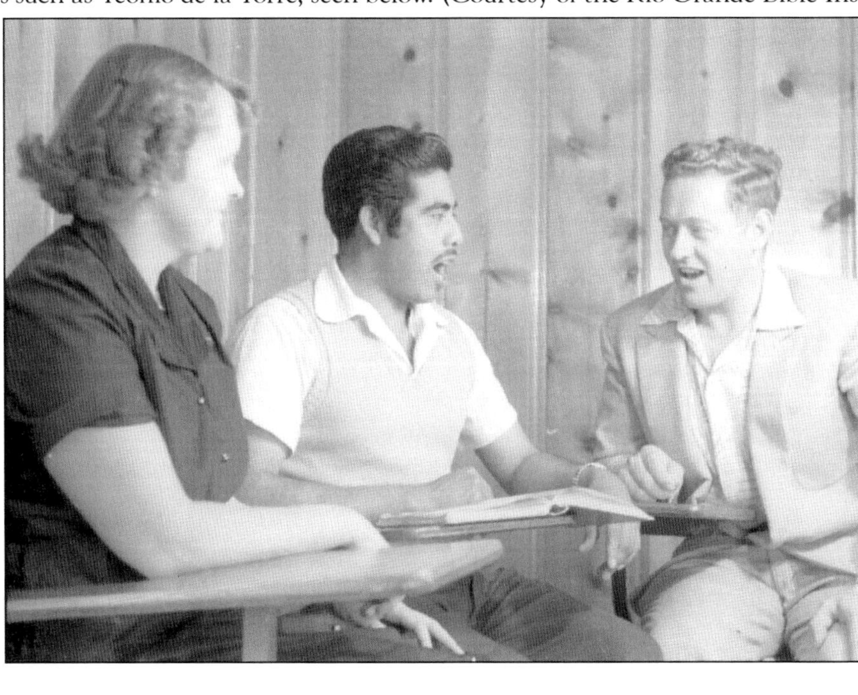

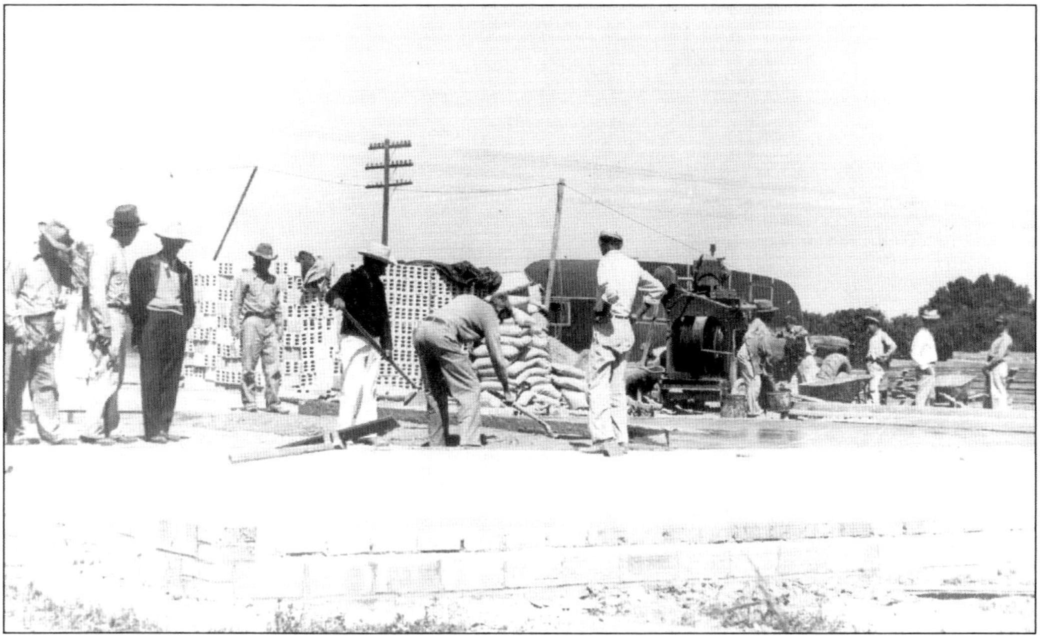

M.C. Ehlert purchased 40 acres on Highway 281 in Edinburg to open the Rio Grande Bible Institute in 1947. The assistance and volunteer work of locals as well as winter visitors, primarily from the Midwest, have built both the school buildings as well as its reputation. The students and supporters of the institute have not only enriched the school itself but also the communities that the students and graduates have reached. The photograph above shows the laying of the foundation of a dormitory. The photograph at right shows Ehlert speaking on the KURV radio station, which is located on the campus. (Courtesy of the Rio Grande Bible Institute.)

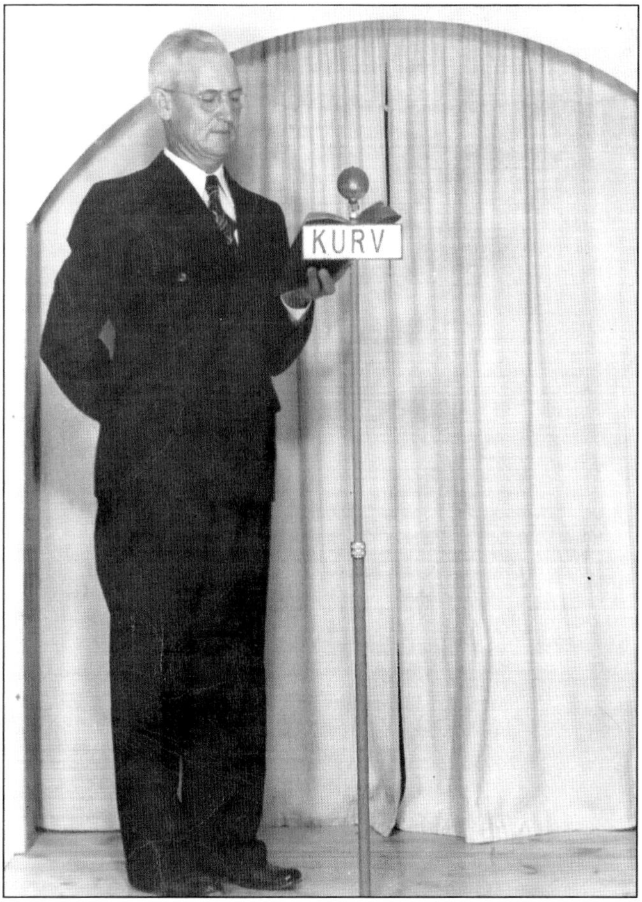

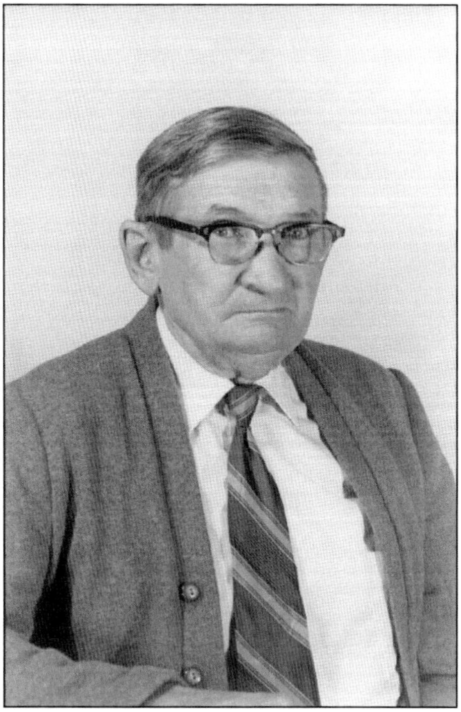

The South Texas Independent School District (STISD) had its beginnings in Edinburg as the Rio Grande Rehabilitation District. The district was originally associated with the Edinburg Consolidated Independent School District. A group of 13 volunteers organized the district, and it was formally created in 1964 by the Texas legislature to provide education to disabled youth who were then excluded from public education. Albert Hughes (left) was one of the original volunteers and the first president of the board of directors. He was instrumental in getting the legislation passed and finding a location for the district's first school, shown below. In 1967, the district became an independent school district and opened another school with the same name in Harlingen. (Courtesy of the South Texas Independent School District.)

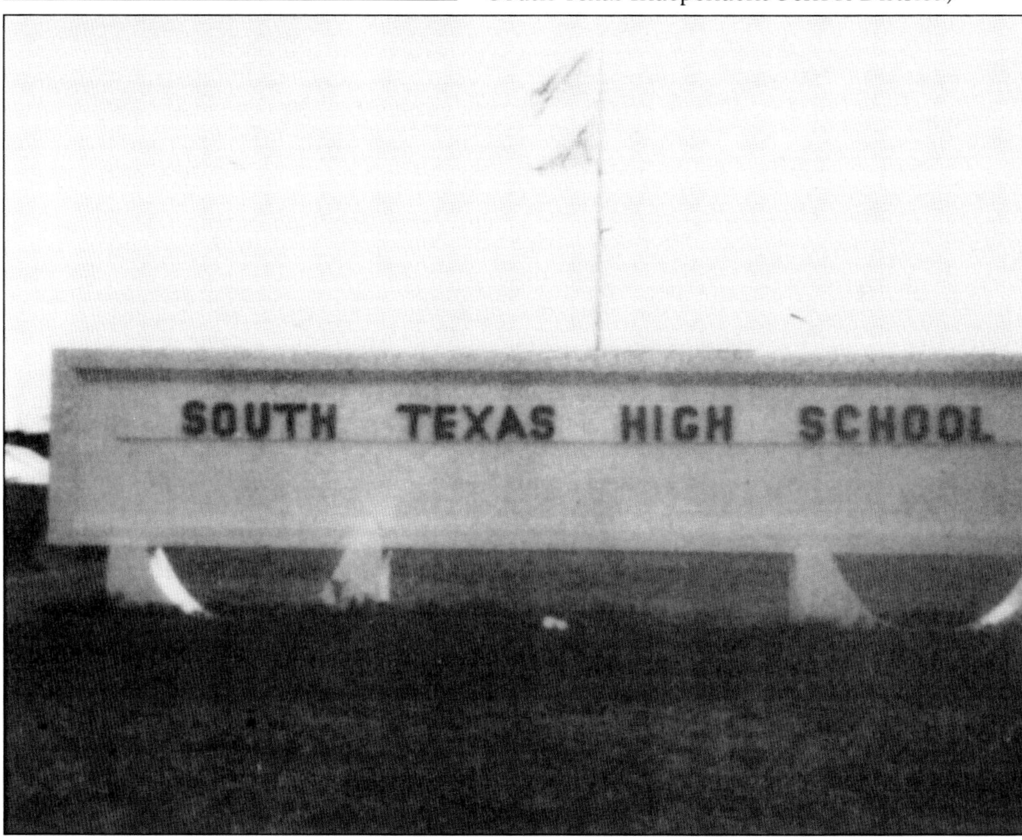

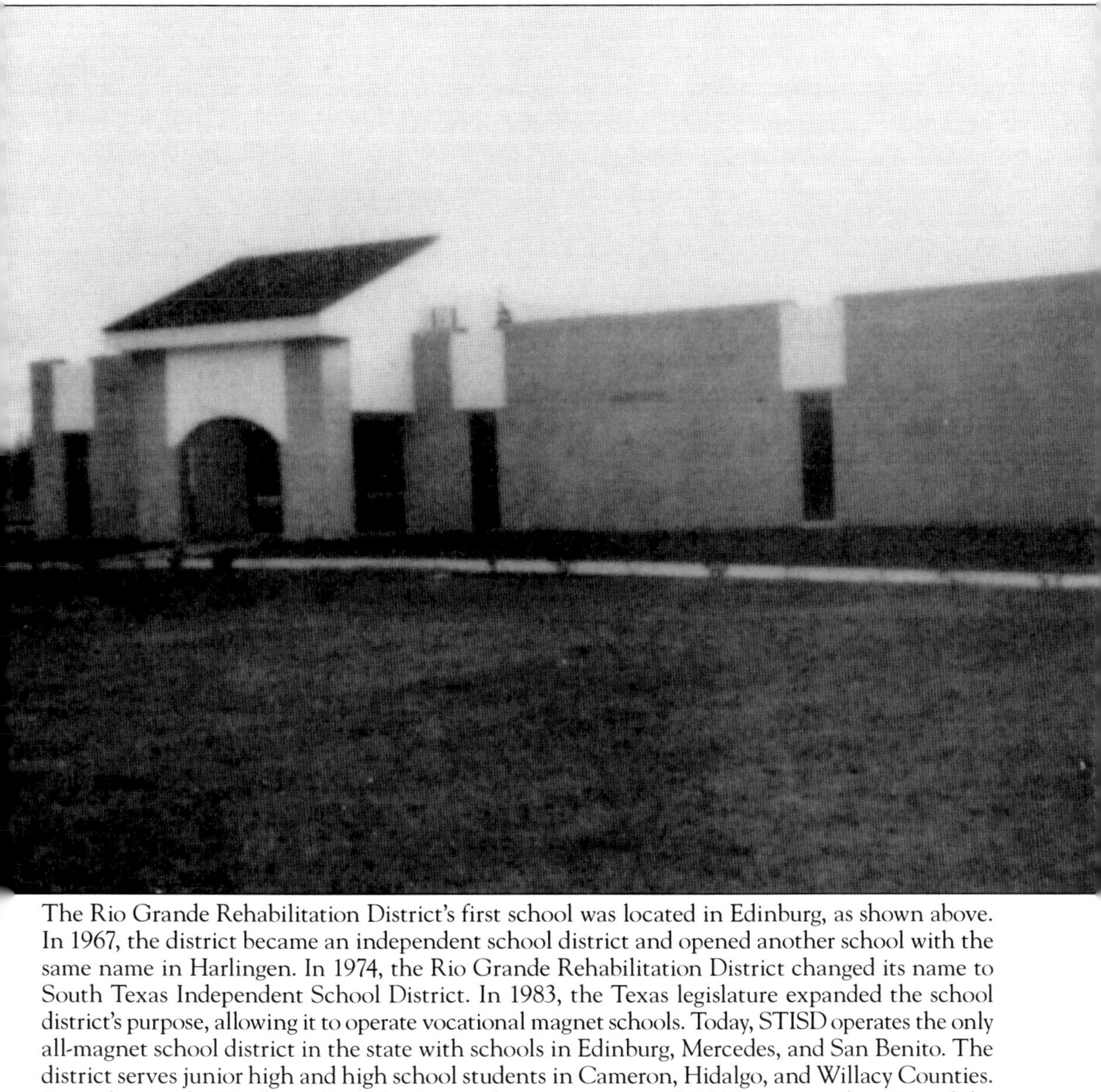

The Rio Grande Rehabilitation District's first school was located in Edinburg, as shown above. In 1967, the district became an independent school district and opened another school with the same name in Harlingen. In 1974, the Rio Grande Rehabilitation District changed its name to South Texas Independent School District. In 1983, the Texas legislature expanded the school district's purpose, allowing it to operate vocational magnet schools. Today, STISD operates the only all-magnet school district in the state with schools in Edinburg, Mercedes, and San Benito. The district serves junior high and high school students in Cameron, Hidalgo, and Willacy Counties. It overlaps with 28 other school districts and serves an area of 3,643 square miles. Two of the schools in the South Texas Independent School District remain in Edinburg—the South Texas Preparatory Academy (STPA), a junior high school; and the South Texas Business, Education & Technology Academy (BETA). (Courtesy of the South Texas Independent School District.)

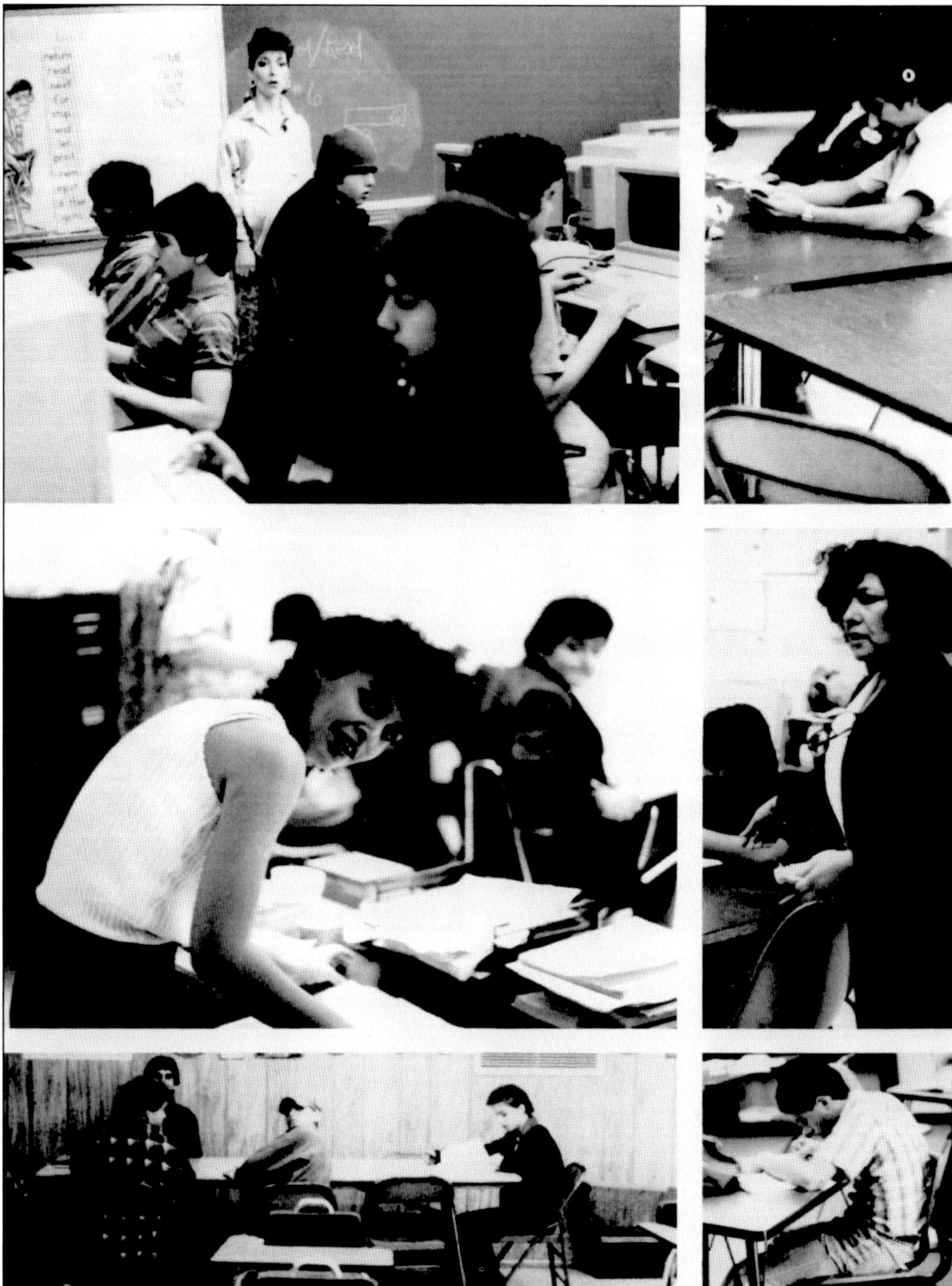

Shown here are classroom scenes from the South Texas High School. (Courtesy of the South Texas Independent School District.)

Five

Edinburg
Gateway City to the Valley

Edinburg became known as the "Gateway City to the Valley." Since the very first settlements established by José de Escandón, much of the growth of the region has taken place parallel with the river. The first road ran along the southern banks of the river connecting the first towns, including Reynosa and Matamoros. After this region became part of the United States, Gen. Zachary Taylor is credited with establishing the old Military Highway along the northern bank of the river in the mid-1800s. Half a century later, when the railroad was built, that too ran parallel to the river. Towns blossomed along its tracks, creating what was advertised beginning in the 1930s as the "longest main street in the world," which ran from Brownsville through McAllen and on toward Rio Grande City. Edinburg took on the role of connecting that long line of towns with cities to the north, becoming the "Gateway city to the Valley." Edinburg is at the beginning of the northern stretch of one of the longest highways in America. US Highway 281 stretches from Brownsville and west toward Hidalgo, where it takes a turn toward the north, running through Pharr to Edinburg, then on to Falfurrias, over 60 miles away, and then north through San Antonio to Oklahoma, Kansas, Nebraska, South Dakota, and North Dakota until it reaches the Canadian border. Edinburg became the central gathering place on this highway before the long trip north, and the first welcoming city after a long drive south.

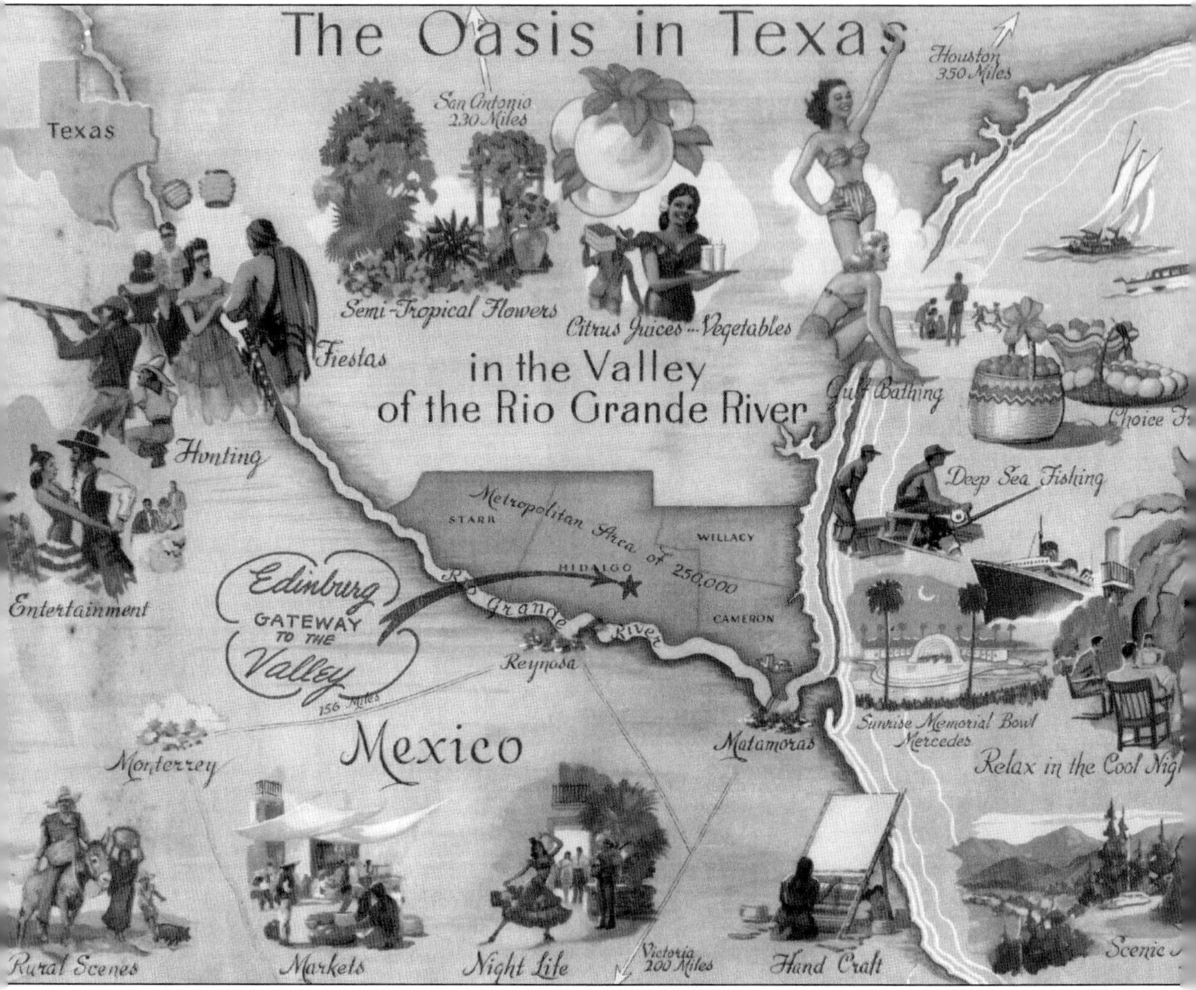

Edinburg took pride in its role as the "Gateway to the Valley." The Lower Rio Grande Valley has been an "oasis" or a "magic valley" attracting tourists for 100 years. This poster from around 1930 extols the virtues of the "Valley of the Rio Grande River" with Edinburg prominently located in the middle. The 1920s and 1930s saw some of the highest population growth of the Valley, due in large part to the Anglo-American land promoters of that time. The Valley was perceived as a last frontier, an area that up until then had been largely ignored by northerners. The map on this page typifies that view, with the four counties of the Valley clearly delineated, San Antonio and Houston vaguely indicated to the north, and the Mexican towns of Reynosa, Matamoros, and Monterrey nearby to the south. The map indicates that the Valley offered everything desired, from flowers and citrus to gulf bathing and deep-sea fishing, to nearby Mexico with its markets, handcrafts, and entertainment. (Courtesy of The University of Texas–Pan American Library.)

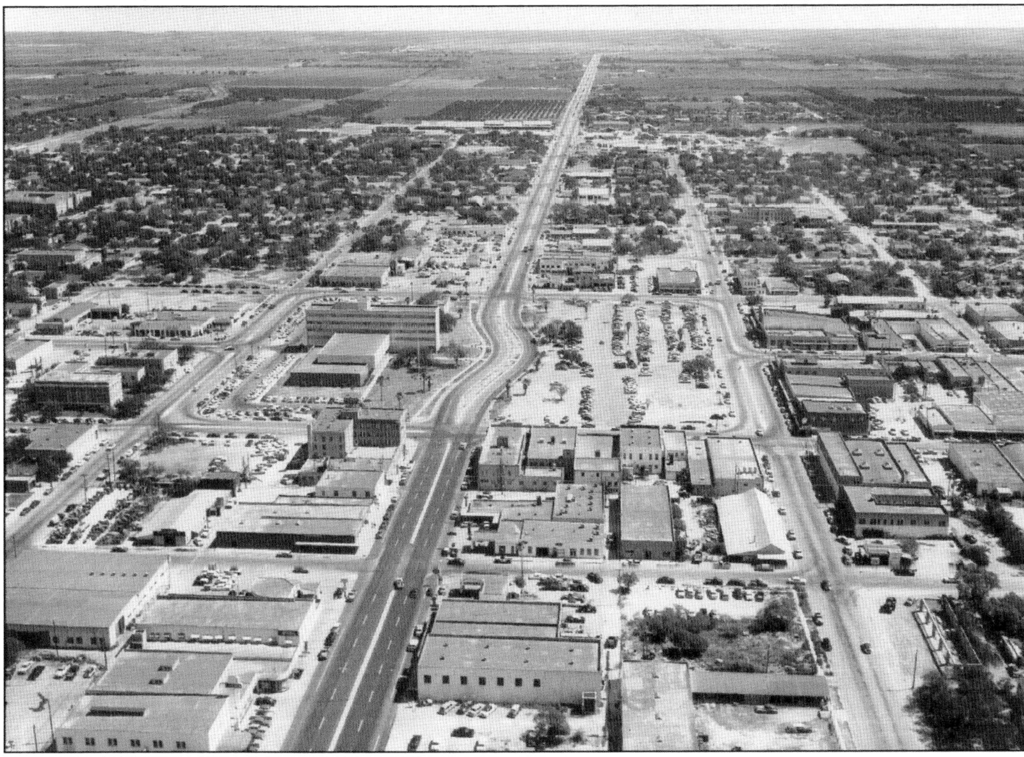

State Highway 66 was originally constructed in 1925 from Edinburg to Pharr. Highway 66 later became part of US Highway 281, leading straight through Edinburg, as seen above. In the 1930s, Edinburg became home to many packing and shipping plants that used this central location to ship their produce to northern markets. In 1954, the highway was expanded to become a four lane divided highway. The median area was planted with palm trees and bougainvillea shrubs. The Edinburg Garden Club also planted bougainvillea around the courthouse square, as shown in the photograph below from Gertrude Schaleben. Traffic has continued to increase after NAFTA (North American Free Trade Agreement) was enacted and maquiladoras prospered. (Above, courtesy of the Edinburg Volunteer Fire Department; below, courtesy of The University of Texas–Pan American Library.)

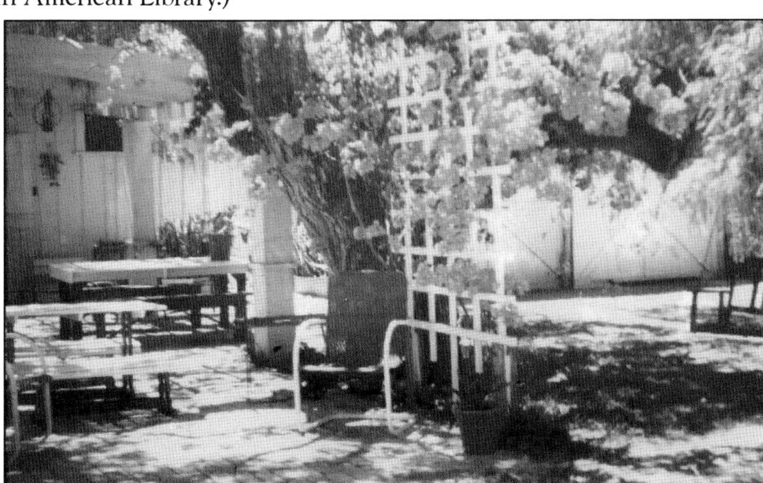

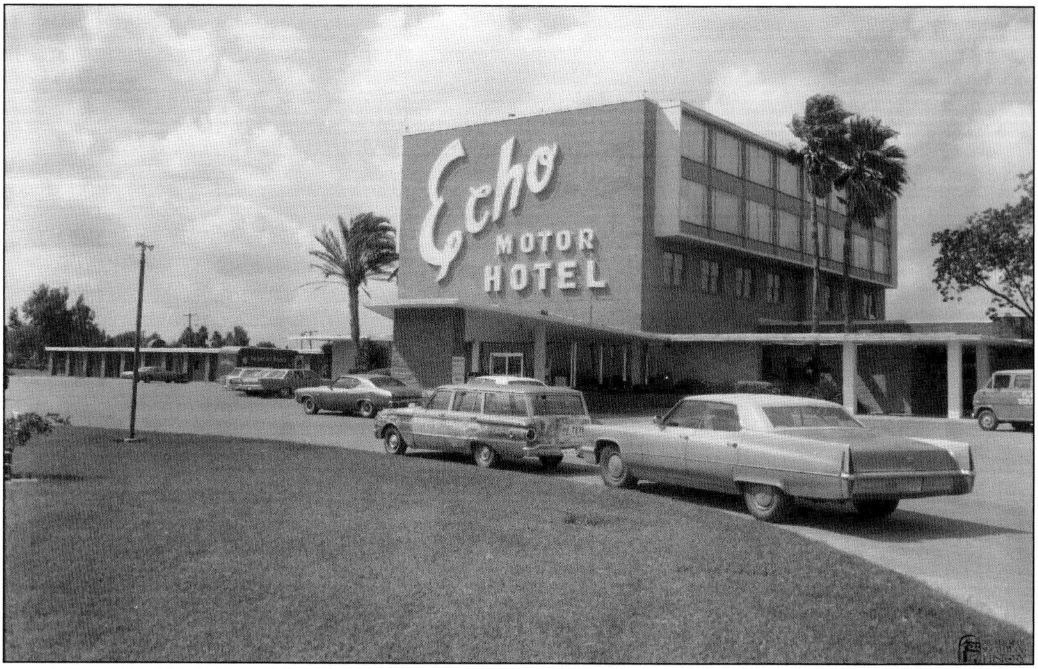

The Echo Hotel is just one example of the ways in which the residents of Edinburg came together to make a difference. In 1955, no major hotel chain would build a hotel in Edinburg. "There isn't enough business" was the most common comment. The residents of Edinburg wouldn't take *no* for an answer. A meeting was held at Sibley's Café, which led to the creation of the Edinburg Community Hotel Organization, their initials forming the name of the hotel. 250 citizens worked together to sell stock, hold weekly sales rallies, and secure additional loans to build the $1 million hotel. More than 1,100 citizens of Edinburg bought stock in support of building the hotel. After four years of hard work, the best-equipped motor hotel in the area was opened in 1959.

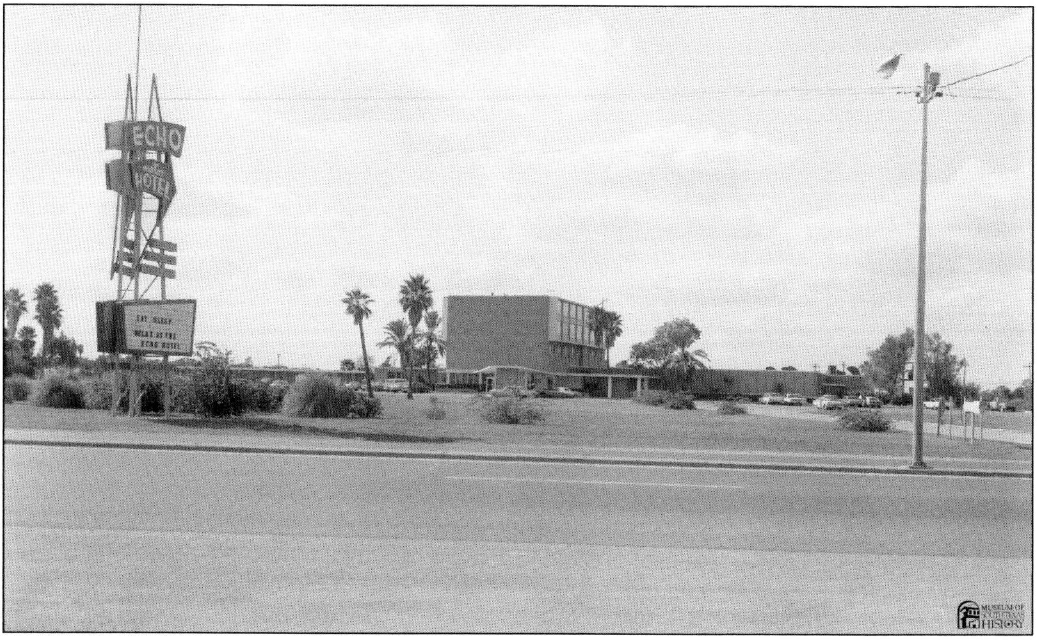

Irrigation canals developed faster than roads were paved, leaving farmers with the problem of getting their produce to market. The first shippers, probably Wade and Newton, had many smaller locations in Valley cities in the 1920s near the railroads, so that the farmer only had to make it as far as the nearest railroad. As the roads developed, centralized packing and shipping locations were built. Crates were used for tomatoes, bushel baskets were used for other vegetables, and watermelons were loaded directly onto the train car, as can be seen in the photograph at right showing D.B. Chapin helping to load watermelons onto a train car in the town of Chapin. The photograph below shows crops in the field already crated and ready. (Right, courtesy of the Museum of South Texas History; below, courtesy of The University of Texas–Pan American Library.)

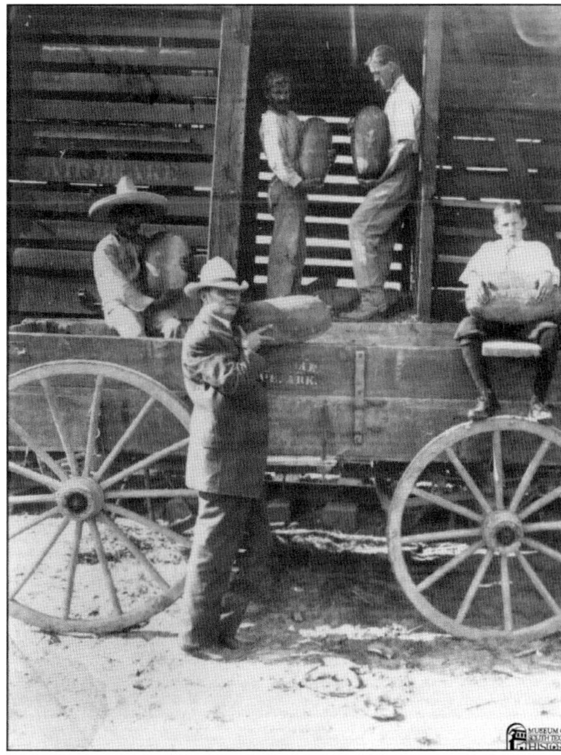

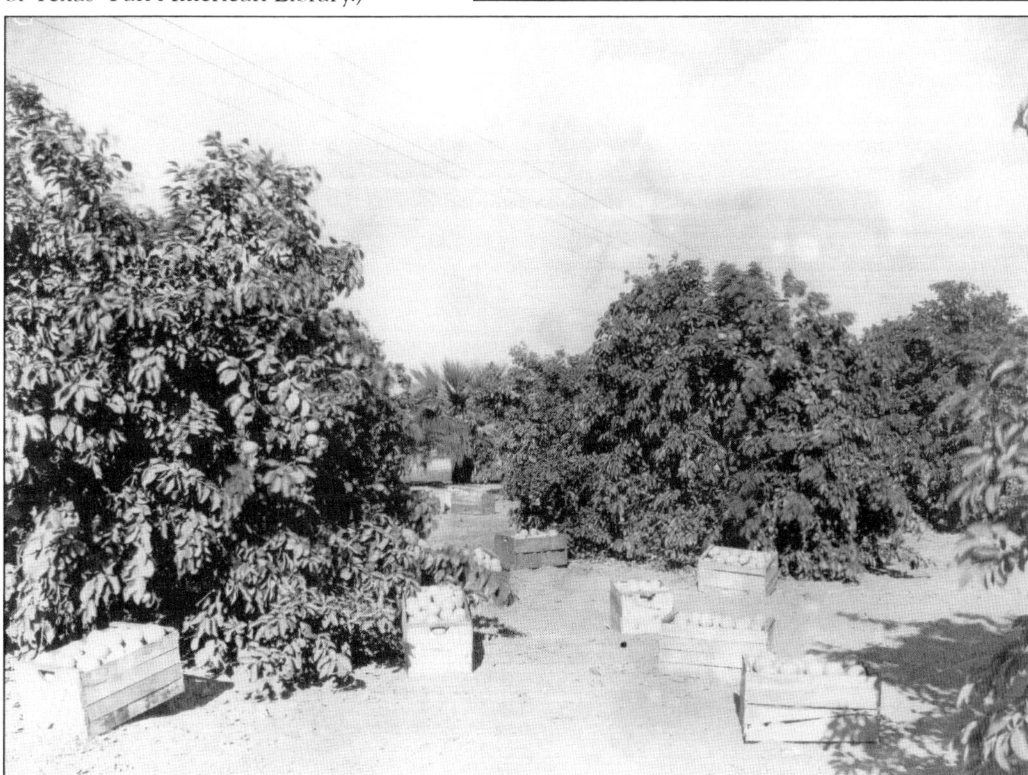

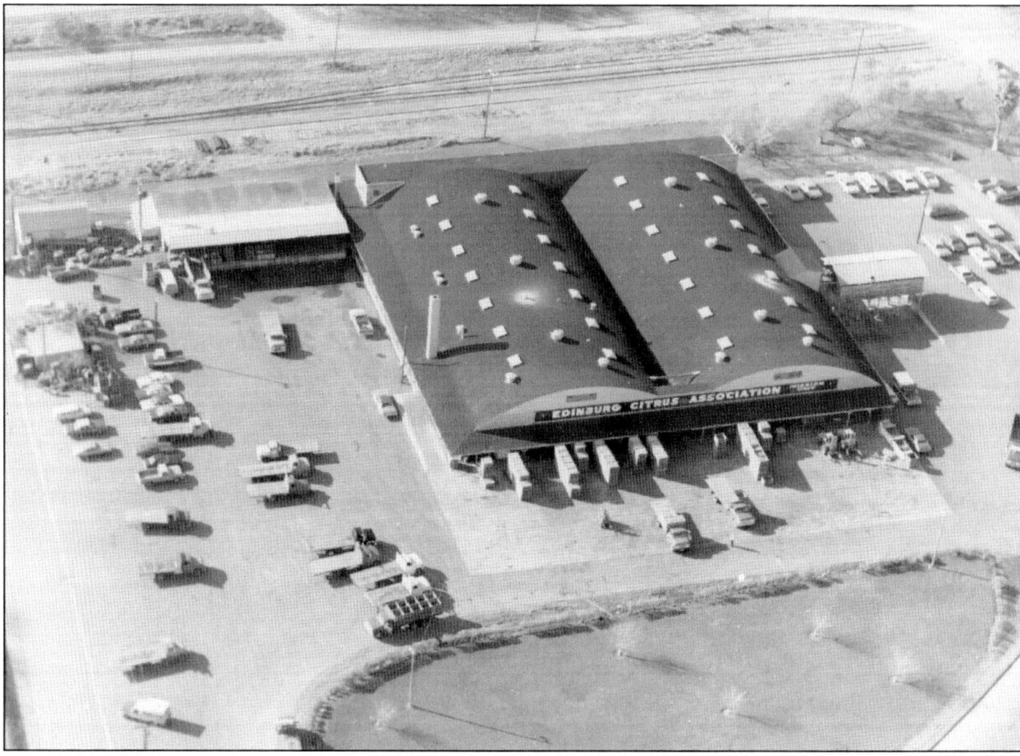

With the construction of US 281, Edinburg finally realized its dream of connecting the Valley with San Antonio and other cities to the north. When Chapin/Edinburg was first established, the founders had envisioned a railroad track that would run through Edinburg on its way north to Falfurrias, and eventually San Antonio. Although that railroad never materialized, the highway did, allowing Edinburg to become a center for packing and shipping agricultural products including citrus, melon, peach, corn, grain, sorghum, sugarcane, cotton, and poultry. The photograph above shows a busy shipping center with trucks ready to be loaded with citrus crates. The photograph below shows the inside of a packing plant as citrus is being sorted and packed. (Courtesy of the Edinburg Citrus Association.)

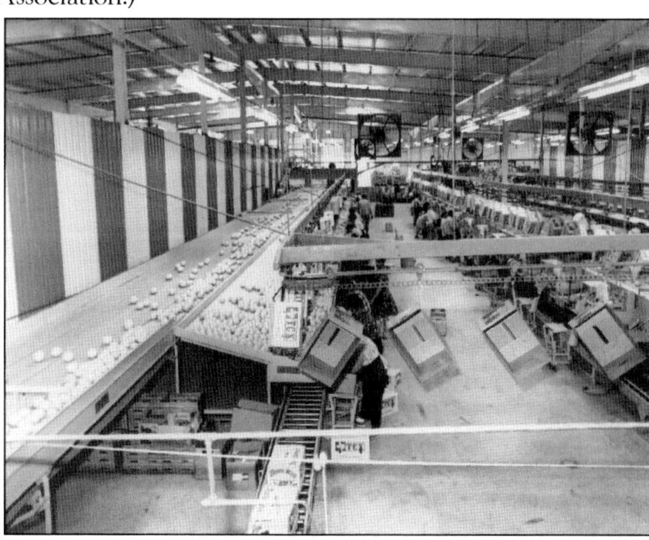

In the 1930s, a number of vegetable and citrus packing and shipping companies flourished. One of the firsts, in 1931 or 1932, was a company organized by Ed Smith, Jack Berry, and Mr. Chesnutt. A year later in 1933, the Edinburg Citrus Association was formed, originally located near the Southern Pacific depot. By 1969, the company was still going strong, and was able to expand to a plant on the north side of Edinburg, reportedly one of the largest and best equipped citrus packing plants in the United States. The shipping label on the right is from the Edinburg Citrus Association. The photograph below was taken in front of trucks from the Edinburg Citrus Association plant. (Courtesy of the Edinburg Citrus Association.)

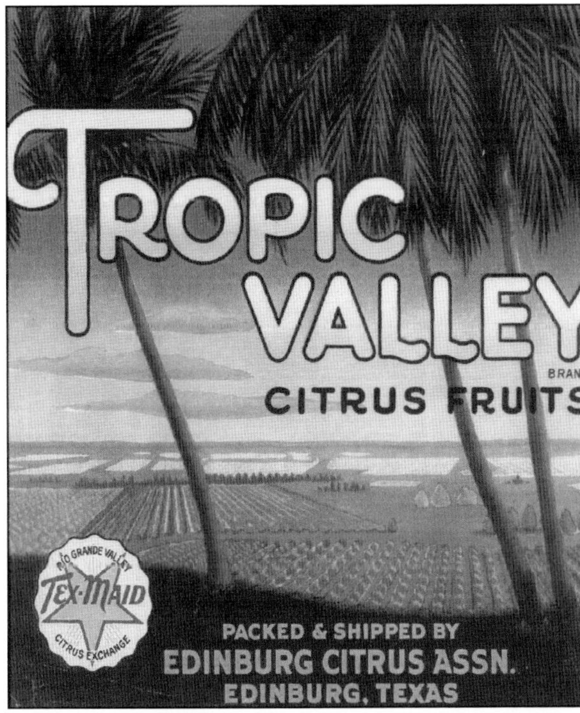

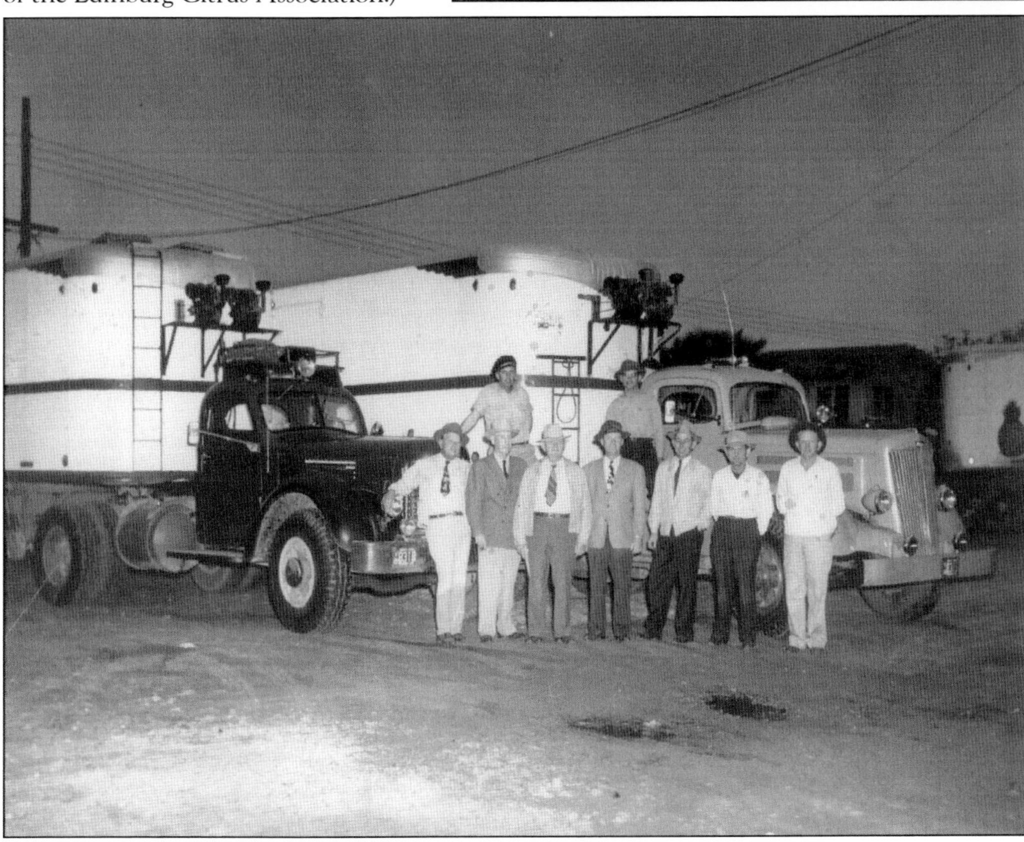

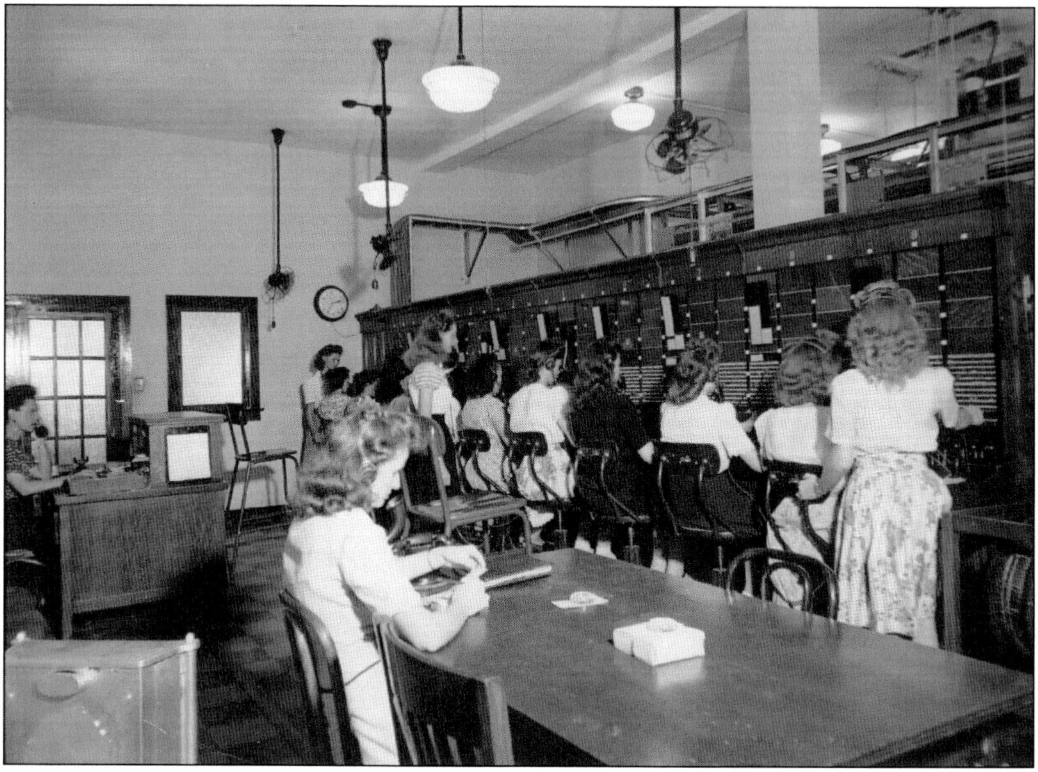

In 1914, telephones were introduced to Edinburg largely through the efforts of a committee led by W.R. Montgomery and Juan de la Vina. The Edinburg telephone office was on the first floor of the American State Bank at Closner and McIntyre. There were approximately 50 telephones, all operating as party lines in which two or more customers shared a line. Mattie Dougherty operated the first exchange day and night. When she could not attend the switchboard, her son, W.R. Montgomery, took over. Initially the telephone numbers were single or double digits, indicating the small number of customers. The sheriff's telephone number was 24. The number to the telephone office itself was (unlucky) number 13, as no customer wanted that number. (Courtesy of The University of Texas–Pan American Library.)

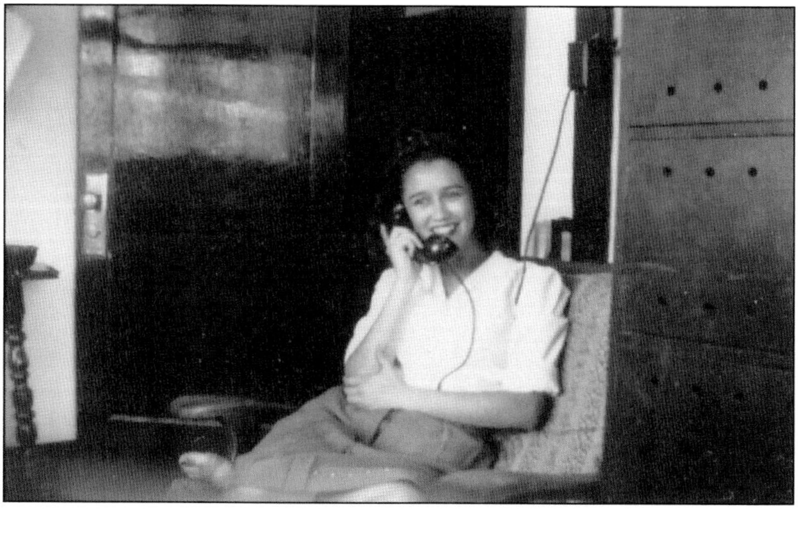

Throughout the years, the county seat has had a number of newspapers. In 1903, James H. Edwards and R.A. Marsh published the first issue of *Hidalgo Advance*. The *Advance* was printed in the Hidalgo jail, and was published in both English and Spanish to promote the county and attract a railroad. The subscription rate was $1 per year. In 1914, a new newspaper, the *Edinburg Valley Review,* began publication. The *Review* has gone through a series of name changes, including *Edinburg Daily Review*, the *Daily Review*, and (currently) the *Edinburg Review*. Other newspapers published in Edinburg include the *Hidalgo Independent*, the *Hidalgo County Sun*, the *Hidalgo County News*, and *Revista del Valle*. (Courtesy of The University of Texas–Pan American Library.)

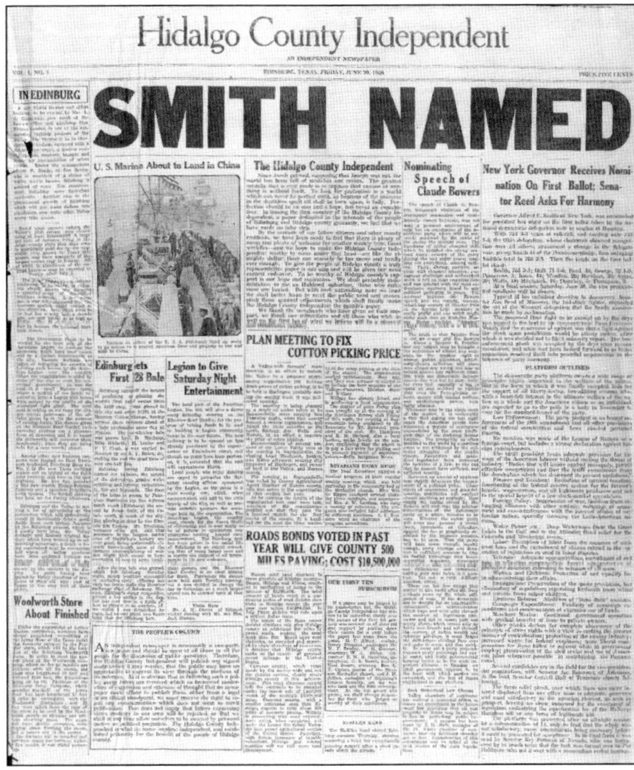

Hidalgo County Independent

AN INDEPENDENT NEWSPAPER

IN EDINBURG

SMITH NAMED

U. S. Marines About to Land in China

The Hidalgo County Independent

Nominating Speech of Claude Bowers

New York Governor Receives Nomination On First Ballot; Senator Reed Asks For Harmony

PLAN MEETING TO FIX COTTON PICKING PRICE

Edinburg Gets First '28 Bale

Legion to Give Saturday Night Entertainment

ROADS BONDS VOTED IN PAST YEAR WILL GIVE COUNTY 500 MILES PAVING; COST $10,500,000

Woolworth Store About Finished

THE PEOPLE'S COLUMN

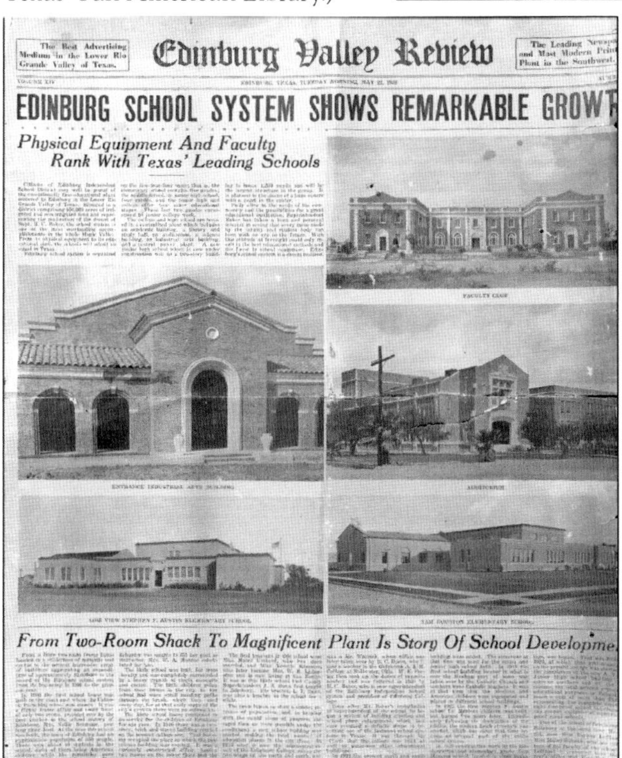

The Best Advertising Medium in the Lower Rio Grande Valley of Texas.

Edinburg Valley Review

The Leading Newspaper and Most Modern Print Plant in the Southwest.

EDINBURG SCHOOL SYSTEM SHOWS REMARKABLE GROWT

Physical Equipment And Faculty Rank With Texas' Leading Schools

From Two-Room Shack To Magnificent Plant Is Story Of School Developme

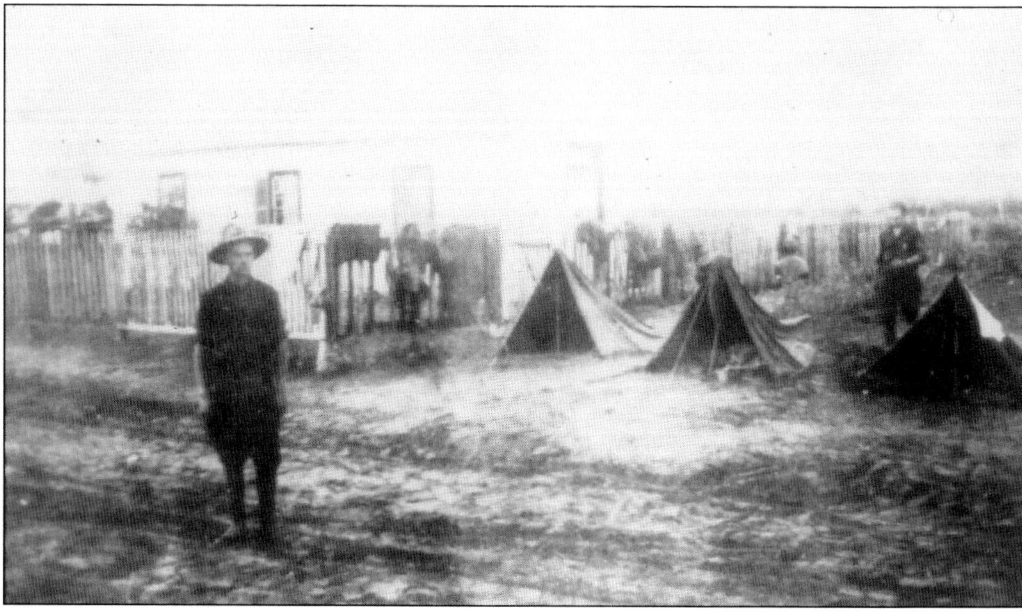

The fathers of the Oblate of Mary Immaculate offered the first religious services near Edinburg from Brownsville. The fathers would stop at Laguna Seca Ranch on their travels throughout the Valley, and chose Laguna Seca to build one of the first Catholic churches in the Valley. The first wedding in that church was in 1896, when Miss Eloisa Vela, the only daughter of the family who ever married, became the bride of William S. Dougherty of Brownsville. The Anglo American settlers in Chapin were primarily Protestant. In 1913, preachers from four different denominations, Methodist, Presbyterian, Baptist, and United Brethren, took turns traveling to Edinburg each Sunday of the month. By 1924, there were three Protestant church buildings. The first Catholic church building was the Sacred Heart, built in 1926.

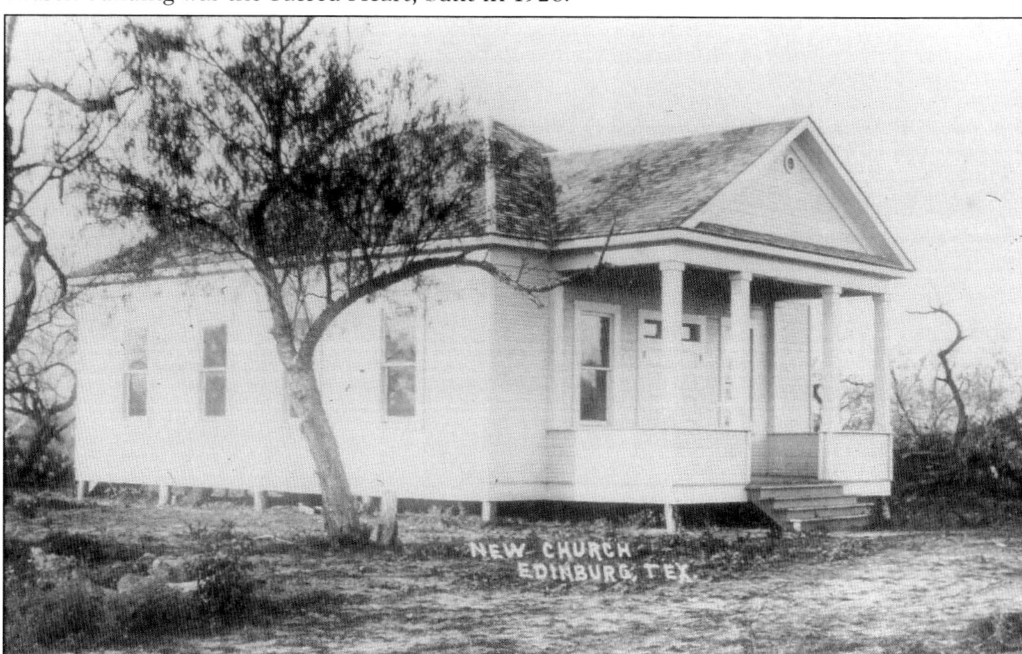

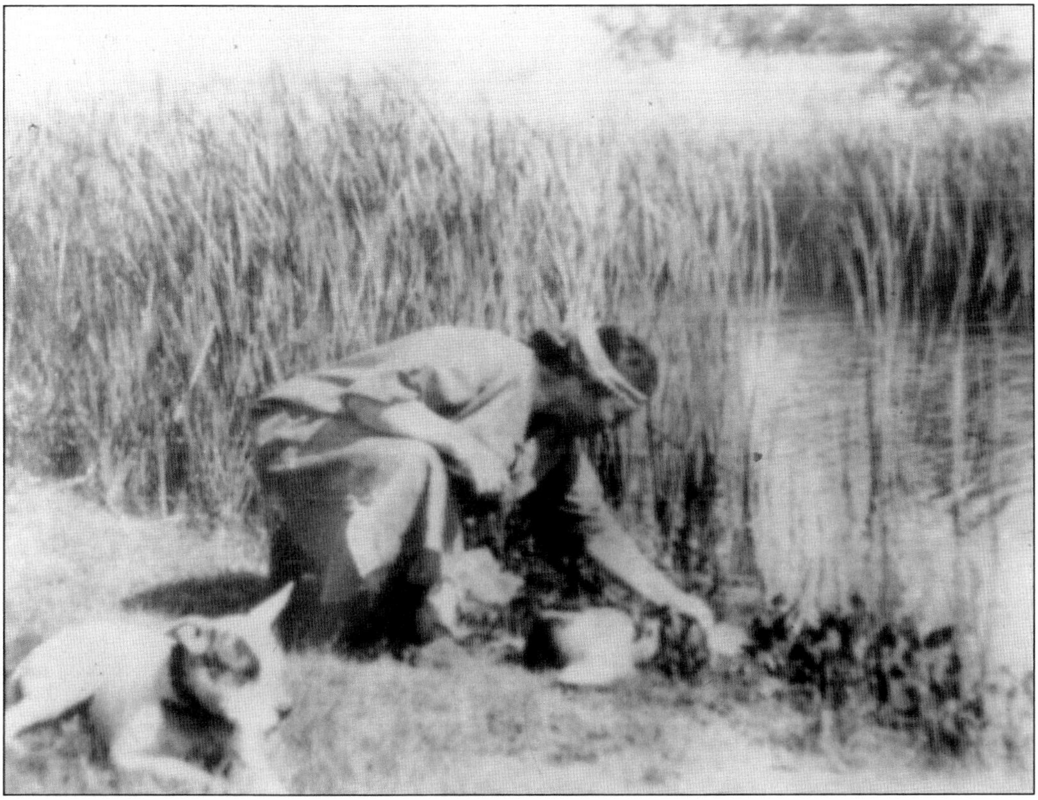

Clubs were a very popular way for people to get together to enjoy each other's company as well as improve themselves and their environment. One of the first clubs in Chapin was La Cultura Roycroft Junta No. 47, a literary club organized in December 1910. The club was soon disbanded, possibly because 5¢ was levied as a fine to any club member who failed to study the lesson. A number of other clubs were organized throughout the years, including the Campfire Girls in 1915. The photograph above shows Mrs. H.O. Schaleben from the Campfire Girls. The image at right is taken from the Edinburg Garden Club scrapbook. (Courtesy of The University of Texas–Pan American Library.)

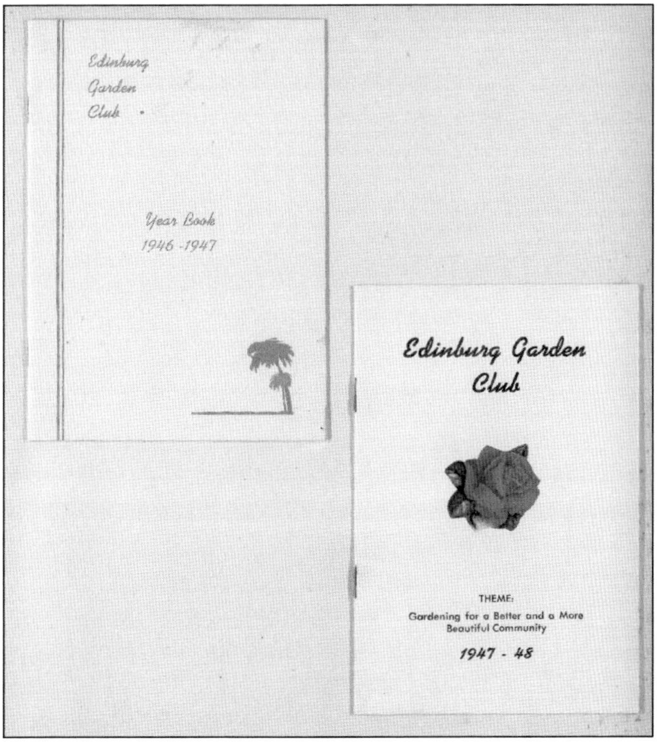

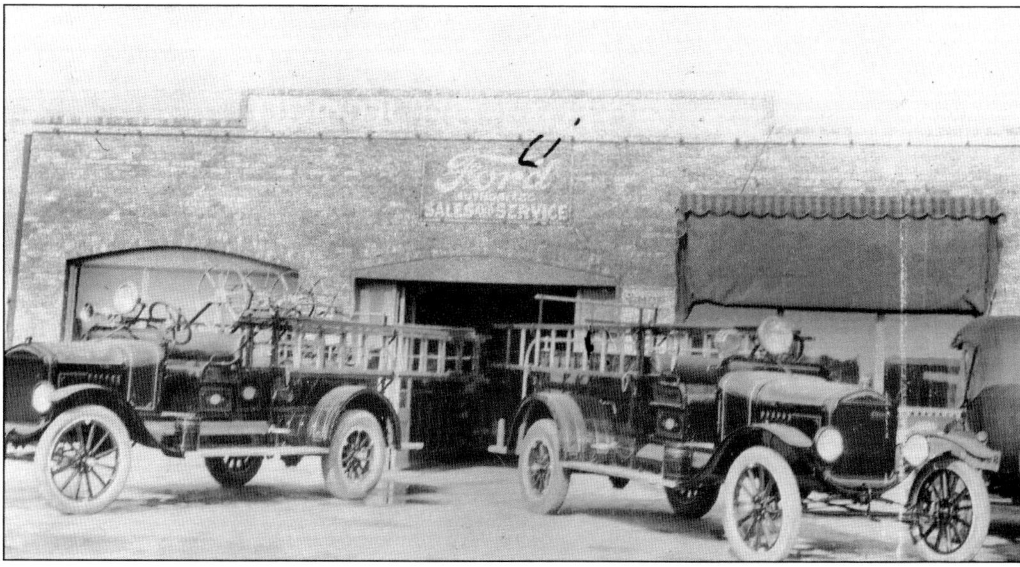

Volunteers formed the first organized fire department in Edinburg in 1921. The city purchased the first fire trucks in 1926, shown above, and built the first firehouse on the east side of city hall (now part of the Museum of South Texas History). An early program that still exists today also provides dormitory housing for volunteer firefighters attending college. Edinburg's volunteer firefighters, however, do not limit their contributions solely to this region. After the deadly and destructive Hurricane Camille hit Mississippi in 1969, two years after Hurricane Beulah, the Edinburg Volunteer Firefighters worked with the Veterans of Foreign Wars to collect and take clothing, food, and money to Mississippi. (Courtesy of the Edinburg Volunteer Fire Department.)

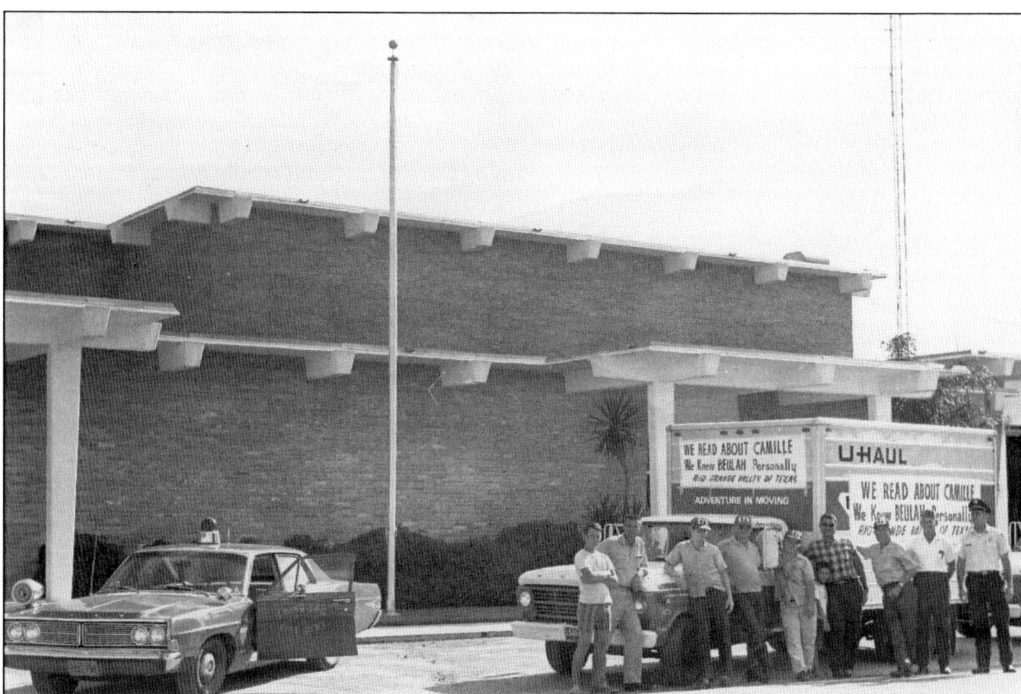

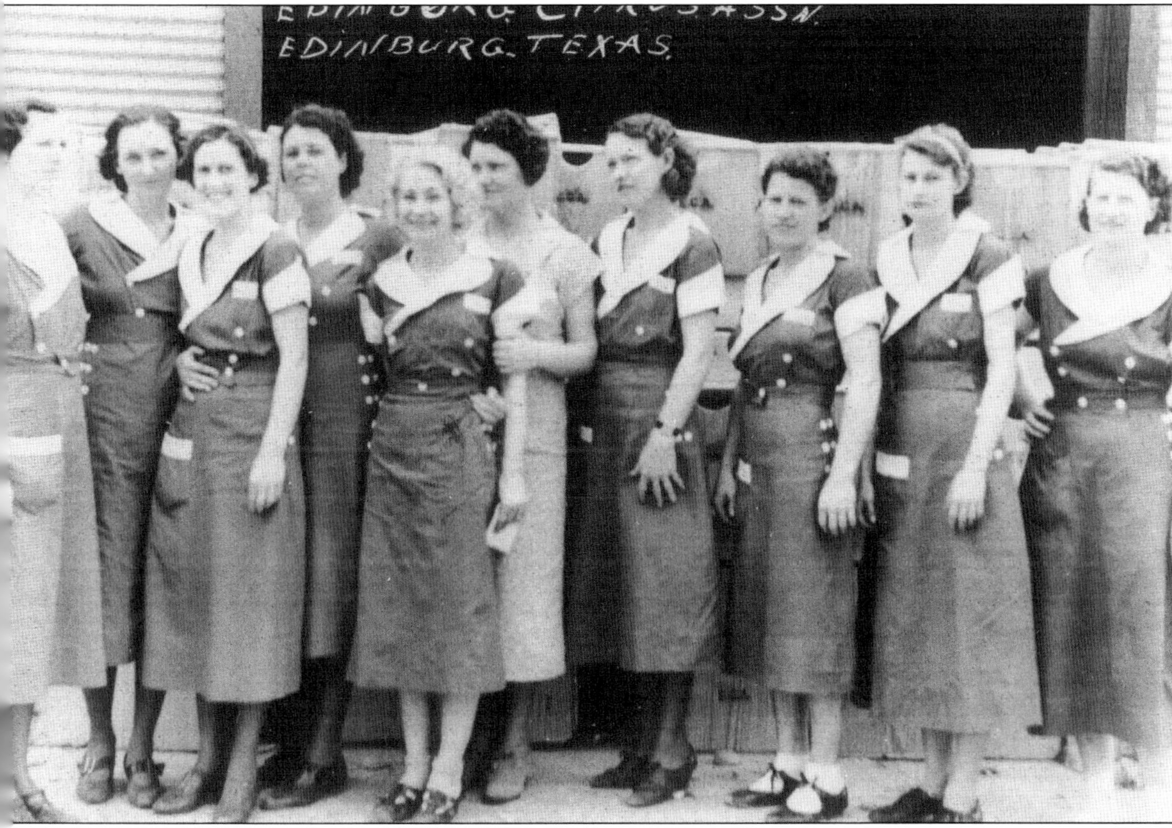

Throughout its history, Edinburg has shown time and again that the community can come together to accomplish great deeds. Edinburg is one of 40 cities in the United States that has won the All America City award three or more times. Each year the National Civic League recognizes 10 cities that demonstrate exceptional civic achievements. Edinburg was named All America City in 1968, 1995, and again in 2000. Edinburg was recognized as being a pro-business community with strong educational facilities, quality of life, and pride in the community. This photograph shows one example of what makes Edinburg worthy of being named an All America City—its labor force. (Courtesy of the Edinburg Citrus Association.)

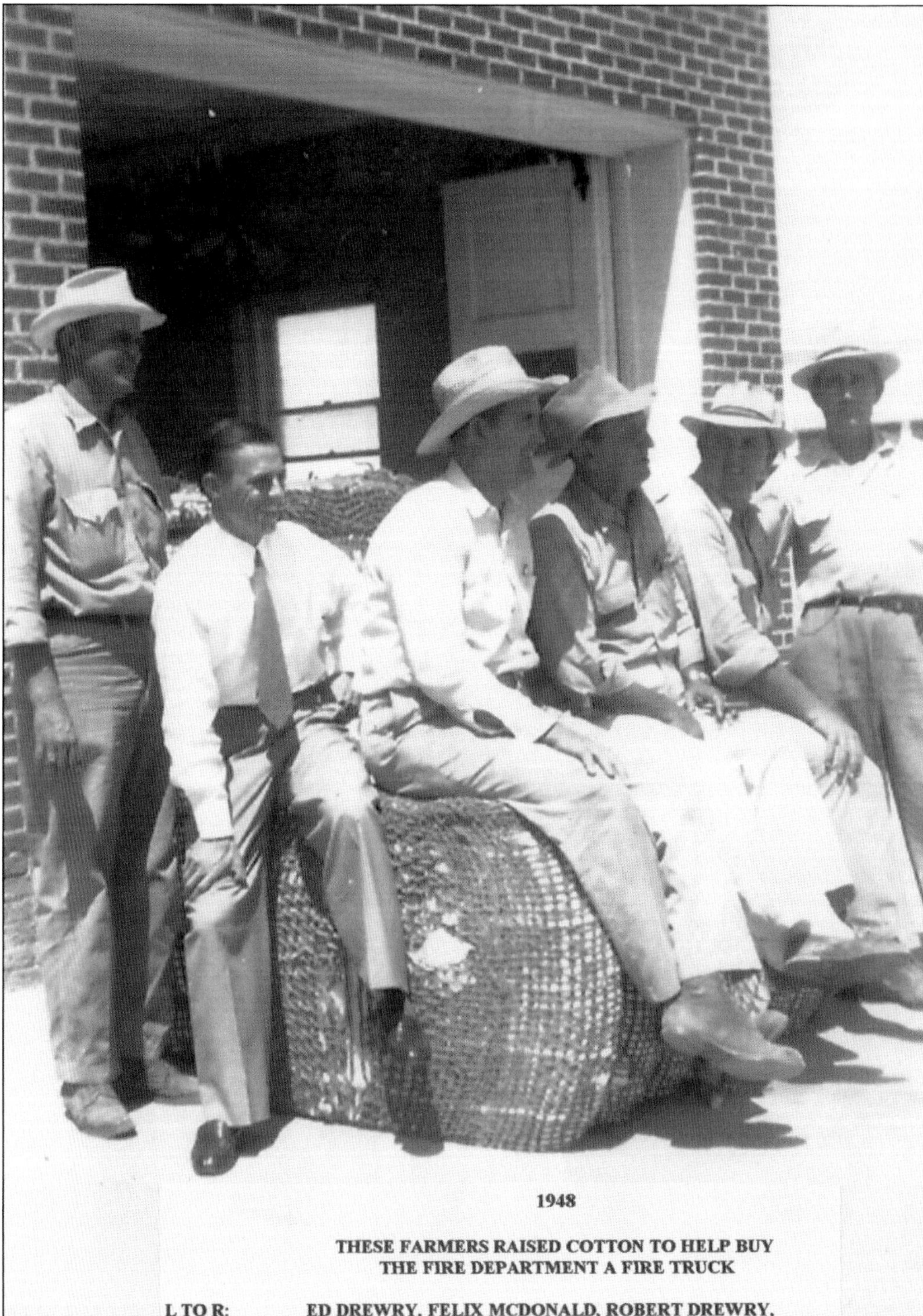

Edinburg's community involvement is depicted in this 1948 photograph. (Courtesy of the Edinburg Volunteer Fire Department.)

Bibliography

Daily Review. Centennial edition. Edinburg, TX: December 7, 1952.

Edinburg Bicentennial Heritage Committee. *Edinburg*. Edinburg, TX: Self-published, 1976.

Gerhardt, Karen and Rod Santa Ana III. *Hidalgo County, Texas*. Charleston, SC: Arcadia Publishing, 2000.

Hidalgo County Centennial Corp. "The Centennial Celebration of the Organization of Hidalgo County in Texas." December 7–13, 1952. Mission, TX: Times Pub. Co., 1952.

Hidalgo County Historical Marker Applications Collection, University Library Special Collections and Archives, University of Texas–Pan American.

Peavey, John R. *Echoes from the Rio Grande*. Brownsville, TX: Springman-King Co., 1963.

Pickens, Thomas Spencer. "The Southern Study in Edinburg Schools." Thesis (MA), Texas College of Arts and Industries, 1941.

Scott, Oran Randolph. "History of Hidalgo County, 1749–1852." Thesis (MA), Texas Christian University, 1934.

Texas State Historical Association. "Handbook of Texas Online." http://www.tshaonline.org/handbook.

Valley By-Liners. *Gift of the Rio: A Story of Texas Tropical Borderland*. American Revolution Bicentennial Ed. Mission, TX: Border Kingdom Press, 1975.

————. *Roots by the River: A Story of Texas Tropical Borderland*, Mission, TX: Border Kingdom Press, 1978.

————. *Rio Grande Round-Up: A Story of Texas Tropical Borderland*. Mission, TX: Border Kingdom Press, 1980.

Vela, Roberto, edited and translated by Antonio H. Vela and Carlos F. Vela. *Memories of Laguna Seca*. 1978.